Teaching India–Pakistan Relations

Teaching India–Pakistan Relations

Teachers' attitudes, practices and agency

Kusha Anand

First published in 2023 by
UCL Press
University College London
Gower Street
London WC1E 6BT

Available to download free: www.uclpress.co.uk

Text © Kusha Anand, 2023
Images © Contributors and copyright holders named in captions, 2023

The author has asserted their rights under the Copyright, Designs and Patents Act 1988 to be identified as the contributors of this work.

A CIP catalogue record for this book is available from The British Library.

Any third-party material in this book is not covered by the book's Creative Commons licence. Details of the copyright ownership and permitted use of third-party material is given in the image (or extract) credit lines. If you would like to reuse any third-party material not covered by the book's Creative Commons licence, you will need to obtain permission directly from the copyright owner.

This book is published under a Creative Commons Attribution-Non-Commercial 4.0 International licence (CC BY-NC 4.0), https://creativecommons.org/licenses/by-nc/4.0/. This licence allows you to share and adapt the work for non-commercial use providing attribution is made to the author and publisher (but not in any way that suggests that they endorse you or your use of the work) and any changes are indicated. Attribution should include the following information:

Anand, K. 2023. *Teaching India-Pakistan Relations*.
London: UCL Press. https://doi.org/10.14324/111.9781800080430

Further details about Creative Commons licences are available at http://creativecommons.org/licenses/

ISBN: 978-1-80008-045-4 (Hbk.)
ISBN: 978-1-80008-044-7 (Pbk.)
ISBN: 978-1-80008-043-0 (PDF)
ISBN: 978-1-80008-046-1 (epub)
DOI: https://doi.org/10.14324/111.9781800080430

Contents

List of figures and tables	vii
Acknowledgements	ix

1   Introduction: education and India–Pakistan relations · 1

2   Education and national identity construction in India and Pakistan · 19

3   Teachers and teacher agency in India and Pakistan · 53

4   Teachers' attitudes towards India–Pakistan relations · 72

5   Teachers' pedagogical strategies to India–Pakistan relations: what happens in the classroom? · 101

6   Conclusion: socio-economic status of schools and teachers · 137

Appendix A Snapshot of each teacher participant in Delhi and Lahore · 157

References	160
Index	174

List of figures and tables

1.1   School SES, habitus and teachers, based on the literature reviewed   17

1.1   Framework used for the categorisation of schools (based on their SES type)   13

Acknowledgements

> Are you comparing India and Pakistan?
> What is the use of this research?
> You are biased towards Pakistan.

This book is a response to these questions, which have regularly been asked by academics, research participants, friends, family members, journalists and so on over the years. However, this book is not limited to these questions; it also provides examples of teachers' voices on the teaching of India—Pakistan relations, based on my doctoral research. I would like to take this opportunity to thank all the readers, students and citizens who have encouraged me in this enterprise and whose questions have enriched this work. This book is dedicated to them.

To my PhD supervisor, Professor Marie Lall: I am grateful for your unwavering support and for the way in which you have continually encouraged my growth. You have always shown up for me and having you as a resource to learn from has been invaluable. I have always felt you were there to lift me up and help me succeed, and I appreciate your feedback throughout this process. My gratitude goes to Pat Gordon Smith who supported me in starting the process and guided me from a sparse outline along the long and winding road to the finish. I also want to thank the teachers who willingly gave their time and enthusiasm to my research.

To my parents and grandparents: Thank you for believing I can do anything I set my mind to. That belief encouraged me to begin and to complete this project. No matter the need, you have always been there for me. I love you all!

To my husband Aman: Thank you for supporting me during this adventure. I do not have enough space to list all of the ways you continually support me. I am forever grateful for the partnership we have. I love you (and our son Kian).

1
Introduction: education and India–Pakistan relations

Every facet of India–Pakistan relations has over the decades been scrutinised and commented upon in detail and contemporary events are examined and discussed with precision. Public knowledge about this complex relationship is considerable. The question before the author, therefore, was how do teachers teach students about the relationship? This book explores different pedagogical aspects that arise in teaching India–Pakistan relations in Delhi and Lahore. National curricula have been used to shape the mindset of the new generations vis-à-vis their neighbour and India–Pakistan relations. Teachers are at the core of learning about India–Pakistan relations in schools today, possessing a direct conduit to children and families (see Chapters 2 and 3). This book consequently situates teachers within the context of reformed textbooks and curricula in both research sites, serving as a rationale for research on how these reformed textbooks have been enacted in the classrooms.

The book has two purposes. First, it aims to present teachers' attitudes towards India–Pakistan relations. Teachers' attitudes could influence their actions and instructional decisions in the classroom. This book consequently reports interests beyond curriculum and textbooks, as teachers' attitudes could also play a significant role in the classroom. Second, the book intends to offer a voice to teachers as they are involved in teaching a politicised version of history and are affected by the changing landscape of education and reformed curricula and textbooks in both countries. This is significant because the voices of teachers are not usually heard.

This book is thus different from other books on India and Pakistan. It is based on teachers' attitudes, pedagogical practices, decisions and responses collected through in-depth interviews and classroom observations at both research sites. The book argues that, despite the education reform priorities espoused by the textbook boards in both countries that explicitly advocate critical thinking and social cohesion, teachers in both research sites face similar issues. Teachers often ignore opportunities in their classrooms to engage with multiple perspectives and stereotypes, both in terms of the portrayal of India–Pakistan relations and in the portrayal of existing inequalities between Hindus and Muslims. Regardless of their attitudes, teachers have to bow to the interests of their school (headteacher) and state.

There are two interpretations of the findings. First, they expose the claim that the textbooks could perhaps contest the societal narratives of memories of partition and the perceptions of India–Pakistan relations. Second, regardless of the textbook change and teachers' views, the Socio-Economic Status (SES) of schools also influences the attitudes of their teachers and determines their pedagogical decisions on how to portray India–Pakistani relations. Based on in-depth data collected in India and Pakistan, this book seeks to provide a holistic perspective upon the attitudes and pedagogical responses of both government and private school teachers to India–Pakistan relations.

In this introductory chapter, the author first gives an overview of the history of India–Pakistan relations and their political ramifications. It then reviews the role of education in India–Pakistan relations. This sets the background for the rest of the book which details individual teachers' responses to teaching India–Pakistan relations. Finally the chapter provides a summary of the theoretical framework, the methodological design and the way in which findings are set out across the rest of the book.

Introduction to India–Pakistan relations

In giving a historical and current overview of how and why India–Pakistan relations took the course they did, the author's focus is upon the broad mainstream of the relationship itself. In order to keep the book to a manageable length, the author discarded any attempt to be exhaustive. This section brings out a fuller flavour of India–Pakistan relations in terms of the wider context of the relationship. The author must at the beginning set out a 'proviso'. This is an 'education book' rather than a 'history' book.

The conflict between India and Pakistan predates the creation of these states out of the British Empire. Under British rule, Hindus and Muslims engaged in the struggle for independence together under one leadership. When it came to power sharing in one governmental structure, however, Muslims became suspicious of Hindu policies; they were not of the majority, the leadership was Hindu and policies also appeared to have a Hindu 'slant'. As a result of the ensuing suspicion and distrust, the Muslims decided in 1906 to form their own party, the Muslim League (Mumtaz and Bluth 2020).

It was in 1930 when the idea for a separate Muslim homeland, based on the 'two-nation theory', was introduced. The rift between Hindus and Muslims then intensified due to communal clashes between Hindus and Muslims. The then viceroy Lord Mountbatten concluded that the only solution was to divide the subcontinent into two separate states, a Muslim Dominion of Pakistan and a secular union of India which was to be predominately Hindu (Mumtaz and Bluth 2020). The process of partition was accompanied by communal violence in which, according to various estimates, up to 500,000 people died (Mumtaz and Bluth 2020).

The British expected that the princely state of Jammu and Kashmir would become part of Pakistan, but the ruling Maharaja[1] failed to make a decision. After Muslim protesters and Pakistani troops entered Kashmir, the Maharaja requested help from the British but was told by Lord Mountbatten that he could not expect British assistance until he formally acceded to India. After the Maharaja signed the instrument of accession, Indian troops entered the territory and evicted the irregular forces from most of the territory (Mumtaz and Bluth 2020). The 1947–8 Indo–Pakistani war over Kashmir, in which around 8,000 soldiers were killed, ended with India controlling about half of the former princely state of Kashmir and Jammu while Pakistan occupied the Northern Territories and 'Azad Kashmir'. A ceasefire line was established and monitored by the United Nations until 1972. It was then renamed the Line of Control (LOC) and manned by troops of the opposing sides. A United Nations mandate to hold a referendum in Kashmir to determine its future has been consistently rejected by India, whereas Pakistan has never accepted that part of Kashmir belonged to India. Three major wars and one minor war

---

1 Maharaja Sir Hari Singh was the last ruling Maharaja of the princely state of Jammu and Kashmir.

have been fought (1947–8, 1965, 1971 and 1999) without either country changing the status quo to its advantage (Mumtaz and Bluth 2020).

The Kashmir dispute is thus one of the intractable global conflicts resulting from the British partitioning of the Indian subcontinent. Kashmir has developed into a 'decomposed' conflict between the two countries (Indurthy 2005). The conflict over Kashmir is less a contest over strategic ground or resources than over competing visions of nationalism and state-building. For India, Kashmir is symbolic of secular nationalism and state-building and of the possibility of a Muslim-majority area choosing to live and prosper within a Hindu-majority country (Ganguly and Bajpai 1994). For Pakistan, Kashmir is symbolic of the impossibility of 'secular nationalism' in the region and thus of the need for a Muslim homeland in the north-western corner of the subcontinent (Ray 2018).

In 2014 the political alliance between the Jammu and Kashmir Peoples Democratic Party and the Bharatiya Janata Party in the state of Jammu and Kashmir has aggravated the ideological differences between the two parties (Ray 2018). The polarisation of the Hindu and Muslim communities in Jammu and Kashmir is not merely political: it is a result of conflicting approaches to dispute settlement, imbued with strong communal undertones (Ray 2018).

In February 2019 40 Indian soldiers were killed in an attack on a convoy of paramilitary forces in Indian-controlled Kashmir. The attack was claimed by the Pakistani militant group Jaish-e-Mohammad (JeM), which has acted as a proxy force for the Pakistani inter-service intelligence services (Mumtaz and Bluth 2020). The Indian government responded with air strikes on what they claimed was a terrorist training camp inside Pakistan. Two weeks later Pakistan retaliated with air strikes in Indian-administered Kashmir; these were followed by direct engagements between the Indian and Pakistani air forces in which two Indian aircraft were downed and one Indian pilot was captured. The confrontation gave rise to speculation about the dangers of escalation to a nuclear conflict. The events of 2019 encapsulate some of the key issues in the tense relationships between India and Pakistan (Mumtaz and Bluth 2020).

Following the terrorist attack on a Central Reserve Police Force (CRPF) convoy in Pulwama in February 2019, right-wing activists targeted Kashmiri students in Dehradun. They approached colleges seeking assurance (via written documentation) that no Kashmiri students would be permitted to gain admission from the next term (Mishra 2019). In addition to this, four members of the Akhil Bharatiya Vidyarthi Parishad (ABVP), a right-wing all-India student organisation affiliated with the Rashtriya Swayamsevak Sangh (RSS), were also arrested in

Rajpur for allegedly attempting to seek a similar undertaking from a private college. The authorities at a Dehradun-based private college also suspended its Kashmiri dean (as demanded by a mob) (Khan 2020).

Over two hundred Kashmiri students are estimated to have left Dehradun since these events. While some students have returned to Kashmir, others have been provided shelter in Chandigarh by an NGO (*The Times of India* 2019). In the midst of a hideous Covid-19 pandemic, the conflict in Kashmir continued unabated. (Khan 2020). The Kashmir issue was put on hold, and maintaining peace in the subcontinent as a whole remained 'problematic' (Khan 2020).

The recent crisis thus presented an opportunity for both the Indian[2] and Pakistani[3] leadership to 'shore up' their nationalist vision for South Asia. The rise of Narendra Modi (Modi) and Hindu nationalism have slowly eroded the idea that India represents home for multiple ethnicities, religious groups and social classes. Pakistan's continuing practice of oppressing religious minorities finds acceptance and legitimacy in the leadership of Imran Khan (Hamidi 2019). Education (via curriculum and textbooks) has been used to lay the ground for systemic discrimination on communal lines. This will be discussed in more detail in the following section.

Schools, textbooks and India–Pakistan relations

Education is a significant tool in the construction of state-promoted national identity. This occurs through the formal process of education in schools where the role of government is central (Adeney and Lall 2005). Education has been used fundamentally to construct a national identity that aims to unify the nation of individuals. Education policy has been recognised as an effective tool to promote and spread the nationalist ideologies of India and Pakistan (Adeney and Lall 2005). The education systems and nation-building processes have been based on the political aims of the government in power at the time (Adeney and Lall 2005) (discussed further in Chapter 2).

---

2 The recent societal trends in India reveal growing communal violence – particularly by emboldened far-right Hindu nationalists targeting the Muslim populace. Some of this violence targets Muslims who eat beef or are even simply accused of eating beef.

3 The election of Pakistani Prime Minister Imran Khan has reinforced the pre-existing nationalist tendencies of the Pakistani establishment, which has often legitimised its rule through the Indian threat. Khan's ability to triangulate Islam, the Pakistan Army and a strong nationalist Pakistani identity have made him a popular leader in Pakistan. However, his defence of Pakistan's blasphemy laws further alienates and oppresses the few minority groups that remain in Pakistan.

Schools are invested with the task of 'socializing the young into an approved national past, the approving agency being the state' (Kumar 2001, 20). Although this is also true in 'older' nation-states where education often reflects official ideology, it is especially valid in postcolonial societies, in which nation-building becomes so crucial that it relegates other concerns to the background. In 'newly formed' nation-states the main purpose of education is arguably not to favour the intellectual development of children; it is above all 'to disseminat[e] a view of the nation's past deemed conducive to the strengthening of "national unity" or the furthering of "integration", whether in the present or the future' (Powell 1996, 190). In this process the teaching of history, as much as its (re)writing, assumes a prominent position.

In India and Pakistan, history textbooks have been used to justify and embed the hostile attitude toward the respective neighbouring country (see Chapter 2). As stated by Aziz and mentioned in Ahmed and Baxter (2007), history in schools, colleges and universities in India and Pakistan is taught in a damaging way. The method employed is an assurance that a nation tends to be unaware of its past, unconscious of its present and unaware of its future (this will be discussed in more detail in Chapter 2).

Textbooks constitute one of the fundamental sources of knowledge for children attending school. Particularly drafted in accord with an official curriculum, they are one of the fundamental tools which determine the restrictions of legitimate knowledge in a state, transfer this knowledge and reproduce it in each cycle (Yilar and Cam 2021). The textbooks contribute to the process of giving shape to what is defined as legitimate and true by society. They help to construct the foundations of authenticity and thus support the reproduction of a basic reference point for the real nature of knowledge, culture, belief and morality (Apple 1990).

In India and Pakistan, a communal interpretation of history lies at the root of the continuing ideological clash between Pakistan's 'Islamic' nationalism and India's secular beliefs, with the espousal of Hindu nationalism by the Bharatiya Janata Party (BJP) introducing a new dimension to this conflict. This is because the history of the subcontinent is closely tied to the question of identity and nationalism (Behera 1996). The India–Pakistan divide may be studied in this context where the construction of a partisan history has been a critical factor in perpetuating this divide (Behera 1996). As Romila Thapar (1993, cited in Behera 1996, 192) puts it

[...] a communal segmentary nationalism draws on an identity which focuses on one group identified by religion and excludes the others ... the argument is that we have a right to be a nation-state or to dominate the nation-state because of our distinct identity. Whether it is the Muslim component of the subcontinent as it was in the pre-partition days or whether it is the Hindu majority or Sikhs in Punjab, this right or this perception of identity is based on how history is perceived. History, therefore, is modulated in order to conform to projecting an identity.

Perhaps that is why some Pakistani rulers have sought to Islamise their history and the BJP strives to Hinduise Indian history to present an exclusively Hindu view of their past (Behera 1996). The ruling regimes in India and Pakistan have often tried to re-write their respective countries' past to suit their present political ideologies and their motives for expounding a revisionist history (a subject discussed further in Chapter 2). This has an impact on their younger generations in terms of sustaining an enemy image of the other country (Behera 1996). Rewriting of history textbooks by different ruling regimes may therefore be viewed in the context of their efforts to project a particular identity or to propagate a particular brand of nationalism to suit their respective political ideologies (Behera 1996).

In India and Pakistan, scholars (Aziz 1993; Kumar 2001; Saigol 2005; Lall 2008; Afzal 2015, 2018) have suggested that history textbooks devote space to depicting conflicts with the state's other as the national narrative to construct the country's identity (against this other). The history textbooks' narratives are silent on the internal conflicts as their purpose was exactly to construct homogeneity and to depict the nation as a natural entity (Guichard 2013). This process is not natural and it was most of the time not harmonious, in that it used force to put together or maintain together with the components of the 'nation' (Guichard 2013). However, the consequences of these internal conflicts are frequently quite tangible in modern society and the silences in textbooks cause a divergence between the history programme and what students actually experience (Guichard 2013). Chapter 2 outlines how education has been used historically to justify and embed a hostile attitude towards the respective neighbouring country.

School is an effective instrument in this context. There is not enough literature looking at teachers' voices in teaching India–Pakistan relations within the respective country contexts, which is the innovative focus of this book. The portrayal of India–Pakistan relations in Indian and

Pakistani textbooks is key, particularly the impact of textbooks on teachers' classroom practices. It is important to understand how teachers negotiate and enact the textbook content on a historical conflict event (Banerjee and Stöber 2016), which helps in providing insights into what the students are learning in such contexts and how this might shape their view of the India–Pakistan relations.

Teachers' voices and India–Pakistan relations

The concept of voice has been widely studied in education and non-education settings. In education, definitions of voice are much more varied and nuanced. As key actors in the education system, teachers (and the incorporation of their voices into decision-making) are often perceived as both the remedy and the cause of problems facing schools today (Gyurko 2012). The voices of teachers have come to represent knowledge and power, position and participation, control and collaboration, leadership and resistance (Conley 1991; Hargreaves 1996; Kahlenberg and Potter 2015). While some researchers define teacher voice more generally as teachers' expressions of opinions, attitudes and ideas, other researchers specify the areas influenced by teacher voice. Many education researchers argue that there has been a dearth of teachers' voices in education decision-making (Hargreaves 1996; Ingersoll 2007).

In India and Pakistan teachers play a significant role in transmitting history in the classroom based on the textbooks used. In classrooms, the role of teachers was traditionally perceived as being restricted to 'implementing the curriculum designed by external agencies' (Durrani and Halai 2018, 539). Teaching was understood as the transmission of knowledge, with learners as passive recipients. Nonetheless, there has been a progressive transformation 'in the understanding of teachers' roles or positions, particularly teacher agency in curriculum innovation as well as the transformation of teaching' (Priestley et al. 2013; Halai and Durrani 2018, 539) (to be discussed further in Chapter 3). Teachers are thus at the heart of our understanding of the role of education in India–Pakistan relations (Nayyar and Salim 2003; National Curriculum Framework 2005; Batra 2006; Lall 2008; Anand 2019). They play a dominant role in the enactment of textbooks in both India and Pakistan. Textbooks have a similar status as teachers place blind faith in written words (Reardon and Cabezudo 2002).

Very limited attention has been paid to the voices of history teachers involved in teaching India–Pakistan relations in India and Pakistan; many scholars (for example, Kumar 2001; Nayyar and Salim 2005; Durrani 2008; Afzal 2015) have only reviewed education policies or the curriculum. Teachers' voices are important, however, as Frost (2008) argues: policy-makers can benefit from hearing teachers' anecdotes and incorporating their experiences in the classroom into policy-making processes. In the context of educational change and reform, teachers, as key local actors or 'street-level bureaucrats' (Lipsky 1980), exercise substantial influence on whether and how major school reforms are implemented in the classroom (Cuban 1998).

The methodological design of the book, positionality and Bourdieu's theory of social reproduction

This section outlines the methodological design and approach in data-gathering methods and the use of thematic analysis as a data analysis lens.

The author is a former teacher and journalist. She has been researching education for over a decade through intense engagement with teachers as part of fieldwork in India and Pakistan. Born and brought up in Delhi, she grew up watching the national television channels in India blaming Pakistan and Muslims for the partition of India. The author remembered her teacher once commenting that 'Pakistan is a dangerous country'. She and others like her got this image of Pakistan from its media portrayal, which left resounding echoes in the minds of Hindus for a very long time.

The author has also read history school textbooks that portray Pakistan and the relations between India and Pakistan negatively. She is aware of the negative attitudes that society and teachers have concerning India-Pakistan relations and the responsibilities of teachers. In general, society and teachers hold each other responsible for the status of ties between India and Pakistan. The author felt that it is important to incorporate the contrast of context and case study approaches to understand teachers' voices and their pedagogical responses. A case study is an examination of a phenomenon such as a person or a group of people (for instance, a teacher or several teachers), an institution (for instance, a school), a programme, an event (for instance, a school curriculum or pedagogical process) (Willis and Turner 2007). To understand these different aspects, therefore, this book deals with Delhi (in India) and Lahore (in Pakistan) as separate cases, identifying them as objects of study (Stake 1995) as well as a procedure of inquiry (Merriam 1998).

These two cities were selected due to competing nationalism and education (see Chapter 2), social base and inter-connectedness[4] and peace activism. The case study method was useful for presenting an understanding of teachers' pedagogical responses to the teaching of India-Pakistan relations, both systematically and coherently (see Chapter 4). The case study methodology, as noted by Yin (2004), is predominantly appropriate when the investigator supposes the framework to be extremely appropriate to the question being researched. This supported the rationale for choosing such an approach as it allowed for an exploration of the teachers' pedagogical responses to teaching India–Pakistan relations. The parallel case study methodology enabled the author to explore the attitudes of teachers towards India or Pakistan (see Chapter 3) and India–Pakistan relations (see Chapter 4 in Delhi and Lahore), as the cases were studied concurrently.

The contrast of contexts method is mainly used in comparative history to focus on the historical exclusivity of every case; in this way, contextual reliability is valued. It is one of the options of the comparative method (Skocpol and Somers 1980). This method is used to represent or evolve theoretical hypotheses and generalisations. The fundamental significance of the contrast-oriented approach is that the 'historical integrity of every case as a whole is carefully respected' (Skocpol and Somers 1980, 75). To preserve historical reliability, the exceptional descriptions of every case are brought out and their influence on the

---

4 Lahore is a city like Delhi, and this helped the author to select the sample from schools of different socio-economic statuses (SES). Historically Lahore has been represented as Delhi's smaller 'sister city' and they are also considered as twin cities (Hameed 2017 Anand, 2019). Life in Lahore is often compared with that in Delhi (Karachi is compared with Mumbai) (Murali 2004). Lahore is the capital of Punjab; Delhi is the capital of India, and both have been Mughal capitals. Delhi and Lahore also have deep historical connections such as Mughal monuments and culture, large education systems and political control (Talbot 1995, Anand, 2019)). As Talbot (1995, 224) explains in 'Divided Cities', in 1947 approximately 240,000 Hindus and Sikhs in Lahore constituted about one-third of the city's population. After partition, these people migrated to different parts of India such as East Punjab, Delhi and elsewhere. Muslims living in Pakistan formed about half of the total population (about 40,000) and they migrated to Lahore. Amritsar in India lost all its Muslims, while Lahore in Pakistan lost all its Hindus and Sikhs. Delhi to this day has many Muslims. Due to similarities between the two cities especially in terms of culture and civilisational heritage, it was particularly pertinent to research these two cities. Delhi and Lahore also connect by languages such as English, Urdu and Punjabi. The English language has been a component of Britain's colonial legacy which India and Pakistan have both inherited. Urdu is another common language that Indians and Pakistanis share and that unites them. Spoken Urdu is mutually intelligible with Hindu, apart from specialised vocabulary. Punjabi is another language widely spoken in Pakistan (Rahman 2004, Anand, 2019). It is the most widely spoken language in Pakistan and the eleventh most widely spoken language in India. Language is shared between Lahore and New Delhi; Lahoris communicate in English and Punjabi, while many residents of Delhi use Punjabi, Hindi and English (Baart 2003, Anand, 2019)). This resolved the language barriers.

social process being researched analysed. This method was extremely appropriate for this book as it enabled a comparison of complete cases, in this instance Delhi and Lahore. Components from the contrast of contexts technique were used; this allowed the historical reliability of every case to be valued and their important characteristics to be contrasted with one another (Skocpol and Somers 1980).

The case histories in this book chosen for illumination lend themselves strongly to this comparative method because they represent contrasting trajectories in teachers' pedagogical responses to teaching India–Pakistan relations. In the case of India, there is an emphasis on secularism in its educational discourse (as per the Indian constitution); in the case of Pakistan, its educational discourse emphasises the values of Islam. These contrasting characteristics were described and compared systematically. Skocpol and Somers (1980) point to a weakness in the contrast of contexts approach – while researchers can provide a rich, broad and chronologically diverse explanation of contrasting case histories, they do not provide any causal explanation for these contrasts. Nevertheless, this book does not simply juxtapose these two case histories to provide contrasting narratives about each; it rather attempts to provide causal explanations for these differences.

This book is based on semi-structured interviews with 21 teachers, each from different types of schools in Delhi and Lahore. Teachers' attitudes were collected through the semi-structured interviews while their pedagogical responses were observed through classroom observations. In India and Pakistan social stratification is in line with the social basis. Ethnicity, caste identity or kinship network associations, gender, patriarchal relations, economic conditions and affiliation (with traditional and modern lifestyles) are the significant factors in social stratification (Alavi 1982; Saigol 1993, 2000; Talbot 1998; Qadeer 2006; Anand 2019). Correspondingly, inequality in income, ownership, non-ownership of property and distribution of wealth are obvious structures of disparity among different socio-economic classes (Gardezi 1970; Juma 1987; Qadeer 2006; Anand 2019). Regarding the association between these socio-economic classes and the prevailing educational opportunities accessible in a country, social scientists and educationists claim that education systems provide a comprehensive range of choices. The education systems that are prevalent in India and Pakistan are the conventional religious-based school system and the modern formal school system (Hayes 1987; Baldauf 2001; Marlow-Ferguson 2002, 1014). The author drafted a socio-economic status checklist (adapted from ASER 2014, 2017; Khattak 2014) to classify schools as per their

Table 1.1 Framework used for the categorisation of schools (based on their SES type)

Type of school (based on socio-economic status)	School composition	
	Physical capital: school characteristics	Human/cultural capital: school ethos
Elite private SES schools	– The buildings are centrally air-conditioned and heated. There are drinking water facilities and an adequate number of separate toilets. – The classrooms have sufficient furniture (chairs and tables) for the students. Each floor has enough electrical coolers with filtration plants to provide clean drinking water to the students. – Elite schools have separate assembly halls; music rooms; swimming pools; large playing fields with different sports courts; and extensive parking spaces for teachers, visitors and students.	– Support Western/secular ideas. – Promote modernity and enlightenment in society. – Believe in collective identity and secularism. – Complete independence from government influence. – Students are graded on the standards of their academic analysis, independent thinking and reasoning. – English as a medium of instruction.
Middle government/private SES schools	– The classrooms have sufficient furniture for students. – Ceiling fans are provided in the classrooms. – There is no adequate system for clean drinking water. – The number of washrooms is adequate, although a few of them are clogged and non-functional and thus remain closed. – All floors are clean; there are offices and medium-sized libraries. – Schools have separate assembly halls and extensive playing fields with a few sports courts. – The classrooms only have blackboards and white chalk as teaching aids.	– Favour progressive education and Western intellectual ideologies. – Support cultural norms and conservative ideological orientations. – Subscribe to the traditional theme of national pride and loyalty. – Show a high amount of trust towards the school as an institution. – Act as a state agent and support its ideology. – Emphasise traditional teaching methodology. – Emphasise the importance of integrating religious or political epistemology into the corpus of modern/secular knowledge. – Hindi/Urdu used as a medium of instruction in government schools and a mixture of Hindi/Urdu and English in private schools.

Type of school (based on socio-economic status)	School composition	
	Physical capital: school characteristics	Human/cultural capital: school ethos
Lower SES government and private schools/teachers	– A few classrooms have sufficient furniture. – Although ceiling fans are provided in the classrooms, on the majority of occasions half of them are out of order; there is also no adequate system for clean and filtered drinking water. – In certain places the electrical wires are hanging loosely without being adequately covered with protective material. – Toilets are clogged and non-functional, and thus remain closed. – The classrooms only have blackboards and white chalk as teaching aids and there are no overhead projectors. – The libraries/labs do not have adequate teaching aids such as microscopes, thermometers, beakers, test tubes, chemicals, charts, maps, models, etc. Moreover, their quantity is significantly insufficient to accommodate all the students.	– Emphasise religious differences between Hindus and Muslims. – Prefer the traditional way of teaching. – Unprepared or inexperienced teaching students of low SES. – Pupils are forced to memorise passages from textbooks. – Blame the pressure of exams. – Prefer a single narrative of events in semi-academic 'textbookese'. – Hindi/Urdu used as a medium of instruction in government schools and private schools.

Source: Anand (2019)

Note: This table is a summation from data sources (the semi-structured interviews and classroom observations) and adapted from the Annual Status of Education Report (ASER) 2014; ASER 2017; ASER 2018; Khattak 2014. A snapshot of each teacher participant in Delhi and Lahore is given in Appendix 1.

socio-economic status. The factors used for classifying the SES of schools were the economic, social and cultural status of the school (see Table 1.1 below for the categorisation of schools). In schools, there are three types of capital. The physical capital encompasses the buildings, books, equipment and the resources needed to deliver a comprehensive and balanced curriculum. The information and skills of the teaching and administrative staff include human capital. Finally, what happens between teachers and students and between peer groups, both in the classroom and in the interactions between teachers and students, constitutes the cultural capital.

Positionality and reflexivity in data collection and analysis

The author's experience of living and working in Delhi helped her to illustrate, as fully as possible, a sense of teachers' pedagogical responses to India–Pakistan relations have developed. During this time she gained a sufficient level of intercultural competency to establish rapport and trust with the participants in Lahore. Despite such competency in Lahore, the author's nationality and limited knowledge of their classroom context positioned her as an 'outsider'. Her position as an insider or outsider was consequently in flux, depending on the particular situation.

The author used a reflective journal to advance her understanding and viewed the situation from the perspective of both sides. She was aware that such discussion is complex as each group might be convinced that the *self* is right and the *other* is wrong, and so construct boundaries to limit the research. She posed questions[5] for herself to stimulate reflexivity regarding conflicting positions, thoughts and actions (Anand 2019).

The author's identity as an Indian Hindu in Lahore challenged the course of recruiting participants. When the author first contacted teachers by phone and email, many voiced hesitation and scepticism about the research topic. Prior to travelling to Lahore, the author connected with teachers via Skype. In response to the email approach, teachers opposed participation, most declaring that they could not participate in research on a political topic. However, after speaking with them on Skype and meeting them in person, participants were more eager to take part in the study. (Anand 2019).

In the semi-structured interviews, the participants used oral narratives they had heard in their families. In these narratives, the other was the aggressor and the self is the victim. The author felt that her emotional experiences could prompt a distortion of the data and acknowledgment of agonising stories.[6] She also embraced debriefing to reduce the impact of an emotional understanding. Such a process

---

5   What are my thoughts on India-Pakistan and the relations between the two countries? How do I feel I understand it?
Will the research be impacted by my knowledge, and if so, how?

6   'My grandparents had tragic memories of India – how Hindus evacuated their homes and murdered our relatives (teacher, Lahore).' (Anand, cited in Naveed et al. 2017, 789).
'We were rich before partition. Pakistan just destroyed everything. These mullahs [Muslims] are responsible for our suffering (teacher, New Delhi).' (Anand, cited in Naveed et al. 2017, 789).

improved critical thinking and acknowledged every feeling that might source judgement as well as a generalisation (Dickson-Swift et al. 2007; Anand 2019). The author used de-briefing meetings (by phone, Skype calls and face-to-face meetings) with her seniors, fellow researchers and acquaintances, which helped to reduce any baseless oversimplifications (Anand 2019).

Reflexivity helped in preparing and tackling the issues of data interpretation in emotional contexts. This strategy helped the author to appreciate inconsistencies, changes and omissions where her positionality or evolving experience had coloured the emotions in her research. Before framing themes and categorising attitudes, the author reflected on the recorded 'insider or outsider' issues in her reflexivity journal (Anand 2019).

In terms of data analysis, the author's reflexivity took the method of reflective memos and notes about the data (Anand 2019). Throughout this process, coded findings were organised, elucidated, incorporated and interpreted (Corbin and Strauss 2008). In memo writing, the author compared notions and patterns which allowed her to develop classifications of attitudes. She tried to conduct the data analysis process with humility, recognising that 'some voices are silenced, and other voices and knowledge dominate the airwaves' (Byrne-Armstrong 2001, 112). She listened to the interview tapes numerous times and logged her impressions of what was going on for the participant, for her and between the two of them as the narrative unfolded (Anand 2019). Some teachers avoided confrontation by embracing their patriotism and forming friendships with the other side (India or Pakistan, Hindus or Muslims). The data displayed a narrative shift in teachers' attitudes towards the other country and India–Pakistan relations (Anand 2019). Assessing it proved to be an interwoven process of analysis and writing-up of the data like the 'fifth moment' in qualitative research when 'messy, uncertain, multi-voiced texts, cultural criticism and new experimental works will become more common, as will more reflexive forms of fieldwork, analysis and intertextual representation of fieldwork' (Denzin and Lincoln 1998, 30).

The author employed reflexivity to highlight particular aspects of her decision-making process throughout the data analysis phase. She referred to the synopses, and summaries, that were drafted throughout the interviews, drawing on what she felt the participants had expressed in response to the interview questions (Anand 2019).

Theoretical framework

In this book, Jean Anyon's analysis of social class and Pierre Bourdieu's idea of social reproduction serve as the theoretical foundation. Bourdieu's sociological theory offers a detailed framework to examine social reproduction through education (Bourdieu 1990). Bourdieu discusses the methods in which the education system has been most responsible for the transmission of social inequality in modern societies (Bourdieu and Passeron 1990). He argues that school provides not only the transmission of technical knowledge and skills, but also socialisation into a cultural tradition (Bourdieu 1990).

Bourdieu says that the educational inequality prevailing in schools can only be explained by examining both economic and cultural relations (Schwartz 1997, 191). Such inequality deflects attention from, and contributes to, the misrecognition of its social reproduction function. In other words, schools are central to this process of production and reproduction, including the social stratification and the sustaining of dominant power. Bourdieu's theoretical framework also explains that interactions between habitus,[7] capital[8] and the field determine the differentiated social relations in society (Webb et al. 2002). The author thus used Bourdieu's conceptualised significant concepts such as field, habitus and capital as features of an interconnected system and applied them to provide an in-depth exploration of differences in teachers' pedagogical responses to teaching India–Pakistan relations (see Chapters 4, 5 and 6).

Chapters 4 and 5 explain how teachers' experiences are constructed by the social class[9] of their school. In this book, SES and social class have been used interchangeably to illustrate their relationship with habitus. Scholars often use social class or social stratification as a measure of SES (Magnuson and Duncan 2006), and a few studies on children's academic performance have often used social class in the place of SES.

---

7   Habitus is acquired through socialisation and assimilation into society or schools, and thus influences how teachers and students construct attitudes (Bourdieu and Passeron 1977). Habitus is a conceptual tool that influences attitudes and tendencies that an individual develops because of their interactions with others and their surfacing actions (Bourdieu 1998; Reay 1998; Nash 2005). It also provides an insight into the dispositions, attitudes and experiences that work as a mediating factor between the individual and their world (Bourdieu and Passeron 1977).

8   Bourdieu's concept of capital refers to the amount of economic, cultural, social and symbolic resources that an individual possesses.

9   Social class is a "societal division based on family income, education, occupation and material possessions" (Spring 2011).

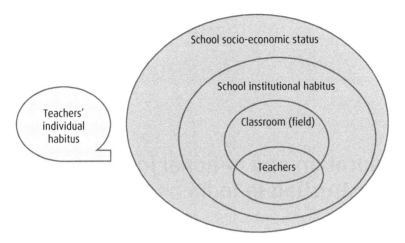

Figure 1.1.School SES, habitus and teachers, based on the literature reviewed. Source: the author.

Figure 1.1 illustrates how the three inner circles—habitus, classroom (or field), and teachers—are individually influenced by the SES of the school in the outer circle. It demonstrates how the school's SES creates institutional habits. An institutional habitus is a collection of biases, assumptions, and viewpoints based on how schools are set up (Reay et al. 2001). It is crucial in understanding how a school, "with its own configuration of ideas, practises, and activities," is universal (Atkinson 2016, 333). The bubble represents how the institutional habitus negates the teachers' individual habitus, which is why it is not transmitted in the classroom field (discussed further in Chapter 5).

Individual habitus is created with emotional dilemmas in diverse social structures (Bourdieu and Passerson 1990). It includes family habitus, which refers to 'the deeply ingrained system of perspectives, experiences and predispositions family members share' (Reay 1998, 527). This partially accounts for why, in this book, teachers' attitudes reveal contradictions. Each teacher's attitudes to his or her socialisation histories – and habitus – are constitutive of diverse social fields that have diverse values (discussed further in Chapter 5).

This chapter has provided a brief overview of India-Pakistan relations, the methodology, and the role of education in the formation of national identities. The next chapter provides a detailed analysis of how education has been used in both India and Pakistan to encourage the creation of national identities.

2
Education and national identity construction in India and Pakistan

This chapter first presents how education has been used to build national unity that results in identity construction in societies (Miller 1988; Gellner 1983) and nationalism (Anderson 1991; Smith 2002). It then presents the literature on the significance of education (the curriculum and textbooks) in the construction of national identity in India and Pakistan (Apple 1993). Schools and textbooks are the primary vehicles through which societies impart national narratives, establishing a clear link between education and nationalism. Textbooks play an important role in constructing a national narrative out of which national identity can be formed (Hussain and Safiq 2016). This chapter then looks at how textbooks published by the National Council for Education Research and Training (NCERT) in India, from 1998 up to 2014, interpret and enact policy objectives or guidelines to depict particularly Pakistan, Muslim and India–Pakistan relations. In Pakistan, the integration of Islam with the Pakistani identity is also reflected in education policies, curricula and textbooks. Finally, this chapter shows how Pakistani textbooks from 1960 to 2009 interpret and put into practise policy objectives or instructions, in this case to portray primarily India, Hindus, and India-Pakistan relations.

National identity construction and education

According to Todorov's theory of identity creation, 'there is a predetermined pattern to the way identities are coded or structured' (cited in Lall 2008, 5). In this pattern, the other is coded as identical to us, and in that scenario he or she is recognised as an equal (Lall 2008). When the other is labelled as distinct from us, this difference is transformed into inequality (Lall 2008). A group of people are bound together by shared qualities to form a nation. (Miller 1988). Hence, creating a shared national past is necessary for nation-building. It requires the creation of ancestor mythologies, historical memories, and a shared culture that can foster a shared sense of national identity. (Miller 1988). Every nation is inevitably imagined since it stretches beyond immediate experience – it embraces far more people than those with whom nationals are individually accustomed and far more places than they have visited (Anderson 1991). Nationalism highlights the 'imagined community' of the nation, as envisaged by Anderson (1991, 9), that is brought about by separating the world into 'us' and 'them' to produce internal coherence. It eliminates differences linked with characteristic features, such as ethnicity, gender, social class, religion, sexuality and language, all of which separate people internally (Gellner 1983).

National identity is learned and internalised through socialisation (Apple 1993). Since education is the most important institution of socialisation after the family, its significance to the construction of national identities is widely acknowledged. Education is an essential tool of 'social control that underlines the protection of the social system (its knowledge, status, stratification and power)' (Freire 1998,7). Every society uses the school and its textbooks as an essential medium to store, transmit and legitimise knowledge, as well as to make sure this is internalised by the young. Education is a necessary instrument of politics as noted by Freire (1988). He goes on to argue that:

> Neutral education cannot exist. It is fundamental for us to know, when we work on the content of the educational curriculum, when we discuss methods and processes, when we plan, when we draw up educational policies, we are engaged in political acts which imply an ideological choice; whether it is obscure or clear is not important. (Freire 1998, 18–19)

Education also acts as a medium of cultural action that indoctrinates conformity and cultivates the youngest generation in the existing order. It is never neutral: the inherently political nature of education relies on those whose interests it highlights, in which form and for what purpose it exists (Freire 1970).

Schools are assumed to have the relative autonomy of the educational system, which 'enables it to serve external demands under the guise of independence and neutrality, i.e., to conceal the social functions it performs and so to perform them more effectively' (Bourdieu and Passeron 1977, 178). By connecting power and culture, the hegemonic curriculum operates in schools by highlighting the political interests fundamental to the selection and distribution of bodies of knowledge (Aronowitz and Giroux 1985, 81). Education is politicised, with differential cultural, economic and political power being part of an 'indissoluble couplet' (Apple 1993, 10). Powerful parties or social movements create educational policies to make their knowledge legitimate, defend their patterns of social mobility and increase their power in the social arena (Apple 1993).

In addition, schools play a significant role in establishing the connection between knowledge and cultural or economic power. They are powerful institutions that are often instrumental in generating structural inequalities of power and access to resources (Apple 2004, 64). Schools are also responsible for the distribution of ideological knowledge and values, wherein the educational system comprises a set of institutions crucial to the production of knowledge (Apple 2001, 21). The curriculum is important in states involved in the construction of national identity (Lall 2008). The disputes on the curriculum range beyond the discussions of 'what content we want to teach to our young' to incorporate multifaceted inquiries 'of who we are' as well as 'how to represent this identity in the curriculum' (Durrani and Dunne 2010, 218). A curriculum is a tool for determining 'relations of power in which the strongest voices are of those who have the most economic, cultural and social capital' (Apple 2004, 229). It is the first medium through which specific pictures of imaginary 'national' values are constructed. 'Official knowledge' is constructed in and through the process of education (Apple 1993, 229).

The curriculum is not a neutral assemblage of knowledge; it is always considered to be a part of 'selective tradition' or some group's vision of legitimate knowledge (Kumar 2001, 10). Apple (1993, 22–3) suggests that 'there is always a politics of official knowledge', whereby politics is incorporated with conflict into neutral interpretations of the world and elite conceptions to empower specific groups over others. The official knowledge is connected to a group's power in the broader political and economic arena. Power and culture are viewed as attributes of economic relations within a society. The curriculum is regarded as a medium by which education can lead to the construction of national consciousness among students (Bernstein 2000). It is an essential source for either producing or reproducing a national consciousness for horizontal solidarity. The curriculum acts as a medium to create vertical hierarchies among distinct social groups within the nation. The official knowledge delivered by the state and distributed among educational institutions establishes distinct identities (Bernstein 2000).

Syllabi, textbooks, and teacher manuals are examples of curriculum resources that are crucial for describing how to conduct lessons in the classroom (Cohen, Raudenbush and Ball 2003). Teachers often use these curriculum materials as tools (Ball and Cohen 1996). The curriculum and textbooks do not supply 'neutral knowledge' because their content reflects complex interplays between power and politics (Apple and Christian-Smith 1991, 22). The curriculum is an important reference point for teachers, predominantly in developing countries, where it is prearranged in the official textbook and teacher guides, frequently the sole resource used by teachers (Alexander and Alexander 2018).

Teachers' pedagogic approaches, strategies and practices consequently serve to enact the curriculum. The curriculum links the macro (formally designated educational goals and content) with the micro (the act of teaching and valuation in the classroom or school) and is predominantly seen as 'a series of translations, transpositions and transformations' (Alexander and Alexander 2018, 16). The official curriculum is implemented and, in the procedure, becomes transformed, as 'teachers and students interpret, modify and add to the meaning embodied in the official specification' (Alexander and Alexander 2018, 16).

As discussed briefly in the previous chapter, the history curriculum is particularly fundamental to the construction of a 'national collective self-concept' and the process of educating 'successive generations about the frontiers of the national community' and its resrelation to the 'other' (Durand and Kaempf 2014, 333). The following sections present the significance of history education in nation-building and the construction of national identity in India and Pakistan. The two countries offer unique insights into the relationship between the history curriculum and national identity construction as they share a common history. It is consequently insightful to explore how interpretations of this history vary across and within each country (Durrani, Kaderi and Anand 2020). The following section also provides insight into how history textbooks are intertwined with the 'politics of memory' in each nation, with a focus on how the nation is imagined in opposition to the "other" and the impacts that such national imaginaries have on social relations both within and outside of each nation (Durrani, Kaderi and Anand 2020).

Textbooks' revisions and national identity construction in India

This section looks at the work of the National Council for Education Research and Training (NCERT) in India, specifically over the period between 1998 and 2014. In particular, it considers how the NCERT interpreted and enacted policy objectives or guidelines to portray Pakistan, Muslim and India–Pakistan relations (Batra 2005; Lall 2008; Guichard 2010; Kumar 2018).

Bharatiya Janata Party (BJP)-driven changes and 'saffronisation' in education (1998–2004)

From 1998 to 2004 the BJP used education policy as an instrument for promoting and spreading its Hindu nationalist ideology. After gaining power, leaders of the BJP occupied the key posts in the education system of the central government and consequently introduced changes in curriculum and textbooks (Taneja 2003). The BJP aimed to inculcate the ideology of Hindutva into future generations. Hindutva[1] is founded on the basis that 'India is a Hindu nation primarily and non-Hindus living in the country have a choice either to accept the majority's domination or leave the country' (Lall 2008, 158). This intolerant opinion is directed at non-Hindu communities, specifically the Muslim community, which are considered to be 'separate' and 'second-class citizens' (Lall 2008, 158). Muslims are also suspected of having loyalties outside India, connected to the Islamic world or Pakistan. The 'exclusivist interpretation of Hinduism'

---

1 In the essay 'Hindutva: Who is Hindu?' Veer Savarkar wrote that 'Hindutva is not identical with what is vaguely indicated by the term Hinduism'. The Hindutva forces also want to amend the Constitution of India, remove keywords and turn India into a theocratic state based upon 'systemic inequality', 'anti-egalitarianism' and 'elitism' – where the Hindus will have supremacy over all the other religious minorities. Hindutva ideologues were inspired by the nationalist, racial, supremacist and cultural values of both Nazism and Zionism. Over the decades that combined influence has become 'culturally internalised' within the Sangh Parivar (Chaudhuri 2020, para. 4; Anand and Lall 2022).

positions itself in opposition to an 'inclusive' and 'tolerant approach' to citizens belonging to different religions (Lall 2008, 158).

The BJP appointed scholars to rewrite the history textbooks because the old textbooks (drafted by Congress) were secular; they did not focus on Hindu achievements nor attempt to increase Hindu pride among learners (Guichard 2010). The revised curriculum and textbooks surrendered precision to meet the nationalist goals and utilised history as an instrument for propaganda. Guichard (2010, 2) analyses the debates and 'the virulence of the arguments; between the opposing parties (BJP and Congress), clearly showing that the controversy was not about scientific and educational concerns but opposing views of Indian history'. Guichard explains that

> it [the discussion] was caused, fuelled and sustained, instead, by deeply rooted, diverging conceptions of the Indian nation and the nation's history. One group defended secular historiography and conception of the nation and the other a Hindu nationalist one. (Guichard 2010, 3)

The controversy provided a medium for the supporters of these two opposing views to reintegrate or represent their arguments (Guichard 2010). The National Curriculum Framework (NCF) 2000 emphasised the battle between competing national identity identities, which had an impact on India's public and political discourse for two decades. (Habib 2005; Lall and Vickers 2009). The NCF 2000 viewed social science as a subject that could deliver general knowledge and teach skills, enabling learners to contribute to their society (NCF 2000, 62).

The NCF 2000 was intended to construct skills and values such as 'critical thinking, reading, interpreting tables, diagrams, and maps, cooperating with others and responding to other problems' (NCF 2000, 62). The phrases 'cooperating with others' and 'responding to other problems' highlighted the values that needed to be established; 'critical thinking, reading and interpreting tables, diagrams and maps' represented the skills that needed to be developed (NCF 2000, 62). The NCF 2000 offered no explanation and association between the values and skills, as mentioned above (Habib 2005). The description of critical thinking was limited to the development of cognitive skills, instead of the critical investigation of hostile social realities to generate social change, as associated with the tradition of critical pedagogy (Habib 2005, 9).

The aim of NCF 2000 was the uncritical glorification of India (Habib 2005). It highlights the 'humane and national perspective and inculcate[s] a sense of pride in the country and in being an Indian'; it also strengthens the national identity and develops an appreciation for cultural heritage (NCF 2000, 62). These objectives were the primary reasons for developing nationalistic and chauvinistic attitudes among the citizens of India. Habib highlights that citizens should not be unquestionably proud of their country; instead they should develop a critical understanding of the conflicts and problems that exist in the nation (Habib 2005). In addition, the NCF 2000 aimed to 'promote communal harmony and social cohesion' by eradicating the rigid social structures and practices to develop a democratic society (NCF 2000, 62). However, it did not explain the ways in which this desired harmony or cohesion were to be brought about. The NCF 2000 thus made no argument on what basis disharmony and disintegration are affecting society, nor on the need to promote critical awareness among learners (Batra 2005).

The aim of BJP through the NCF 2000 was

> blatant distortions and even hatred … not for simple narrow political gain but to enable a slow insidious reconstruction in the public mind and public domain of what India is and what it should be. Exclusions and denials of rights and liberties of religious minorities, Dalits and all women were a singular part of that agenda.
> (Setalvad 2005, 8)

The BJP sought 'fundamentalisation' of education in distinct spheres and levels through documents or textbooks. These measures were performed to promote the superiority of Hindu culture over others and to threaten religious minorities such as Muslims (Lall 2008, 176). The main objective of the subject of history, as part of education, was highlighted as the development of the 'national spirit' and 'national consciousness' by instigating pride among the youngest generations about India's past or distinctive religio-philosophical ethos, presented as Hindu (Lall 2008, 176).

In response, the Communist Party and left-wing historians introduced various campaigns against history textbooks (Lall 2008). Polarisation reached a height in 2001 when Arjun Singh, who was to be appointed Education Minister under the Congress-led coalition government in 2004, criticised the BJP for 'talibanising' the writing of history (Lall 2008, 176). The BJP defended the case by 'claiming that it had actually helped to free history from the vestiges of colonisation: far from attempting to talibanise education', the goal of their action was in fact 'de-Macaulisation' (Lall 2008, 176).

During the general elections of 2004, the BJP-led coalition party lost its power to the Congress-led United Progressive Alliance (UPA). The UPA government then undertook to 'detoxify' school education (Guichard 2010, 5). The revised curriculum and textbooks were published between 2005 and 2007 by the National Curriculum Framework 2005; they were focused on promoting an unbiased and more accurate view and of history. The textbooks sought to provide a more neutral view of history; they strove for historical accuracy and adopted ideas from both political parties, reducing the level of textbook controversy (Guichard 2010, 5) as a result. These developments are discussed in more detail below.

Congress and 'de-saffronisation' of education (2004–14)

The National Council of Educational Research and Training (NCERT) framed another document, known as the National Curriculum Framework (NCF) of 2005, under the leadership of Professor Krishna Kumar, the former director (2004–10) of the NCERT. The NCF 2005 highlights a widespread break and a paradigm shift from the NCF 2000 in several critical ways. The document has been established through an intricate process of 'curriculum deliberation' (Kumar 2018, 154) – a process that has continued for years and served to shape one of the most progressive curriculum documents in India (Gupta 2015). The NCF 2005 has been commended by its supporters (Sadgopal 2005; Setalvad 2005; Thapar 2005) for being the consequence of hard work by individuals who would like to see India on the path of democracy, justice, peace and secularism.

The paradigmatic change in India's educational landscape highlights, with specific reference to social studies, a shift from 'traditional social studies' (Leming 1994, 153) to 'critical social studies' or 'social studies for social change' (Hursh and Ross 2000; Kumar 2018, 154). In the NCF 2005 social science was considered an important method of delivering knowledge to construct a fair and peaceful society. The central principle of the document was to encourage teachers to raise students' awareness (NCF 2005, 50). It also connected the curriculum to critical thinking and developing a critical awareness of the social reality among learners (NCF 2005).

The NCF 2005 aimed to deliver social, cultural and analytical skills (NCF 2005, 50) and to assist learners in adapting to interdependent social reality, instead of inducing a concept of nationalism. It targeted social change and democratisation by emphasising 'concepts and the ability to analyse sociopolitical realities rather than [focusing] on mere retention of information without comprehension' (NCF 2005, 50). It adopted the 'normative dimensions of social science' and focused on the evolution of human values such as freedom, trust, mutual respect and respect for diversity (Thapar 2005, 56; NCF 2005, 51) – concepts crucial to the foundation of a peaceful and just society.

In addition, the NCF 2005 established a connection between the local and the global via the national. It focused on teaching history through references, with the help of local understanding when considering the national events, and then connecting Indian history with evolution in other parts of the world (NCF 2005). This approach had the potential to broaden learners' minds, enabling them to accommodate and assimilate the multiple perspectives of historical events or processes (NCF 2005, 3). As Setalvad (2005, 9) explains:

> NCF 2005 has consciously divided the critical issues of structural denials to large sections of our population any forms of education … that have not simply been perpetuated over the last 58 years, but have sharply grown through the years after 1992 with the withdrawal of the State from its basis Constitutional Mandate – to ensure UEE (Universalization of Elementary Education) to each Indian child, regardless of gender, caste or community.

The aim of 'Universalization of Elementary Education (UEE)' was to foster democracy (as a way of life) by integrating respect for constitutional values of plurality and secularism into learners (Setalvad 2005). The NCF 2005 promoted 'constructivism' as a mode of pedagogy without considering the requirement to build rich resources in schools and to hire professionally trained teachers (Setalvad 2005, 9).

The series of textbooks, which the Congress government issued in 2006, was intended to represent a mainstream style of Indian history with less historical assumptions and interpretations. Textbooks provided a detailed account of distinct historical topics, such as urbanity in the Indus Valley Civilisation (IVC)[2] and an understanding of how Hindus evolved in their interpretation of history (Bhattacharya 2008). Textbooks were intended to moderate the impact of 'textbook culture by counselling learners to think critically' (Guichard 2010, 74). However, in these textbooks, the unclear topics that require partisan lines (such as beef consumption) are left out. By omitting controversial topics, these

---

2   The Indus Valley Civilisation (IVC), or Harappan Civilisation, was a Bronze Age civilisation within the north-western regions of South Asia. It is a territory that spread from northeast Afghanistan to Pakistan and north-west India.

textbooks reduced the learning of students who should instead be introduced to such topics and encouraged to debate them academically in an unbiased way (Guichard 2010, 11).

Neeladri Bhattacharya, the principal consultant for the history textbooks, recognises the former textbooks (published by the NCERT under the BJP Government in 2000) as a 'narrative of the nation' in which '[t]he idea of the unity of India was projected back into the past and history was read as a gradual unfolding of the nation' (Bhattacharya 2009, 106–7). He explains that in designing the third set of textbooks they tried to problematise the nation and its unfolding in the historical narrative in numerous ways, in order to propose that 'the territorial boundaries of the nation-state need not be the only valid unit of historical study' (Bhattacharya 2009, 106). This was done by changing the focus of the narrative, shifting its focal point away from the nation. The textbooks are designed to emphasise that diverse communities 'have specific histories that cannot be encapsulated within the story of the nation' (Bhattacharya 2009, 106–7). Textbooks also distanced themselves from the nation as a unit of analysis by turning to the history of everyday life (Bhattacharya 2009, 106–7; Guichard 2010).

Additionally, the NCF 2005 altered how people thought of themselves as citizens by integrating citizenship education into critical pedagogy and human rights frameworks, giving students 'an opportunity to reflect critically on issues in terms of their political, social, economic and moral aspects' (NCF 2005, 23). In so doing, it sought to encourage students to accept 'multiple views on social issues' through 'democratic forms of interaction' (ibid). This, along with the constructivist approach to learning, created ample space for students to participate actively in the construction of knowledge through 'negotiation of meaning' (NCF 2005, 17) and 'sharing of multiple views' (ibid) as part of a collaborative process. This in turn made it possible for a teacher to go beyond the textbook and to accept more than one 'right' answer from the students. Scholars (Guichard 2010; Setalvard 2005; Thapar 2005) have only evaluated the NCF 2005 with regard to its guidance and aims; their work thus lacks a detailed analysis of the new curriculum and textbooks in relation to the depiction of the other faith (Muslims), other country (Pakistan) and India–Pakistan relations. The following sections present how the NCERT textbook portrays Pakistan and India–Pakistan relations and how it is used by teacher participants.

In the history textbook (T1),[3] the chapter titled *Understanding Partition: Politics, memories, experiences* (pp. 376–404) presents the reasons for the partition of India and the creation of Pakistan.

> The name Pakistan or Pak-stan (from Punjab, Afghan, Kashmir, Sind and Baluchistan) was coined by a Punjabi Muslim student at Cambridge, Choudhry Rehmat Ali, who, in pamphlets written in 1933 and 1935, desired a separate national status for this new entity. No one took Rehmat Ali seriously in the 1930s, least of all the League and other Muslim leaders who dismissed his idea as a student's dream. (T1, 386)

The chapter begins by presenting partition experiences, narrated by people who had experienced partition, to an Indian researcher in 1993:'how those who had lived more or less harmoniously for generations inflicted so much violence on each other in 1947' (T1, 377). In the same textbook and chapter, partition is not depicted as an event of religious strife between Hindus and Muslims, but as a complex historical event, the consequence of of multiple social and political factors. The section titled 'Partition or Holocaust?' does not equate violence during partition with the Holocaust, but it does use the term 'ethnic cleansing' (T1, 376). It begins with the causes that resulted in the partition of India and the 'harrowing experiences of ordinary people during the period 1946–50 and beyond' (T1, 376). The textbook explains why partition, like the Holocaust in Germany, is remembered.

> The narratives just presented point to the pervasive violence that characterized Partition. Several hundred thousand people were killed and innumerable women raped and abducted. Millions were uprooted, transformed into refugees in alien lands. The survivors themselves have often spoken of 1947 through other words: 'maashal-la' (martial law), 'mara-mari' (killings), and 'raula' or 'hullar' (disturbance, tumult, uproar). Speaking of the killings, rape, arson and loot that constituted Partition, contemporary observers and scholars have sometimes used the expression 'holocaust' as well, primarily meaning destruction or slaughter on a mass scale. (T1, 380–1)

---

3   *Themes in Indian History*. III. NCERT. Delhi. (12th Grade).

Nationalism scholars (Giesen 2004; Greenberg 2005) have noticed the association between traumatic events, national identity and cultural trauma theory. They highlight a framework for interpreting how traumatic events become trauma narratives (Debs 2013). There is a generational outcome whereby the hostility of a painful and traumatic historical event can only be taken up by a generation detached from the experience (Giesen 2004; Greenberg 2005). As with the Holocaust, this seems to be predominantly factual for those who survived partition; numerous historians have their associations with the children of partition survivors (Butalia 1998; Chakrabarty 2002).

Additionally, Greenberg (2005) and Geisen (2004) contend that it frequently requires more time to recollect events like the Holocaust and the Partition. For instance, it took time for the Holocaust to become recognised as a social experience and to acquire national specific connotations in the United States (Alexander 2013), Israel (Alexander and Dromi 2011), and Germany from being merely "a historical fact" (Debs 2013, 638) as it was described by historians like Reitlinger (1953). (Giesen 2004). In a process whereby strong mediators choose, modify, or transform trauma narratives and connect them to current frames, the cultural trauma-based narratives are therefore important for the development of national identity (Anand 2019).

In addition, the textbook outlines the reasons for the partition of India by highlighting the two-nation theory and discusses Britain's divide-and-rule policy. The strategy of 'divide and rule' is a tool used in history to sustain imperial rule (Sandhu 2009). This policy recognises previous ethno-religious separations in society and subsequently influences them (ethno-religious separations) to avoid ruling through outsiders. The British implemented this strategy to reinforce the Raj (Sandhu 2009). India is depicted as a country where there were no communal difficulties before the British. The British, the Muslim League and Muhammad Ali Jinnah are criticised for 'sowing the seeds of communalism' in the country. The dominant message is the sacredness of a unified India (Sandhu 2009, 10).

This version of partition as an event that was done to us by the other, an event that could and should have been avoided were it not for the British and the Muslim League and Jinnah, resonates with the narrative in the earlier textbook. It is also a popular line of rhetoric in India. However, causal associations between the occurrence of partition and the contemporary communal difficulties between Hindus and Muslims would be useful for students (Anand 2019).

The textbook also depicts the role played by the Hindu Mahasabha[4] in British India. It provides a history of the electoral politics between the Muslim League[5] and the Congress, making reference to the Lucknow Pact,[6] the Pakistan Resolution and the growth of the Rashtriya Swayamsevak Sangh (RSS).[7] The textbook declares

> The origins of the Pakistan demand have also been traced back to the Urdu poet Mohammad Iqbal, the writer of 'Sare Jahan Se Achha Hindustan Hamara'. In his presidential address to the Muslim League in 1930, the poet spoke of a need for a 'North-West Indian Muslim state'. Iqbal, however, was not visualising the emergence of a new country in that speech, but a reorganisation of Muslim-majority areas in north-western India into an autonomous unit within a single, loosely structured Indian federation [*sic*]. (T1, 386–7)

There is relatively little introduction to Muhammad Ali Jinnah. Only a limited description of his vision is provided, along with discussion of reasons for forming the Muslim League. The Muslim League is placed in one box and the Hindu Mahasabha in another (T1, 385). There is a gap and omission in the discussion of the actual partition negotiations between Pakistani nationalists and Indian right-wingers, and the formation of the Muslim League (1906) and the Aga Khan-led Simla Deputation are both omitted. However, the author does provide some questions to urge students and teachers to engage critically with historical events:

> Some scholars see Partition as a culmination of a communal politics that started developing in the opening debates decades of the

---

4   Hindu Mahasabha is a Hindu nationalist political party in India, formed to protect the rights of the Hindu community in British India. It was 'founded in 1915' and is described as 'a Hindu party that remained confined to North India. It aimed to unite Hindu society by encouraging the Hindus to transcend the divisions of caste and sect. It sought to define Hindu identity in opposition to Muslim identity' (T1, 385).

5   Muslim League, also known as All India Muslim League. It was founded in 1906 to safeguard the rights of Indian Muslims at the time of the partition of British India (1947).

6   The Lucknow Pact was drafted by the Indian National Congress (headed by Bal Gangadhar Tilak) and the All-India Muslim League (headed by Muhammad Ali Jinnah). The meeting at Lucknow marked the reunion of moderate and radical wings of the Congress. The pact dealt with the structure of the government of India and the relationship between the Hindu and Muslim communities.

7   Rashtriya Swayamsevak Sangh (RSS) is an Indian right-wing and Hindu nationalist organisation. It is regarded as the parent organisation of the Bharatiya Janata Party (BJP). The RSS is one of the principal organisations of the Sangh Parivar group.

twentieth century. They suggest that separate electorates for Muslims, created by the colonial government in 1909 and expanded in 1919, crucially shaped the nature of communal politics. (T1, 383)

What was the League [Muslim League] demanding? Was it demanding Pakistan as we know it today? (T1, 387)

The textbook portrays Mahatma Gandhi[8] as 'a voice in the wilderness' in his opposition to partition.

The textbook also depicts how North Indian Muslims felt about partition in comparison with those in Punjab and Bengal. It urges students to read Saadat Hasan Manto,[9] especially the section entitled 'Regional Variations (T1, 397). The section 'Fiction, Poetry, Films' (T1, 398) briefly describes Manto (in a box); it encourages teachers and students to be critically engaged and to explore the short stories, novels, poems and films about partition (those that define and unite Indo–Pakistani history). The partition of India is extensively depicted by case studies and oral histories which endeavour to illustrate the narratives on India–Pakistan relations critically for readers. The textbook encourages teachers to discuss the stories they have heard about partition in their families or societies (T1, 382). Exercises in the textbook (T1) also require students to work in groups to summarise the issues on partition addressed in the textbook and to conduct research (for project work) on partition.[10]

The textbook portrays the different perspectives of the conflicting parties (India or Pakistan) by describing the role of stereotypes in India and Pakistan.

India-haters in Pakistan and Pakistan-haters in India are both products of Partition. At times, some people mistakenly believe that the loyalties of Indian Muslims lie with Pakistan. The stereotype of extra-territorial, pan-Islamic loyalties comes fused with other highly objectionable ideas: Muslims are cruel, bigoted, unclean, descendants of invaders, while Hindus are kind, liberal, pure, children of the invaded. The journalist R.M. Murphy has shown that similar stereotypes proliferate in Pakistan. (T1, 381)

---

8 Mahatma Gandhi was the leader of the Indian independence movement against British rule.
9 Saadat Hasan Manto was an author. He became famous for writing short stories about South Asian history.
10 'Discuss… Find out more about ways in which people supported one another and saved lives during Partition' (T1, 400).

The relationship between Pakistan and India has been profoundly shaped by his [Gandhi's] legacy of Partition. Perceptions of communities [Indians and Pakistanis] on both sides [India and Pakistan] have been structured by the conflicting memories of those momentous times [partition/migration]. (T1, 382)

In addition, the oral narratives[11] are used to encourage students to 'try and imagine how the same stories would be narrated by different communities' (T1, 382). In the section entitled 'Some partition experiences' (T1, 377), the oral histories of Pakistani or Indian informants are presented, challenging students to understand how those who had lived harmoniously for generations could inflict such violence on each other. These sources are as follows:

I am simply returning my father's karz, his debt. (T1, 377)

In this source, an Indian man confronts the librarian at the Punjab University Library about the motivations for his generosity. The librarian explains that the man belongs to Jammu, where during partition an old Hindu woman protected his father's life. The librarian says he is reimbursing that debt.

For quite a few years now, I have not met a Punjabi Musalman. (T1, 378)

In source 2, a former male staff member (who belonged to the Pakistan High Commission in Delhi) asks directions from a Sikh man in Delhi. The staff member introduces himself as Iqbal Ahmed from Lahore. The Sikh man whom he addresss, Sardarji, exclaims, 'Stop! Stop!' Mr Ahmed thought that he would be stabbed, but he was hugged instead. 'It's been years since I met a Punjabi Musalman,' Sardarji explained. 'No, no! You can never be ours.' (T1, 379)

The oral history outlines not only migrants' experiences of postpartition, but also a spectrum of positions from a Pakistani perspective towards India/Hindus/Sikhs. The sources above in the T1 also attempt to

---

11 Oral history is a narrative approach that gathers personal reflections of events from individuals or groups and illustrates how these events affect the individual group being studied (Creswell 2013, 74).

encourage teachers and students to reflect[12] on peoples' attitudes, and the ways in which they identify themselves/others in sources. This is because oral history education enables teachers and students to introduce historical evidence from the underside, shift the historical focus, open new areas of inquiry and challenge assumptions about the past. Oral history has long been a crucial pedagogical tool whereby different civilisations teach their citizens about the past (Llewellyn and Ng-A-Fook 2017). However, considering the critical nature of India–Pakistan relations, it might be helpful for textbooks to provide a basic introduction to Pakistan. It would be beneficial for students to learn about Pakistan from the more balanced textbooks rather than from other sources – such as community storytelling or oral histories, films and the media – where the potential for subjective interpretation is quite high (Banerjee and Stöber 2016).

The textbook contrasts two hostile narratives of the conflict-ridden history of India–Pakistan relations (particularly the partition of India and the role of stereotypes). In doing so it presents these narratives side by side on two columns of each page, separating them through a blank space designed to encourage pupils to develop their own understanding of the contested past. The intention underlying the textbook is for students to become equipped to acknowledge, understand and respect (without having to accept) the narrative of the other. (Adwan et al. 2016, x) Perhaps, by exposing students to narrative plurality as well as diversity concerning the past, this method is believed to be democratic. It also creates chances for dialogue as well as reconciliation by encouraging students to question as well as critique and to reconsider exclusive, seemingly irreconcilable cluster narratives and predetermined truths (Anand 2019).

History is thus not presented just as a narrative, but as a subject of inquiry and debate, a new approach in the context of Indian schools. The textbook also stipulates practical activities. It addresses the partition of India and Pakistan by requesting teachers and students to discuss the historical documents. However, the textbook does not list the documents to be selected or suggest how to implement them didactically in the classroom (as discussed further in Chapter 5). This implies that the

---

12 Questions such as:
'1 What do each of these sources show about the attitudes of the men who were talking with each other?'
'2 What do you think these stories reveal about the different memories that people carried about Partition?'
'3 How did the men identify themselves and one another?' (T1, 379).

curriculum provides the flexibility to teachers to engage students in examining broad social issues through a lens of ideological and critical perspectives (Anand 2019).

In general, the history textbook is descriptive and leaves out the contentious issues. In addition, it says nothing about disputes between Muslims and Hindus. The textbook's goals are to promote equality and portray the nation as secular (Guichard 2010). The silence represents an explicit decision taken by the Congress government. The textbook has thus diminished the learning of students by omitting details of controversial issues (Guichard 2010). The process of ending incitement, hatred and misrepresentation of the other (country or faith) in sustained violent conflict can indeed become challenging (Fitzduff and Stout 2006; Bar-Tal 2013). The partition of India requires attention because familiarising students with this critical historical event, even at a young age, might be beneficial. Otherwise their young minds will have to access information from various other sources (Bannerjee and Stöber 2016).

This section shows that the United Progressive Alliance (UPA)[13] textbooks presented a more neutral view, preserving historical accuracy while borrowing ideas from both political parties in India. The textbook intended to disrupt the authority of both historian and textbook, empowering the student to formulate new ideas about the topic. The textbook content on partition resonates with the objectives of NCF 2005, namely to teach by providing multiple perspectives and opportunities for critical engagement with the topic (Chhabra 2016, 243).

The textbook depicts more neutral and positive images of Pakistan and Muslims. There may be various reasons for this. First, the textbooks may be predisposed to such an approach by the liberal intellectuals involved in curriculum planning and textbook production (Guichard 2010). The textbook associated with 'Congress rule' depicted India as a composite culture where communalism symbolised one of the major challenges facing modern India and one of the root causes of partition. The national 'we' of the 'seculars' is depicted as inclusive, comprising Hindus, Muslims and other groups (Gottlob 2007). Second, the unstated aim of NCERT is that if the India–Pakistan conflict remains poorly understood and under-analysed, it may not be questioned (Haydock 2015). The choice of a 'rhetoric of silence' (Laurence 1983, 10)

---

13 The United Progressive Alliance (UPA) is a coalition of centre-left political parties in India. It was formed after the 2004 general election.

underlying official textbook work has been determined by several considerations which are reinforced by faith or a political pretext, connected to the advantage of the passage of time (De Baets 2015, 18).

In the textbook itself, the unsettled postcolonial historical past is either omitted outright or is reduced to a list of names and dates to avoid controversy (Bentrovato 2017). It presents the explanation of historical events in contrast with the moving language and condemnations that appeared in the previous NCERT textbooks (published before 2005). The textbook reflects on oral histories or memories, positions of memory politics and symbolism, making them subject to debate in the classroom (Banerjee and Stöber 2016). This section raises queries about the insufficient engagement of Indian textbooks with the partition of 1947. This implies that classroom discussions should emphasise the causes of the partition of India, while the violence that took place during this period is not adequately addressed. The classroom could be an ideal place for sensitive debates rather than exposing the young mind to an argumentative rhetoric of the outside world that is quite visible in the case of India–Pakistan (Tripathi and Raghuvanshi 2020).

The generalisations above mask contextual nuances and shifts across time. In all contexts, the history curriculum and textbooks have undergone revisions, prompted not solely by pedagogical or academic interests but also by a strong political agenda. Nevertheless, the NCERT textbooks series 3 (under the Congress government) in India were groundbreaking in terms of offering multiple perspectives on history and encouraging students to engage critically with textbook topics. Yet even these textbooks made little difference to the dominant pedagogy of transmitting information as predefined truths, particularly within an examination-oriented system (Durrani, Kaderi and Anand 2020).

In Pakistan, the integration of Islam with the Pakistani identity is also reflected in education policies, curricula and textbooks. Islam is used to converting a multilingual and multi-ethnic population into a nation (Aziz 1993; Rosser 2003; Dean 2005; Nayyar and Salim 2003; Lall 2008). The following section discusses how textbooks in Pakistan, from 1960 to 2009, interpret and enact policy objectives or guidelines to depict particularly India, Hindus and India–Pakistan relations.

National identity and education in Pakistan

During the ruling of (Zia) (1977–88), the curriculum was Islamised. The regime filled the education system with invariable Islamic content, which served as a part of the national policy and executed an entire amendment of the curriculum and textbooks (Lall and Vickers 2009). The 'Islamisation' of the school curriculum heightened the 'sectarian divisions' between Sunni and Shia (Lall and Vickers 2009, 179). The education policy under Zia stated nine national aims of education, four of which highlighted the political agenda of Islam. The ideology of Islam was determinedly integrated into school textbooks and highlighted the Islamic orientation of Pakistani nationalism (Lall and Vickers 2009).

As part of this approach, textbooks were revised and rewritten to Islamise the content and give greater emphasis to an Islamic view of historical events (Nayyar and Salim 2003). They presented Islam 'not simply as a belief system but a political ideology and a grand unifying worldview that must be accepted by all citizens' (Ahmed 2012, 45). Saigol (2005, 120) argues that the Zia era used 'religion as an instrument of homogenization and control became centre stage … Almost all the official sites of knowledge production were put to reimagining an Islamic nation' (Rosser 2003). Zulfikar Ali Bhutto started the practise of erasing, disparaging, and disrespecting the non-Islamic heritage of the subcontinent and identifying it with the "other," which peaked during Zia-ul-Haq. (Rosser 2003). The reimagining of Pakistan as an Islamic state was achieved through the removal of the citizenship of the non-Muslim citizens of Pakistan (Saigol 2005).

Under the leadership of Zulfikar Ali Bhutto, the National Education Policy (NEP) of 1992 attempted to review the marginalisation of non-Muslims as a component of the 1979 policy. This policy marked the extension of the trend to disregard the downward decline and status of non-Muslims in education (Rehman and Zia 2010). The educational system had been reorganised by Zia's interpretation of the Islamic doctrines, such as the 'Ideology of Pakistan'; it suggested that teachers become representatives of the Muslim Ummah by delivering teachings about social sciences (Rehman and Zia 2010). The national education policy of 1992 also ignored the status of non-Muslims in education (Rehman and Zia 2010). It declared that 'the ideology of Islam forms the genesis of the State of Pakistan. The country cannot survive or advance without placing the entire system of education on sound Islamic foundations' (Government of Pakistan 1998, 2). Islam is the foundation for monitoring social practices as well as regulating the evaluative beliefs of Pakistanis (on the function of philosophies see van Dijk 1995). This policy therefore constructed the hegemony of Islam as a discursive framework. However, it neither illustrated which Islamic principles and values would underline the educational philosophy nor specified recognised which aspects of Islam were required in creating 'the good Muslim'.

The policy also insisted on a commitment to Islam to defining the textbook content, and thus excluded the non-Muslim citizens of Pakistan (Vogt 1997, 10). Textbooks used 'totalisation' for fixing the meanings to incorporate all kinds of differences (Naseem 2006, 451). The metaphor of 'oneness' presents the nation as disregarding all differences based on religious belief, regional background, gender and ethnicity. The content of the textbooks disclosed 'that they are insensitive to the religious diversity of the Pakistani society' while 'Islamiyat is not taught as one subject but permeates the teaching of Urdu, English and Social Studies as well' (Lall 2008, 14). The national education policies of the 1980s and 1990s revised the textbooks of Pakistan Studies (as part of the process of greater Islamisation). Hindus and non-Muslims were portrayed as wicked and disloyal, and secular knowledge was likewise viewed with extreme distrust (Hoodbhoy and Nayyar 1985, 174–5).

In 1999 the chief of the army, Pervez Musharraf, overthrew the government of Nawaz Sharif in a military coup. The enforcement of army rule disconnected Pakistan from the world and interrupted the provision of internal help for social development, including in the national education sector (Ziring 2005). In 2001 Musharraf took the office of president and outlined his priorities for good governance: political stability and economic recovery. He initiated the Education Sector Reforms (ESR) by outlining the need for educational reforms and the de-Islamization of the textbooks used in public schools (Lall and Vickers 2009, 188). The events of 11 September 2001 were critical for President Musharraf. He obtained international legitimacy for his government by entering into an alliance with the US and the UK known as the 'War on Terror' (Kronstadt 2004, 112). The various economic benefits were followed by an alliance involving grants and loans to aid economic and social development, which consisted of specific funding from USAID for the national education sector. USAID dedicated $100 million to education development between 2002 and 2007 in Pakistan (Kronstadt 2004). Musharraf defined his approach as 'enlightened moderation', seeking to represent Islam as compatible with modernity and to portray the image of Pakistan as a moderate, tolerant and forward-looking society (Kronstadt 2004, 8; Lall and Saeed

2019). He could not take any revolutionary step forward, as it was difficult to reply to the pre-1970 curricula in the presence of enormous orthodoxy disseminated during the intervening decade of the 1980s (Kronstadt 2004).

The National Curriculum Document (2006) issued by the Government of Pakistan was based on the aims of the National Education Policy (1998–2010). The objective of the document was to frame the school curriculum to 'inculcate among the students the sense of gratitude to Almighty Allah and the sense of patronising behaviour patterns of national character' (Behuria and Shehzad 2013, 10). The additional aims were to spread unity of the Muslim Ummah and to develop and practise the 'Ideology of Pakistan'. This highlights the fact that the philosophy of the curriculum or textbook was based on Islam and the ideology of Pakistan framed under the Parliament Act of 1976 (Behuria and Shehzad 2013, 10).

The national curriculum of 2006 provided a list of guidelines for teachers, noting an urgent need for 'continuous awareness [of] the modern concepts introduced in the educational field' and for a 'proper orientation to establish a commitment to the Islamic beliefs and principles as enunciated in Quran and Sunnah' (Government of Pakistan 2006, 10). In 2007 protests occurred among the Islamic parties regarding the new curriculum's aims of teaching pre-Islamic history, something that could integrate chapters on Hinduism and Buddhism. Instead opponents claimed that Pakistan's history should begin with Mecca and Medina in place of the Mohenjodaro and Harappan civilisations (Engineer 2007). The national curriculum of 2006 also attempted to recognise the ethnic and religious diversity of Pakistan and aimed to prepare young people for global citizenship as befits citizens of a democratic society (Hussain and Boquérat 2012). The curriculum and textbook sought to 'define enlightened moderation' (Hussain and Boquérat 2012, 9) and to

> inculcate awareness about the multi-cultural heritage of Pakistan to enable the students to better appreciate the socio-cultural diversity of Pakistani society and get used to the idea of unity in diversity in [their] national context. (Hussain and Boquérat 2012, 1)

The national curriculum included an explicit commitment to exploring the role of religious minorities in Pakistan by identifying 'the major features of Pakistan's culture and commonality in regional cultures leading to national integration and cohesion' (Hussain and Boquérat 2012, 13). Teachers were advised that the point of their teaching was not only to prepare students to do well in examinations but also 'to successfully face the challenges of a global society and develop their social consciousness to the extent that they become the agents of social change' (Hussain and Boquérat 2012, 14). The explicit guidance on teaching strategies for Pakistan studies within the school was also markedly progressive. Teachers were exhorted to engage students of varying interests and abilities in cooperative learning and discussion, stimulating their active participation and avoiding 'the spoon-feeding style of traditional classroom teaching' (Hussain and Boquérat 2012, 15).

The National Education Policy (NEP) of 2009 under the leadership of Asif Ali Zardari introduced the chapter on Islamic education in the textbook. The vision of Islamic education in the national curriculum was regarded as the transformation of society by Islamic and human values, as envisaged in the Constitution of Pakistan (Government of Pakistan 2009, 4). The NEP 2009 demanded that Islamiyat should be a compulsory subject, instead of delivering it by religious teachers in the curriculum for early childhood education to higher secondary levels, stretching it up to degrees in every global and professional institution (Shakil and Akhtar 2012). This mandatory measure was intended to transform society into a more tolerant and peace-loving one, capable of finding solutions to life's problems within the teachings of the Holy Quran and Sunnah (Shakil and Akhtar 2012).

An Islamic study was also introduced as an elective subject in the 9th to 10th and 11th to 12th Grades (Shakil and Akhtar 2012). It acknowledged 'unresolved' debates about 'how to accommodate non-Muslim minorities' (Government of Pakistan 2009, 9). There was also recognition that 'globalisation' had made little impact on the education system ('a desired response has been missing') (Government of Pakistan 2009, 5). A key aim of the education system was articulated as:

> To raise individuals committed to democratic and moral values, aware of fundamental human rights, open to new ideas, having a sense of personal responsibility and participation in the productive activities in society for the common good. (Government of Pakistan 2009, 11)

The policy of 2009's rhetoric conflicted with the ideological orientations of policy-makers, writers of textbooks and teachers committed to the more overtly theocratic Islamic Pakistan Studies (PS) curriculum (Rehman and Zia 2010). Regarding recommendations, the education policy of 2009 outlined that the curriculum and textbooks should include content on Islam or any Islamic school of thought and cultural or linguistic minority (Rehman and Zia 2010). This policy recommended that 'all who live in Pakistan are equal without regard to race, ethnicity, religion or denomination' (Government of Pakistan 2009, 4). Although a separate ethics book was published for non-Muslims, the oppressive depiction of non-Muslims in Muslim students' textbooks was left in place (Rehman and Zia 2010, 32). The decentralisation of education (see Rehman and Zia 2010; Shakil and Akhtar 2012; Behuria and Shehzad 2013; Kronstadt 2004; Lall 2008) encouraged by the curriculum raised questions about potential issues of uniformity of the curriculum and the consequent impact on national identity and cohesion. Therefore, adding new material to the curricula might have had a negative impact on national identity and integration.

Under this policy, the Pakistan Studies textbook of the 9th[14] and 10th Grades[15] emphasises the Pakistan ideology and the notion that Islam is the basis of Pakistan. The textbooks factually begin with this concept – it is the title of the first chapter – and use it to portray the five pillars of Islam, violating the constitutional clause that non-Muslim students do not have to study Islam. The Pakistani identity is equated with Islam, to the exclusion of non-Muslims (Afzal 2015). The textbooks depict India or Hindus in derogatory language (Afzal 2015; Banerjee and Stöber 2016; Afzal 2018). The positive associations are only used for the self, such as 'equal' or 'brotherly' (P1, 6; P2, 20). This dichotomy is discussed in more detail in relation to the partition of India, both before and after the partition (Banerjee and Stöber 2016). The textbooks portray the self (Pakistan or Muslims) as victims and the other (Hindus or India) as perpetrators before the partition (in the section titled 'Background of Pakistan Resolution'):

> The Muslims wanted to secure themselves against the domination of Hinduism. The Hindu parties were making demands for Ram Raj. Hinduism was constantly trying to merge Islam into it like other issues. If the united subcontinent had got freedom, it would have been a permanent form of Hindu Authority because modern democratic system believes in majority government. It was a must to get rid of the dominance of the Hindus and it was possible only if the subcontinent was divided. (P1, 20–1)

---

14 *Pakistan Studies*. Punjab Textbook Board. G.F.H. Publishers: Lahore (9th Grade) (P1).
15 *Pakistan Studies*. Punjab Textbook Board. Gohar Publishers: Lahore (10th Grade) (P2).

In addition, the textbook notes:

> The Muslims were given less status in the society. They could not lead a dignified and graceful life in the Hindu Society that believes in caste system, colour and creed and the Hindus could never agree to give the Muslims equal status [*sic*]. (P2, 21)

According to the textbook, before partition the entire non-Muslim population was conspiring against the Muslims. While discussing the 'Pakistan resolution' in the section on 'Jinnah–Gandhi talks 1994', P1 depicts 'Quaid-e-Azam's[16] reply to Gandhi' (in the section 'Reply of Quaid-e-Azam' to 'Proposals made by Gandhi') as follows:

> Quaid-e-Azam adjudged that the style adopted by Gandhi is nothing but cheating and hypocrisy and cunningness. He emphasized that the British must settle the issue of Pakistan before the freedom of India because Congress and Hindus could not be relied upon. (P1, 25)

Then again, when describing the services rendered by Quaid-e-Azam, the authors refer to the conspiracy by Hindus, mentioned in the chapter called 'Making of Pakistan' (P1, 48), as follows:

> It was the fruit of his efforts that the Muslim League met with success in 1945–46 Elections. He [Quaid-e-Azam] made all the conspiracies of the Hindus and the British unsuccessful. At last, Lord Mountbatten presented 3rd June 1947 Plan promising to establish Pakistan and Pakistan came into being on 14th August 1947. (P1, 48)

These stereotypes signal the pervasive use of the strategy of positive self-presentation and negative other presentations in the textbooks (Anand 2019). Hoodbhoy and Nayyar (1985) also point out that the depiction of Jinnah in Pakistan Studies textbooks is made to fit into the view of Pakistani history towards an Islamic state. Jinnah is always referred to by the title 'Quaid-e-Azam' (Great Leader) and depicted as the 'Ambassador of Hindu Muslim Unity' while Gandhi is portrayed as a 'shrewd politician' (Banerjee and Stöber 2016, 155).

In the characterisation of aspirations attributed to the other (India or Hindus) – for instance, while discussing the 'causes of separation of East

---

16   Quaid-e-Azam is also known as Muhammad Ali Jinnah, the founder of Pakistan.

Pakistan' – the authors list two causes: 'poor economic condition' and the 'negative role of Hindu teachers' (P1, 126). Textbooks do present the political difficulties between East and West Pakistan that were the fundamental cause of the secession, but nonetheless place more significance on foreign conspiracies and the Hindu role in East Pakistan. They also describe the status of Muslims in pre-partition India (Afzal 2015):

> The British, dominated by prejudice enmity, dismissed all the Muslims from government jobs especially from Army and shut the doors of employment to the Muslims. Despite having the required qualification for some job, the Muslims were deprived of it. On the other hand, the Hindus were offered jobs even if they had less qualification as compared to the Muslims. (P1, 8)

The argument elaborates that

> The Muslims were deprived of their properties [pre-partition]. Their properties were confiscated. Some Muslim landowners were turned out of their lands. Their properties and lands were allocated to the non-Muslims. The Muslims became tenant cultivators instead of the owners of the land. Sir Syed Ahmad Khan has depicted this miserable condition of the Muslims in the following words: 'No calamity has descended from heaven that had not searched the house of the Muslims before it comes down to the earth'. (P1, 9)

These impressions about India mostly remain with ordinary people of Pakistan for their lifetime unless they are prepared first to 'de-learn' and afterwards 're-learn' the lessons taught in childhood (Tripathi 2016).

The textbooks present history in a one-sided manner (Afzal 2015; Anand 2019) and portray India from a unilateral perspective.[17] The local or self-community (Pakistan or Muslims), by contrast, is characterised in a more positive light – as a victim defending itself in contradiction to the actions and negative purposes of the other (India or Hindus). The lack of recognition of the other country (India) is presented in a historical

---

17 Unilateral narratives depict the other as rivals planning to abolish or control them. These narratives request individuals to be ready to sacrifice existence for the shared good. They are nationalised products that derive from the educational policies and values of a country. This is due to the discriminatory stress on historical occurrences based on a unilateral perspective rather than fiction (Rotberg 2006).

narrative emphasising the degree of their victimisation (Wohl and Branscombe 2008). These images of India or Hindus as the enemy are created at an early age and remain in people's memories; they reinforce the partition or anti-India attitude and refuse to allow space for peacebuilding (Afzal 2015; Anand 2019).

This is due to two reasons. First, nationalist historical discourse is typically based on the dichotomy of 'us versus them', which conveys the official narratives, often portraying the other as a historical enemy. The contact between the self and the others is frequently designated as domination. The others are held responsible for poverty and poor living conditions. This locus is often accompanied by a particular scheme of argument: contact with various 'others' posed a threat to our very existence (Klerides 2008, 156). These loci are used as a strategy of negative presentation that aims to foreground the negative implications for us of contact with 'them' (Klerides 2008, 156). This is part of the strategy of positive self-presentation that serves to promote positive images of us, facilitating the identification of readership with nationalist discourse (Klerides 2008, 156).

Second, cultural differences and diversity within the nation are, as Klerides has noted, 'often repressed, forgotten or backgrounded in national identities, inter-national differences tend to be foregrounded, remembered and emphasised' (Klerides 2008, 13). Through this emphasis on 'alterity' as well as the labelling of 'strangers', the nation nurtures its own vanity, claims itself superior, promotes its own religions and hides its negative actions, as well as projecting its own inconsistencies (Klerides 2008, 13).

The tradition of a positive depiction of 'us' as well as a negative depiction of 'them' is a critical aspect of 'ethnocentrism'. This practice is frequently demonstrated in stereotyping which reduces 'us' and 'them' to an insufficient, modest, vital feature signified as intrinsic, fixed by nature (van Dijk et al. 1997, 175). The learners recite the narrative that 'we' (Muslims and Pakistanis) are good and others (Indians, Hindus, non-Muslims) are bad.

> The textbooks treat Muslims and Pakistan as the victims of conspiracies of the West, India, Hindus and the British. History is presented as a linear, singular narrative, without sources of information or multiple (or for that matter, any) types of evidence presented. (Afzal 2015, 2)

Historical events are not placed in a larger context and serve to assert the main nationalistic narrative (Anand 2019).

The textbook also introduces the two-nation theory from the beginning of the chapter. The two-nation theory called 'Two-Nation Theory: Origin, evolution and explication' (P1, 10), is described as follows:

> In the perspective of the Sub-continent, Two-Nation Theory means that two major nations, the Muslims and the Hindus, were settled there. The two nations were entirely different from each other in their religious ideas, way of living and collective thinking. Their basic principles and way of living are so different that, despite living together for centuries, they could not intermingle with each other. The Indian Muslims fought the war of freedom on the basis of the Two-Nation Theory and after accepting this theory as a historical fact, two separate states, Pakistan and India, came into existence. This theory is the basis of the Ideology of Pakistan. (P1, 9–10)

The two-nation theory, that Hindus and Muslims were always two separate nations living in a united India, is defined as absolute and permanent; how it evolved as a concept is glossed over (Afzal 2015). The textbooks assert the 'two-nation theory' from the beginning of the books and present both Jinnah and Iqbal as firm believers in it (although history records that they were not always so). The textbooks also depict Sir Syed Ahmed Khan, Dr Allama Iqbal,[18] Chaudhary Rehmat Ali and Quaid-e-Azam as firm believers in the two-nation theory.

> Dr. Allama Muhammad Iqbal said: 'The Muslims would not allow that their religions and social rights are usurped. Therefore, I would like to see the Punjab, Northwest Frontier (Khyber Pakhtunkhwa), Sindh and Balochistan put together into a single state'. (P1, 10)

> Quaid-e-Azam was a firm advocate of Two-Nation Theory. He gave the Muslims the state of a separate nation in every respect. He said: 'Musalmans are a nation according to any definition of a nation, and they must have their homeland, their territory and their state'. (P1, 10)

Pakistan Resolution was passed on 23rd of March 1940. In his Presidential Address Quaid-e-Azam said:

---

18 'Dr Allama Muhammad Iqbal presented the idea of a separate state for the Muslims' (P1, 10).

> The Hindus and Muslims belong to two different religious philosophies, social customs and literatures. They have different epics, different heroes and different episodes. To tie together two such nations under a single state, one as a numerical minority and the other as a majority, must lead to growing discontent and final destruction of any fabric that may be so built for the government of such a state. It would be better for the British Government to announce the partition of the Sub-continent by keeping in view the interests of the two nations. It would be a right step religiously as well as historically.(P1, 11)

The textbooks describe the 'two-nation theory' by making 'specific reference to the economic and social deprivation of Muslims in India' (Government of Pakistan 2006, 2). The textbooks (in Lahore) continue to incorporate anti-Indian or anti-Hindu discourses into the construction of students' national identities. The negative depiction of India illuminates the purpose of the hidden curriculum (Hussain and Safiq 2016). The textbook content emphasises the defining representation of Pakistan as its Islamic identity and the defence of Pakistan is equivalent to the defence of Islam. The Islamic identity of Pakistan is established throughout the Pakistan Studies textbooks, often to the exclusion of religious minorities. Some textbook passages imply – or directly state – that Pakistan's Islamic identity, or Islam itself, is under threat, which creates the possibility that the reader could come to view the influence of religious minorities as threatening and 'forge an identity exclusively based on Islam and derived in opposition to India' (Afzal 2015, 2).

As far as reasons for partition are concerned, topics such as 'Pakistan resolution 1940' and the 'Background of Pakistan resolution' imply that the textbook offers narratives separating 'us' from 'them'. Outlining the reasons for the partition of India, P1 claims:

> In the second half of the nineteenth century and during the beginning of the twentieth century, the Hindus continued their attempts to wipe out the language, culture and the civilization of the Muslims. It seemed clear that if India got freedom as a single country, the culture, the civilization and the language of the Muslims would always be in danger. (P1, 2)

It elaborates on the two-nation theory by positioning anti-Indian/anti-Hindu discourses (committed to a writing practice prevalent in the Zia era). P1 discusses the 'history of Pakistan', where the authors of the textbook refer to the 'unjust division of Radcliffe' (93) and hold Sir Radcliffe responsible:

> Sir Radcliffe not only deprived the Muslims of their areas and rights but also created the problem of Kashmir issue. He planted a seed of enmity between the two nations that is still a bone of connection between the two nations. (P1, 93)

The textbooks use stronger and constantly negative language about the Radcliffe border award (Afzal 2015). The authors also refer to the 'rehabilitation of refugees' (93), 'administrative problems' (94),[19] 'distribution of assets' (94),[20] 'division of the army' (95),[21] 'the river water issue' (95)[22] and 'issues of states' (96),[23] where India or Hindus are held responsible.

Moving on to the 'Indo-Pak War 1965' (P1, 114), the textbook again attempts to hold the other country (India) responsible. It lists the reasons as follows:

> Pakistan was established against the wishes of Hindus, so they have never accepted Pakistan from the bottom of their hearts. Wonderful progress and stability of Pakistan constituted a major concern for

---

19 'After the establishment of Pakistan, the Muslims living in India decided to come into their new homeland as they found their lives unsafe there. Millions of families journeyed towards Pakistan leaving all of their belongings in India. These homeless, ruined, miserable and distressed Muslims were accommodated temporarily in refugee camps ... Rehabilitation of the Refugees was a great challenge. The world has not seen such a large scale of migration anywhere else' (P1, 93–4).

20 'The Indian rulers did injustice in the proportional distribution of the assets too. They continued to avoid giving Pakistan its due share. They used every possible device to destroy the economy of Pakistan. They withheld agreed share of Pakistan's assets. At the time of partition, Rupees four hundred billion were deposited in 'Reserve Bank' of the United India ... A meeting between the representatives of both the countries was held in November 1947. An agreement was made. Both the countries confirmed the agreement, but it has not been implemented so far' (P1, 94–5).

21 'After the Sub-continent was partitioned, it was also necessary to divide military assets proportionally, but justice was done in this division too. India wanted to weaken Pakistan so that it was forced to be a part of India' (P1, 95).

22 'The partition of the Sub-continent affected the natural flow of the rivers. According to international law, the natural channel of the river is maintained and two or more countries through which a river flows can benefit its waters' (P1, 95–6).

23 'During the British rule, there were 635 Princely states in India. When the time of freedom approached near, the people started to think about the future of these states. In Cabinet Mission Plan, the rulers of these states were asked to participate in the constitution-making process for their future status as well as protection of their interests. ... No immediate step was taken by the states of Hyderabad, Junagarh, Manavadar and Jammu and Kashmir. Indian Armed Forces occupied these states through military action. It increased the feelings of distrust towards of India' (P1, 96–7).

them [*sic*]. So they started launching aggressive actions against Pakistan. (P1, 114–15)

The Kashmir conflict is the real cause of War 1965. India occupied Kashmir against the will of the Kashmiri people. Kashmiri people are in favour of accession to Pakistan, but India has always avoided holding the promised plebiscite in Kashmir in accordance with the resolution passed by the Security Council. As a punishment for supporting Kashmiri people morally and raising Kashmir issue all over the world, India imposed war on Pakistan in 1965. Pakistan extended moral support to the people of Kashmir and raised the Kashmir issue all over the world not like which India did [*sic*]. (P1, 115)

The textbooks focus on historical events and dates; no explanations are given. Many subjective statements are made, ascribing no basis, justification or source (Afzal 2015). The textbooks also give the reasons for the conflict between Hindus and Muslims:

The main dispute between Pakistan and India is the Kashmir issue, without its solution the relations cannot be improved. Better ties can be established between both countries in all fields if it is resolved. Pakistan has always showed a positive attitude but India is not serious about resolving this issue. (P2, 31)

For resolving the water issue the Indus Water Treaty was signed between India and Pakistan in 1960 is still violating this treaty [*sic*]. (P2, 31)

Some betterment relationship appeared in Pakistan and India in 1990. Mutual trade and travelling facilities were increased. No effect can be fruitful without the solution of Kashmir issue amicably. Pakistan is firm in its stand that the Kashmir issue should be settled according to the resolutions of the United Nations, but it should be done in accordance with the wishes of the helpless Kashmiris. (P2, 32)

The textbooks depict the self (Pakistan or Muslims) as the victim and the other (India or Hindus) as the perpetrator. The story of how Hindus and Muslims co-existed and intermingled is not told (Hussain et al. 2011, 4–5). The Kashmir issue is represented in an emotional tone, depicted as evidence of the bad intentions of India towards Pakistan (Hussain et al.

2011, 4–5). The conventional, single-narrative method has been favoured as an approach to foster unity in Pakistan. This concern is demonstrated in research indicating the prominence of traditional, nationalistic single narratives in textbooks in post-conflict countries (Lerch 2016), despite global trends towards denationalisation (Hansen 2012).

In terms of India's role in the separation of East Pakistan and the emergence of Bangladesh (P1, 124), and the dispute over the separation of assets with India post-partition, the textbook simply observes:

> India succeeded in achieving her objectives and East Pakistan appeared on the map of the world with the name of Bangladesh on 16th December 1971. (P1, 125)

It then discusses how India did not hand over all the cash assets intended for Pakistan as part of the partition.

> East Pakistan suffered always poor economic conditions. Before partition of India, Hindu industrialists and landlords were the cause of economic sufferings of West Bengal. Now [after partition], once again Hindus dominated the economy of East Pakistan. Despite all the efforts, it remained backward economically as compared with the other provinces of Pakistan. (P1, 125–6)

The chapter entitled 'Ideological Basis of Pakistan' also describes the economic deprivations faced by Muslims in India.

> When the war of freedom (1857) was over, Muslims were oppressed very badly. Although the Hindus supported the Muslims in this war [war of freedom in 1857], but [sic] they declared only the Muslims were responsible for all their actions in the war. Thus, they acquitted themselves of any responsibility. The Muslims were the targets of the wrath of the British. So they suffered a lot and faced serious consequences. (P1, 8)

There are also instances of bias against and intolerance towards the beliefs, attitudes and customs of religious minorities throughout the textbook (P1). Significantly, this rhetoric is directed at Hindu people as well as their customs (such as Hindus' ill-treatment of widows and the less fortunate). Two examples of 'polemic historiography' and religious distortion from the textbooks are given below:

Hinduism persistently tried to absorb Islam into itself like it had done with other systems (of belief). (P1, 21)

Because the Muslim religion, culture and social system are different from non-Muslims, it is impossible to cooperate with Hindus. (P2, 31)

Overall, the textbooks offer a standard narrative that aims to safeguard Muslim values and shape the collective memory of learners (Afzal 2015). They delegitimise India or Hindus and present Pakistan or Muslims in a glorifying light, as well as the only victim of the conflict. The textbook narratives are grounded on actual events, but the selection is biased to convene the contemporary societal needs (Liu and Hilton 2005; Southgate 2005). Textbooks perpetuate a narrative of conflict and historical grievances between Muslims and Hindus, while the potential for conflict resolution and reconciliation is ignored. To summarise, the textbooks portray Hindus and India as the eternal other and enemy (Hussain and Safiq 2016; Afzal 2015; Anand 2019). India is depicted in an emotional tone. More neutral presentations of India do not take an emotional tone and restrict themselves to factual arguments (Hussain and Safiq 2016; Afzal 2015; Banerjee and Stöber 2016; Anand 2019).

In Pakistan, textbooks support the political agenda of the state by manufacturing an enemy in the minds of Pakistani youth. In Pakistan Studies (P1 and P2), Hindus and India are labelled as the eternal other and enemy (Hussain and Safiq 2016; Afzal 2015; Anand 2019). India is depicted in emotional words and phrases. The negative tone represents a framework of conflict and presents the other country (India) as a violent enemy, bent on destroying or dominating the self-community (Banerjee and Stöber 2016).

The aims of the reform (National Curriculum of 2006) outlined by the Ministry of Education were narrow. Rather than significantly altering the historical narrative, they tinkered around the edges, aiming to remove problems such as negative language. The reform was further weakened in the conversion of the curriculum to the textbooks (Afzal 2018).

Historical errors, distortions and biases, pervasive in the old textbooks, consequently persist in the textbooks. The improvements mainly relate to the language; they consist of removing negative references and softening the tone (Afzal 2018). In the Pakistan Studies textbooks prejudiced statements are presented as facts, devoid of any references or contrasting points of view. Despite this textbooks reign supreme in classrooms and the board's exams are based, forthrightly and completely, on these books. The exams reward rote memorisation of the textbook material (Afzal 2018).

Conclusion:

This chapter has reviewed the ways in which India and Pakistan use their shared history to construct a national identity and promote social cohesion within their respective countries. The history curriculum in each country has undergone revisions with changes in government, adapted in support of political ideologies (Durrani, Kaderi and Anand, 2020). In particular it has examined how school textbooks of Delhi and Lahore depict the other country (India or Pakistan) and India–Pakistan relations. This chapter has examined how Pakistani textbooks present an idea of Pakistan and an image of India that is historically inaccurate and underwrites cultural animosity to advance state interests. The chapter has then examined how, in the Indian context, the narrative is not so simple. Nevertheless there remains a purposeful evasion of the issues of India–Pakistan relations and partition in Indian textbooks.

The portrayal of the other country (India or Pakistan) in the school textbooks of Delhi and Lahore varied for several broad reasons. First, the impact of partition on individual and public memories drove the societies apart and led to the development of images of the other as a hostile enemy. Second, the government parties in power in both countries use memory politics for their respective aims and have the power to influence textbooks in different directions. Textbooks are thus also shaped by different pedagogical concerns and strategies (Banerjee and Stöber 2016). Third, diversified and decentralised schooling systems – for example, governmental, private or community-based – possess diverse interests and different producers of textbooks. Apart from being politically instrumental, textbooks are also shaped by different pedagogical aims, concerns and strategies (Banerjee and Stöber 2016).

The classroom is an ideal place to initiate critical discussion on such multifaceted issues before young minds are exposed to the argumentative rhetoric on the issue so prevalent in the outside world (Tripathi 2016). In classrooms, teachers play a significant role in enacting the textbooks and sociocultural depictions of historical events. It is important to understand how teachers negotiate and enact the textbook content on a historical conflict event while living in a conflict context (Banerjee and Stöber 2016); this helps to provide insights into what students are learning in such contexts and how this might shape their view of the other (India/Pakistan). Chapter 5 highlights how teachers from both countries are embracing or rejecting the narratives by drawing on their understanding of the collective memory of the historical trauma and on their self-preserving beliefs about the self and the other. This in turn can create opportunities or obstacles in the teaching of India–Pakistan relations in a way that advances or hinders students' historical and ethical understanding. It is significant for teachers to comprehend that textbooks are not free from any bias; they should supplement students' learning through primary and secondary sources as well as the textbooks to provide a balanced discussion of India–Pakistan relations (Banerjee and Stöber 2016; Hussain and Safiq 2016). However, it is important to comprehend the position and role of teachers in India and Pakistan, which will be covered in more detail in the following chapter.

3
Teachers and teacher agency in India and Pakistan

Chapter 2 reviewed the literature on how textbooks lead to the construction of national identity. The contribution of the curriculum and textbooks are just two factors influencing the formation of national identity in India and Pakistan. Schools have a pronounced impact on the efficacy of curriculum and textbooks in the construction of national consciousness, a situation that must be examined by considering teachers' attitudes and pedagogical responses. This chapter first defines teacher agency and critically reviews post-colonial literature on how teachers approach the curriculum. It then reviews how teachers negotiate and enact the textbook content on a historical conflict event. This helps to provide insights into what the students are learning in such contexts and the ways in which this might shape their view of the other. Finally this chapter reviews the role of teachers in the construction of national identity. It further attempts to explore the agency of teachers in textbook planning, organising and delivery through efficacy, practice and leadership in India and Pakistan.

'Agentic triad' of teacher agency, power and identity

In order to understand teacher change, professional learning and the impact of school reforms, it is fundamental to think about who teachers are and what they do. As theoretical lenses with practical implications, the concepts of identity, agency and power have been valuable in seeking to comprehend the ways in which teachers think, act and learn – as well as how they accommodate or resist change in their classrooms and schools. Each of these concepts has distinct bodies of work, with its own histories, tendencies, diverse delineations and arguments. The concepts have frequently been considered in tandem and intermittently all three have been considered together (Lasky 2005). Hargreaves (1996) indicated that good teaching includes moral purpose, political consciousness and emotional investment. Hargreaves' ideas are central to the understanding of how identity, agency and power relate to who teachers are (identity), what they feel they can and must do (power and agency) and how they can implement change.

Teacher identity is manifold rather than singular, fluid rather than static. It is also socially situated rather than an isolated or individual state. Bukor (2015) highlights how both professional and personal identities emerge from attitudes drawn from a teacher's own history and experience. A teacher's outward manifestation of their professional identity does not always reflect their personal history. Teacher identity has been associated with emotion, predominantly when it conflicts with other forces (Yoo and Carter 2017). In answering the question of who teachers are, Kelchtermans (2009) purposefully eschewed the term identity to avoid its static and essentialist connotations. He preferred to use the terms professional self-understanding (encompassing self-image, self-esteem, job motivation, task perception and future perspective) and subjective educational theory (professional knowledge and beliefs) to describe the ongoing process and products of the teacher becoming. Kelchtermans held these terms as both consolidative (constituting a theoretical whole) and analytically separable (Sherman and Teemant 2021). To him they offered an articulation of professional identities through teachers' enactment of their values, beliefs, ideals and self-images in the contexts of their classrooms, schools and collegial milieus.

The professional identities are not isolated – nor are they fixed or singular (Soreide 2006). They can best be understood as 'personal interpretive frameworks' (Kelchtermans 2009, 384) upon which teachers can draw to make meaning and take decisions. This articulation of teacher identity owes much to 'symbolic interactionism', which states that individuals' beliefs and meaning-making leads them to act in particular ways. Teachers can have multiple interpretive frameworks that they bring to bear in different contexts and situations; such frameworks can share beliefs, values and assumptions (with different emphases or priorities) or can be contradictory. Teachers can – and do – experience tension between these contradictory frameworks (Guerra and Wubbena 2017).

Foucault (1995) presented power not as something a person has, but nonetheless something that operates in societies in various ways, through regimes of discipline and self-governance and deriving from the interplay of power and knowledge. Bourdieu (1990) entwined symbolic power to legitimacy and social or institutional stand-up, predominantly where the effective power of speech acts (such as commands) was concerned. Power is commonly treated as a concrete concept, but it is theorised as fluid, socially mediated and ephemeral even while having real world influence. The concept of power in educational research is prominent in critical theory. Major works focus on education as liberation, as an ideological force of social control and reproduction (Apple 2004) and, in the form of critical pedagogy, as a basis for democratic engagement and social change (Apple 2018; Giroux 1988).

Teachers wear many hats and occupy numerous roles (e.g. classroom leader, assessment conductor, professional development participant). Biddle (1986) has observed how roles entail both responsibilities and abilities or actions. These roles may be recognised either formally (as in an organisational position) or informally (as in a socially sanctioned role). Here, drawing on the symbolic power noted by Bourdieu (1991), an articulation of power as actions taken based on the legitimacy and authority of a formal role – or, in short, legitimate action (Herndl and Licona 2007). Viewed in this way, roles can account for a few Foucauldian power dynamics, such as teacher power over others (legitimate action based on role), institutions' power through teachers (role requirements) and teacher internalisation of power as self-regulation (performance of roles). In the case of teaching, prescribed curricula provide an unambiguous illustration of the relationship between power, knowledge and legitimacy (Powell et al. 2017).

Like identity and power, defining the concept of agency involves a great deal of complexity and controversy (Hitlin and Elder 2007). Though sometimes understood as the capacity to act or make decisions (van Lier 2010), agency is generally defined as that and/or something more. Described by Ahearn (2001, 12) as the 'socioculturally mediated capacity to act', it may be seen as action negotiated through the ecological affordances and limitations of context (Biesta and Tedder 2006) or as action enabled relationally through collective coordination (Campano et al. 2020; Devine and Irwin 2005). Agency has been articulated in terms of freedom (Sen 1985) and professional autonomy (Molla and Nolan 2020). Within educational research, agency has been described as crucial to early-career teacher learning (Turnbull 2006), ongoing professional development (Dover et al. 2016), teacher professionalism (Molla and Nolan 2020), and teacher resistance and conflict (Achinstein and Ogawa 2006; Paris and Lung 2008). Agency is often held to be a dynamic that emerges between an individual and their context rather than a capacity: it is framed as something that is *done* rather than that is *had*. Bridging individual and context-mediated views, the ecological theory of agency (Biesta and Tedder 2006; Priestley and Beatty 2012) holds that teachers' agentive action occurs through the affordances and limitations of their school environment.

Some research has considered how teachers' identities related to their reactions to school reforms (Buchanan 2015; Ketelaar et al. 2012; Lasky 2005; Sloan 2006), how agency and teacher identity influenced each other over time (Day et al. 2006; Tao and Gao 2017) and how the positioning of teachers by themselves and others enabled or constrained their ability to act (Kayi-Aydar 2015). These studies exhibit a variety of definitions of identity and agency. Yet they all seek to understand what teachers do in terms of who they are. Teacher agency can be understood in the interplay of individual beliefs, values and ideals with institutional roles, authority and institutional action, producing (or not producing) authentic action (Sherman and Teemant 2021).

In the preceding paragraphs, identity has been articulated as a subjective interpretive framework and power as legitimate action derived from a role or authority (Sherman and Teemant 2021). Agency is emerging in the interplay between these two elements. Drawing on Bandura (2001), teacher agency is articulated in terms of moral agency, an action that adheres to a teacher's ethical or moral beliefs, values and assumptions. This can be understood as moral coherence or authentic action. As with identity and power above, this articulation represents deliberate and pragmatic bracketing of one portion of a much larger idea to focus on concrete implications for teacher change (Sherman and Teemant 2021). Agency can only be understood in terms of identity and power. To that end, the following sections present the triadic model.

The agentive triad shows how agency can passage power and identity to produce agentive action, how power can limit agency and identity, and how identity can be a source of resistance able to influence legitimate roles and actions (Sherman and Teemant 2021). There are three broad points to consider about the agentic triad. First, they are all dynamics, relations between things and ways of describing things that happen. They occur indirectly, through other things. As Foucault (1982, 788) said, 'power exists only when it is put into action', and so it is also with identity and agency in this model. People may have roles and responsibilities, but power emerges as they enact them. People may also have attitudes and values, but identity emerges when they employ them as interpretive frameworks. They may act, but agency emerges in the interplay between identity and power. Second, the agentive triad emphasises agency's role in authentic action – that is, by not elevating agency over identity and power. Rather, agency is found in the interplay of identity and power. Third, taking a note from complexity theory (Opfer and Pedder 2011), the roles and identities from which these elements arise are part of complex systems that continuously and recursively influence one another.

The triad presented here is a 'mock restriction': it engages with the dynamics between these elements without getting lost in the complexity and possible permutations that would arise from consideration of other potential influences, such as material conditions like facilities, class sizes and curricular materials. Though these influences would probably differ from context to context, these three elements would be consistently present (Sherman and Teemant 2021).

Identity and power intersect in conflicts and roles. If an interpretive framework accords with a role, there is a nested identity position. In this case, there is no distinction between power and agency: legitimate action happens to be authentic or agentive. There is an equilibrium between identity and role (Sherman and Teemant 2021). Furthermore, when changes are made to the role, for example through externally imposed classroom reforms, they are likely to be adopted if they do not conflict with teachers' identities (Coburn and Woulfin 2012; Sherman and Teemant 2021). In a 'discordant' identity position, the subjective interpretive framework of an individual – specifically their framework of right and wrong – does not completely overlap with the responsibilities of their roles; that is, the actions they are expected to carry out. In education, this is a common situation with standardised testing regimes that teachers may not believe in but which they are nonetheless required to carry out (Buchanan 2015; Lasky 2005; Sloan 2006). Roles can circumscribe the legitimate actions a teacher can take, even going so far as to dictate the emotions that teachers can legitimately express (Sherman and Teemant 2021).

Teachers' identities may fall outside this boundary. Conflicts such as this can exert a strong emotional toll on teachers (Lasky 2005), violating their moral integrity (Yoo and Carter 2017). Such tensions require resolution moving towards equilibrium, meaning that something must give. Either who the teachers are (their identity) or what they do (their role) must change (Sherman and Teemant 2021). The ability selectively to employ or create new interpretive frameworks suggests that there is a sort of agency at play in teacher identity. A teacher may not be able to prevent a moral framework from being compromised or negated in one context, but may be able to preserve it for another (Sherman and Teemant 2021).

The agentive triad model serves as a theoretical tool for guiding or supporting teacher growth and agentive action, and for understanding the dynamics between institutionally legitimised roles and teacher identities (Sherman and Teemant 2021). Chapters 5 and 6 will go into more detail about this. The chapter's next section provides a review of the literature on how teachers and textbooks interact.

Teacher agency and textbooks

Chapter 2 presents how textbooks portray India–Pakistan relations and this section provides a theoretical understanding of teachers' use of curriculum materials and textbooks. This will help to explain teachers' pedagogical responses, discussed further in Chapter 5. A body of literature explores how teachers interpret and enact curriculum materials in classrooms considering their attitudes, information and experiences (Davis 2006). In the classroom, the curriculum is either interpreted, recognised, renegotiated or resisted. At this level, teachers can participate in the transformation of the culture that they are endeavouring to transmit. Students read a textbook in multiple ways. For instance, they can read a textbook and accept it at face value, they can read and appreciate the ideologies it contains or they can read against it (Apple 1993). The curriculum consists not only of 'what we want to teach to our young', but also 'how we perceive ourselves to be' and 'how this identity [is] to be represented in the curriculum' (Pinar 1993, 10).

The real experiences of students relate to the way in which the curriculum (real or received) is delivered in the classroom, however, as well as to the 'unintended learning' that happens due to the structure of the curriculum, textbook and school (Kelly 2009, 20). The curriculum preserves the dominant social relations and groups 'in a way that implies that there are no alternative versions of the world, and that the interpretation being taught in school is, indeed, undisputed fact' (Sleeter 2011, 281). Bernstein (2000, 85) observes that the social and political construction of knowledge is

> how a society selects, classifies, transmits and evaluates education knowledge, interprets being public, reflects both the distribution of power and the principles of social control.

Gaps between the officially planned and the real or implemented curriculum occur at different stages in all educational systems (Resh and Benavot 2009). The central regulation in curricula challenges teachers' professional autonomy and damages their morale (Rosenholtz 1987; Taylor 2013). Strong evidence exists to show the influence of teachers' curricular approaches on their professional progress (Eilam and Poyas 2012; Eisner 1990) as well as how teachers' curricular approaches influence student learning and motivation (Eisner 1990; Erickson and Shultz 1992; King 2002).

The following sections include a critical review of the literature related to curriculum fidelity (curriculum-transmission), adaptation (curriculum-development) and enactment (curriculum-making). They also assess the association between teachers' approaches to the curriculum and teachers/students' cognitive and affective growth, since teachers' curriculum approaches certainly influence the results that teachers achieve.

Curriculum fidelity: teachers as transmitters

The fidelity approach limits the curriculum to 'a course of study, a textbook series, a guide [and] a set of teacher plans' (Snyder et al. 1992, 427). It includes suggestions for enhancing knowledge, modifying the curriculum and defining the role of teachers. Curriculum modification consequently leads from 'the centre to the periphery in linear and systematic stages, leaving no role for teachers apart from delivery' (Snyder et al. 1992, 427). Curriculum modification also monitors a top-down approach to materials growth (Kelly et al. 1996). A top-down curriculum is concentrated on organisational requirements and fails to inspire teacher development and active learning. In this situation teachers become transmitters who obey classical humanism intended to deliver static information and values of achievement (Anand 2019). Such an approach replicates the classical model of Tyler (1949) that identified objectives, content and methods of attaining and evaluating prescribed learning outcomes. The transmission agenda reproduces behaviourism by practising predetermined content.

Schools guide teachers to transmit knowledge considered necessary to society; however, this knowledge is ordered in a method that facilitates the production of practical experience required to develop markets, control production and labour (Apple 1993, 22). Social and economic authority in schools is implemented using different connotations of knowledge. The formal corpus of school knowledge can be termed social and economic control (Apple 1993). Schools not only control teachers but also their meaning. They help to preserve and allocate what is supposed to be 'legitimate knowledge' that 'we all must have', referring to cultural legitimacy on the knowledge of groups (Bourdieu 1977, 167). The values that are incorporated into schools can encourage children to be more resistant to prejudice, bigotry, racism and lack of tolerance, which may otherwise result in conflict (Anand, 2019).

Schools are also used as a network to transmit attitudes, philosophies and principles that make societies more disposed to violence (UNESCO 2006, 167). Education can cause armed conflict through government policies, which may be due to the use of a 'national' language of instruction considered inappropriate by minority groups; schools thus become a vehicle for cultural supremacy (UNESCO 2006, 169). The UNESCO report inspects the impact of a school on an adult or young learner, who can modify individuals either to be 'more receptive towards the appeals of radical groups' or 'more resistant towards a government that appears as hostile' (UNESCO 2006, 169). The curricula and textbooks can create a rigid division of students by group identity; it can also incorporate negative attitudes towards other groups. In some instances schools are thus responsible for subjecting students to violence (UNESCO 2006, 167). However, teachers can assist students to learn to solve conflicts by using dialogue and rejecting violence.

UNESCO's report of 2006 argues that schools are creating a high level of violence and regularly socialise young citizens into some violent groups (UNESCO 2006). They are also known as places in which children receive skills for their future lives (including learning to value and respect the variety of the community); these in turn develop their ability to view themselves as part of a comprehensive community, to promote social cohesion and peaceful resolution of conflict (UNESCO 2006, 171). There are indeed different ways of teaching about conflict – but this does not imply that everything leads to the diminishing of conflicts or to the reduction of contending attitudes.

Curriculum-adaptation: teachers as translators

The curriculum-adaptation is a 'process whereby adjustments in a curriculum are made by curriculum developers and those who use it in the school or classroom context' (Synder et al. 1992, 410). It also includes discussions among teachers and external curriculum developers for presenting curriculum revisions essential to the equivalent curriculum to local settings. The teacher's role has also become active by altering the curriculum to suit his/her classroom context. Teachers play an essential role in the process because their 'knowledge, experience and skills affect the interactions of students and materials in ways that neither students nor materials can' (Cohen et al. 2003, 4).

The adaptation approach uses the official, hidden and null curricula, which result in the teacher curriculum version (Ben-Peretz 1990). The official curriculum is a sequence of learning that dictates purposes, content, instruction and assessment, but the hidden curriculum is the knowledge that happens without being premeditated in the official curriculum (Pollard and Triggs 1997). The null curriculum occurs when teachers draw upon indispensable ideas, values, abilities and knowledge that are absent from the official curriculum. The adaptation method thus encourages interactions between teachers, students and the curriculum. It is an approach that empowers teachers to structure the curriculum by their contexts (Snyder 1990).

Curriculum enactment: teachers as mediators or adaptors

Curriculum knowledge is constructions of 'the enacted experiences [that] students and teachers create' (Snyder et al. 1992, 410). External knowledge is 'viewed as a resource for teachers who create curriculum as they engage in the ongoing process of teaching and learning in the classroom' (Snyder et al. 1992, 410). Curriculum change is about neither curriculum application nor adaptation, but is rather 'a process of growth for teachers and students, a change in thinking and practice' (Snyder et al. 1992, 429). The teacher's role thus changes from consuming, adjusting and adding external curriculum to curriculum development and creation (Clandinin and Connelly 1992). Curriculum enactment reproduces the powers of liberalism, by tackling learners' requirements, the benefits they hope to obtain and the issue of individual growth. It is supported in the process model; here students discover educational spaces relevant to themselves and the public, rather than touching on pre-specified aims that scarcely address their requirements or skills. The curriculum offers learners with the prospect of constructing a curriculum from their actions under the teacher's guidance (Shawer 2010).

Curriculum enactment offers an opportunity for skilled teachers to develop a curriculum (Parker 1997). It also allows teachers who engage in curriculum development activities to acquire professional skills. Curriculum enactment corresponds with professional development for teachers through learning, focusing on the context of teaching itself. The enactment method reproduces social constructivism (Wells 1999) for connecting active learning, social and consecutive production of multifaceted cognitive plans and students' benefits and requirements (Richardson 1996). Teacher leadership shows that efforts to understand teacher-leadership inside educational, organisational systems have been carried out for over two decades with no significant success. Teachers have a limited role in the determination of curricula within their work settings (Cochran-Smith and Zeichner 2005).

The mediating role of teachers in education policy and its delivery has been changing. Many researchers have been studying the combination of teachers and policies (Eisner 1999), but only a few have analysed teachers' understanding of local knowledge using an interpretive and constructive perspective. The teachers themselves always stay in the background. In contrast the policy-makers, operating at either provincial or national level, retain a higher profile; they submit the policy they frame on to teachers to implement in schools (Ball and Bowe 1992, 102).

Little research has been carried out about the voices of the teachers, who may be overwhelmed 'beyond their control' or 'autonomous resistors' (Ball and Bowe 1992, 102). Teachers can achieve agency differently, from context to context, depending upon specific conditions of opportunity and constraint. The crucial factors in this are the attitudes, morals and attributes that teachers mobilise within specific contextual situations (Novelli and Sayed 2016). The following section outlines the background on how teacher agency is both facilitated and restricted in India and Pakistan.

State policy, curriculum and teacher agency in India and Pakistan

In India, Poonam Batra has written significantly about teacher agency (2005, 2006, 2011), which she recognises as the most unaddressed issue in Indian education reform (Brinkmann 2016). While Batra does not offer a single definition of what teacher agency entails, she highlights issues such as the system that views teachers as passive recipients expected mindlessly to implement predefined content designed elsewhere and that fails to engage with teachers' socio-political context or their imbibed socio-cultural beliefs (Brinkmann 2016). Teacher agency also encompasses the empowering of teachers as 'public transformative intellectuals', guided by critical social opinions and research-based learning theories. Such valued intellectuals can think and act unconventionally, resist state ideological pressures, engage actively with social change and adapt their teaching to local needs, ensuring that all children learn (Batra 2005).

Furthermore, in India, 'rational agency' is fundamental to enable transformative action. This links back to a fundamental barrier to Learner Centred Education (LCE) implementation highlighted by the literature on Indian teachers – that of low teacher agency (Batra 2005; Dyer et al. 2004). However, most educationists do not clearly define the mechanisms of teacher agency, nor discuss how this can be concretely achieved. Dyer et al. (2004) describe how teachers fail to see themselves as 'change agents' – they do not believe in the possibility of change nor in their own capacity to bring it about.

The Government of India's Bordia Committee report (2010) highlights the importance of promoting teacher agency 'through proper training, setting norms of teacher behaviour, strict monitoring and supervision, and taking exemplary action where norms of behaviour are flouted' (2010, 29). However, these measures seem to be designed rather to curtail than to enhance teacher agency – exemplifying how this notion may be co-opted in government discourse in a manner that impedes its objective if the concept is not properly understood. In Pakistan, in the classrooms, the role of teachers has been traditionally perceived as one restricted to 'implementing the curriculum designed by external agencies' (Durrani and Halai 2018, 539). Teaching was understood to be the transmission of knowledge, with learners as passive recipients. Nonetheless, in recent years there has been a progressive transformation 'in the understanding of teachers' roles or positions, particularly teacher agency in curriculum innovation as well as transformation of teaching' (Durrani and Halai 2018, 539).

In the past two decades, researchers have suggested an over-reliance on textbooks in the educational system in India and Pakistan (Sarangapani 2003). Here textbooks do not function merely as a measure of practice or habituation, but have a central, overarching effect on the learning situation. They effectively displace the agency of the learner and the teacher through the production of 'ought-to-know' knowledge that must be digested in the form of a set of right answers. Textbook culture thus symbolises a wider culture of focusing on one type of 'official knowledge' – a type strictly regulated both by the teacher and the textbook in both countries (Anand 2019).

In India, as discussed in Chapter 2, NCF 2005 attempted to address issues that accompany textbook culture. It called both for diversification in terms of resources (and moving away from one textbook) and for an attempt to conceptualise a 'good textbook'. The report claimed that a good curriculum resource

> leads the child to interact with their environment, peers and other people rather than be a self-contained transferrer of knowledge as a finished product. (NCF 2005, 38)

The outlook and design of the NCF 2005 demanded that the schoolteacher have an alert mind in the classroom. It re-defines the teacher's role as one in which he or she should think differently, reflect, make choices and construct an atmosphere where learners could think critically (Batra 2005). This framework also suggests methods for avoiding over-reliance on textbooks and not limiting knowledge to the textbooks' content, thus re-empowering both teachers and students. According to Kumar (2018), the NCF 2005 has been effective in changing the discourse on education in a system-wide manner. There is still some confusion regarding what this fundamental transformation in pedagogy actually entails in terms of actual classroom teaching and learning, despite the fact that teachers are now more receptive to the idea. Schools and teachers look for help as they try to interpret the message of the new curriculum framework, which could be due to a lack of training.

In Pakistan, the curriculum is a message and teachers are the media in schools (McCutcheon 1997). The religious identity of teachers and students is present in the hidden curriculum. The report submitted by the Ministry of Education of Pakistan on the National Professional Standards for Teachers in Pakistan (Government of Pakistan 2009, 10) suggested that

> If Pakistan aspires to compete successfully in the global knowledge economy by converting the raw talent of its people into productive asset, it has to create a world-class educational system from pre-school school to postgraduate level. A world-class educational system is not possible without world-class teachers, who instruct, inform and inspire their students to qualify learning, and quality

learning is contingent upon quality insufficient funding as well as coordination links amidst national and provincial governments, losses caused by terrorists and security concerns.

Teachers perpetuate the salient features of their ethnic identity when asked about the Pakistani national identity (Anand, 2019). The following section explores the agency of teachers in the process of textbook delivery in India and Pakistan through efficacy, practice and leadership.

Teacher efficacy in India and Pakistan

In terms of self-efficacy, in India, the National Curriculum Framework (NCF) 2005 described teachers as 'passive agents of the state who can be persuaded and trained to translate the vision of the NCF 2005 in classrooms' (Batra 2005, 44). Teachers have long blamed the social conditions of learners, such as 'bonded child labour, migration of children during school, the retention of children for domestic chores', for absenteeism and high drop-out rates (Ramachandran et al. 2000, 36). According to the NCF 2005, a teacher should also act as a 'state agent who must be oriented to the perspective of the curriculum' (Batra 2005, 43–50). It highlights that the role of teachers is to create 'an enabling learning environment', one in which

> children feel secure, where there is the absence of fear and [which] is governed by relationships of equality and space for equity … Often [this] does not require any special effort on the part of the teacher, except practising equality and not discriminating against children. (NCF 2005, 77–8)

The guidelines set out by the framework demand that teachers and learners should critically view a society in which identities are constructed by their caste, gender and religious or linguistic groups to engage in any form of social interaction (NCF 2005, 78).

In addition, the NCF 2005 reviewed the 'issues of social exclusion' and declared there should be no discrimination based on caste, gender, ethnicity or religion. It suggested that teachers 'should be sensitive and informed about distinct social dimensions and should promote self-awareness among themselves and learners' (NCF 2005, 51), using the support of preparation, training and student assistance. In a study, teachers' classroom practices were observed to shed light on the poor performance of Dalit children. The teachers perceived the learners to be 'good for nothing'; they also believed that 'whatever benefits are provided, these people [students] will not improve; even stones would respond, but not these kids' (Anitha 2011, 89). Ramachandran et al. undertook field-based observations which revealed that

> many teachers accept practices such as child marriage, withdrawal of girls at menstruation and untouchability in school as cultural practices of communities to which they must be sensitive. (Ramachandran et al. 2000, 36)

According to Batra (2005), the NCF 2005 offered only a limited explanation as to how teachers can be equipped to encompass excluded social narratives, experiences and voices to make them attainable in the classroom. It also lacked information on how to reverse and resist efforts of short-term ideological encouragement of educational policymakers to integrate the process of teaching (Batra 2005). The NCF 2005 only considered the teachers' understanding of social issues; it did not go into the portrayal of teachers' views of historical narratives to achieve social harmony and cohesion in society.

In Pakistan, the curriculum urged teachers to practise their efficacy and appreciate that every student is 'a member of a Muslim nation'. It continued with the observation that, 'in accordance with the Islamic tradition', every student must be 'honest, patriotic, and *janbaz mujahid* [that is, life-sacrificing in a specifically religious sense]' (Nayyar and Salim 2003, 11). Every student was directed to remember that '[the] national culture is not the local culture (or local customs), but rather the culture and the principles underlying the terms of Islam' (Nayyar and Salim 2003, 11). Teachers in Pakistan hold authority as a primary medium to influence the ideas and attitudes of learners. Many expressed low self-efficacy as they have a low level of awareness and understanding of religious minorities and their beliefs (Nayyar and Salim 2003). Nayyar and Salim further assert that 'what is important in the exercise is the faithful transmission, with no criticism or reevaluation, of the particular view of the past implicit in the coming to fruition of the Pakistan Ideology' (2003, 165).

At the school level, teachers of history are often incorrect and behave in a contradictory way. They do not describe 'real' history through a fear of jeopardising their jobs. The significance of educational input impacts on the quality of teaching as well as learning, such as the skills of teachers and learning resources (Nayyar and Salim 2003). Teachers are also regarded as change agents, mentors and academic leaders of society.

They are supposed to listen to negative remarks from parents, and it is believed that the bad performance of learners is based on a failure of teachers (Muhammad 2002). When students fail and receive low marks in examinations, the teachers are held responsible for their performance, without considering the fact that learners are also associated with the school administration, parents and teachers.

Teaching practice in India and Pakistan

As far as teaching practice in India is concerned, the NCF 2005 focused on the principal challenges in the 'delivery of quality education to transform the role and performance of teachers' (NCF 2005, 22). Various references were made to the role of the teacher in delivering 'a safe space for children to express themselves and simultaneously to build in certain forms of interactions' (NCF 2005, 22) as well as to the requirement 'to build the capabilities and confidence in teachers to autonomously plan their teaching in response to children's learning' (NCF 2005, 19). The framework also provided some suggestions of ways to integrate this into practice, making points such as 'teachers need to plan lessons so that children are challenged to think and try what they are learning' (NCF 2005, 20). The NCF 2005 suggested the processes and interventions required to construct relevant knowledge, as well as the connections within school and in wider society that help to prepare and support teachers (NCF 2005).

According to Batra (2005), the NCF 2005 depicts teachers as the mediating agents, depending on which textbooks (either good or bad) are being negotiated. The hidden belief is that textbooks (in singular or multiple form) help to develop secular values as well as to establish questions about social sensitivity. No teacher can single-handedly revise the curriculum in India (Batra 2005). However, the image of curriculum reform depends on an understanding of the original situations in which children are educated, through the 'folk pedagogic practices' as well as the 'behaviourist frame' of traditional teacher education (Batra 2005, 43–4). Within this framework, learners are trained to learn by rote to pass exams, after which the information becomes a 'forgotten memory' (Batra 2005, 43).

In addition, teachers' classroom interaction, focused on their 'personal theories and understanding', frequently becomes constant learning (Batra 2005, 43). Examinations also demanded learners to 'reproduce' and 'summarise' facts in an essay format. These essays evaluate the student's knowledge of the textbook content of instead of their comprehension of, and ability to analyse, general concepts (Kumar 2001, 458).

Kumar recognises this as confusion among teachers and learners between understanding and memorising content for examinations (Kumar 2001, 13). In this method, equal importance and emphasis were given to an individual period in history; learners are expected to memorise dates and figures without evaluating the interdependencies and the nature of history (Guichard 2010). History is often perceived by students as a boring subject[1] and understanding is only shaped by textbooks. This results in the manipulation of the nation's young generation by the BJP or Congress (Guichard 2010, 39).

In Pakistan, teaching practice and education quality are reduced because the learners are exposed to rote memorisation for passing exams (Hayes 1987). The classroom atmosphere does not encourage learners to become involved in cognitive learning, nor to use their judgement or critical abilities (Government of Pakistan 2006). The quality of teachers is acknowledged to be based on their level of professional competency, which includes knowledge, skills and attributes brought to the classroom. It is accepted that the quality and competency of teachers are determined by the quality of their initial or in-service education. About 90 per cent of teachers in public schools have been trained as teachers. The influence of teacher training using pre-service and in-service programmes was not visible in the achievement of learners. In fact, the quality of education delivered by schools and public sectors is often criticised (Government of Pakistan 2006, 2009).

A study conducted by UNESCO (2006) suggests that learner achievement illustrates the quality of the education system that oversees both student and teacher education. The quality of education delivered in the government schools was reduced, a result of the low level of teacher competency, lack of classroom support, absence of a system to assess learner achievement, lack of supervision, inadequate resources to promote critical thinking and weak government and administration (UNESCO 2006). There is a strong emphasis on the engagement of the

---

1   Other than the interplay of exams, textbook content and the lack of teacher freedom, it is important to discuss how history is treated as a subject. In her book *The Construction of History and Nationalism in India: Textbook, controversies and politics*, Sylvie Guichard states that history as a subject experiences issues due to the textbook culture. In India, 'hard science' subjects (such as chemistry, physics, biology and mathematics) are rewarded more for their value to society; social sciences are considered secondary (Guichard 2010, 36). This bias is present in the parent, teacher and student attitudes towards the 'soft sciences' (Guichard 2010, 36). History as a subject does not receive sufficient emphasis, and thus it is not critically taught in classrooms.

private sector (Government of Pakistan 2009, 2006; Gulzar, Bari and Ejaz 2005) as a major part of delivering education. In the private sector, institutions are trying to promote teaching practices in the classroom; these are often regarded as participatory and intuitive. Such practices focus on developing conceptual understanding, critical thinking and problem-solving skills in the classroom (Saleem 2009; UNESCO 2006).

Teacher leadership in India and Pakistan

As far as teacher leadership is concerned, Kumar (2001, 452) writes about 'textbook culture' and explains the importance of textbook material in Indian classrooms. Kumar's views provide insight into the significance and complexity of the NCERT controversy. He suggests that there are two types of education system: first, one in which teachers have no opportunity to shape their curriculum for learners using the available resources; second, one in which teachers are tied to the textbook and have microscopic freedom in altering the curriculum or selecting resources. Teachers continue to teach learners from textbooks, expecting exams to be based on them alone (Kumar 2001). In India, the education system relies on the second type; textbooks are a symbol of bureaucratic authority. Teachers who drift away from teaching the textbook will not be accepted or hired, unlike those prepared to sacrifice their academic freedom.

Based on Kumar's interpretation, teachers have been forced to teach the version of history represented in the textbooks by Congress or the BJP (Kumar 2001). The NCF 2005 presented education as a critical catalyst in the process of developing social transformation, but it failed to establish a link to the support of the teacher (Batra 2005). No research has yet been undertaken on the attitudes of Indian teachers of history or social sciences towards their classroom practices; whether they themselves would prefer to explore learning through critical analysis over rote memorisation and to promote identities in a democratic society through pedagogic methods other than rote learning (Batra 2005).

In Pakistan, teacher absenteeism and leadership are regarded as major issues in the effective delivery of education. Since the Punjab Schools Roadmap began a monitoring process, teacher attendance in urban schools has improved (Habib 2005). The Directorate of Staff Development announced the Continuous Professional Development Program in 2004 (in 36 districts of Punjab), seeking to provide an in-service and professional development programme for primary teachers. This initiative covers a decentralised approach to teacher training, providing at least one community support centre for every region in which district teachers cover about 10 to 15 schools (Habib 2005). Salaries for teachers are commensurate with those for teachers in private schools, reflecting pay-for-performance incentive structures and making it possible to remove absent and non-performing teachers irrespective of their qualifications, training or experience (Andrabi et al. 2010).

This initiative was begun by improving the curriculum at a national level in 2006. Since the devolution, the provinces have implemented changes to the new curriculum. Research in Africa and South Asia (including Pakistan) shows that too much coverage can affect the cumulative learning among learners. As a result, students fail to master the basic skills despite years of instruction (Pritchett and Beatty 2012). Therefore, instead of changing the curriculum, it is crucial to speed up instruction in the classroom to develop familiarity with basic concepts at elementary levels. The national education policies provide a little discussion on the ways in which to integrate professional leadership, ethics or values among the teachers. The integration of traditional and Islamic values offers a medium to promote national cohesiveness, unity and inculcation together with the Muslim Ummah in Pakistan (Zia 2006). Professional ethics or values also need to be compared and viewed from different perspectives, such as the global world, contextual social or cultural norms, national education aims student needs and future developments.

Concluding remarks: 'top-down' reform denies teacher agency

Scholars mentioned in this chapter have emphasised that the achievement of school reforms is integrally linked to the extent to which teachers can translate such reforms into effective classroom practices to serve students' learning needs better (DuFour 2002; Parise and Spillane 2010; Sebastian et al. 2017). This chapter has shown how pedagogical models are developed by a central team with little input from practising teachers; these are then expected to be implemented rigidly by teachers with little attention to the actual process of change, the complexities of ground realities and what teachers themselves know and think about their own classroom practice. Reformers often tend to be unrealistic in what they expect teachers to do, and how quickly they expect change to take place. Both teachers' agency and professional autonomy have been cited as key missing pieces in Indian and Pakistani educational reforms (Batra 2005; Dyer et al. 2004; Sriprakash 2012; Durrani, Kaderi and Anand 2020).

Teachers' pedagogical perspective is also affected by the conflict between the government's pedagogical aspirations and reality (discussed in more detail in Chapter 5).

While the government's aspiration is for a child-centred pedagogy, constraints in implementation must also be considered. These include a lack of resources, inadequate infrastructure, centralised curriculum, strict examination timetables, inconsistent distribution of materials and irregular teacher support, as pointed out by Sriprakash (2012), Smail (2014) and Kumar (2005). All of these handicap teachers seeking to explore the child-centered pedagogy and to implement it fully fledged.

Teachers themselves are pivotal in the consistency and operation of education reforms, yet they play no role in policymaking nor in processes of curriculum or pedagogical reform. The agency and voice of teachers are valuable concepts, but these are often neglected in their own professional development programmes, leading to a disconnect between the system and the teacher (Calvert 2016). Yet teachers' classroom practices can crucially influence the transmission of national identity through curriculum and textbooks, an issue that will be discussed further in Chapters 5 and 6.

4

Teachers' attitudes towards India–Pakistan relations

Attitudes are cultural constructs that are essential to the way individuals think, feel, and act. (Rivalland 2007). They can be – and often are – the outcome of an individual's background and life experiences and, because of teachers, they occur in socialisation forms within schools (McLachlan et al. 2006). Teachers' attitudes, knowledge of textbook content and teaching practices are connected (Vygotsky 1980; Foote et al. 2004); such a link serves as a contextual filter by which teachers check their classroom experiences and interpret their teaching practice (Wilcox-Herzog 2002).

This chapter presents a range of attitudes shown by teachers towards either India or Pakistan or to India–Pakistani relations in general. Their attitudes were collected by asking participants questions such as: 'What do you know about the other country (India or Pakistan)?' and 'What are your views on India–Pakistan relations?' However, their reactions were obtained by asking straightforward questions about attitudes towards India or Pakistan under conditions of the protracted conflict and its associated socio-psychological climate of intolerance. In these conditions, teachers were wary of expressing opinions that differed from the attitudes endorsed by their society.

The thematic analysis resulted in three types of attitudes: secular or pro-Indian or Pakistani attitudes; communal or anti-Indian or Pakistani attitudes; and mixed or blended attitudes (both secular and communal). The attitudes were broadly consistent across gender, age, experience and qualifications. The different socio-economic status (SES) groups (of schools) did reflect some variation in the attitudes of teachers, as mentioned in Chapter 1. The last section of this chapter highlights the sources (for example, family, media, society, school and textbooks) that shaped and refined the teachers' attitudes towards the other country (India or Pakistan) and towards India–Pakistan relations.

Secular attitude: narrative of common cultural traits and suffering or migration

Secular attitude involves the perception of universal suffering or recognition of the suffering of the other side (India or Pakistan and Hindus or Muslims), which could in turn stimulate sympathy and reduce the negative attitude towards them (Salomon 2004; Staub 2005; Vollhardt 2009). The concept also implies that there are common traits between Indians and Pakistanis or Hindus and Muslims. Nor does a secular attitude deny religion in society; it rather separates the social institutions over which religion can or cannot exercise control. Such an attitude involves high degrees of tolerance and diversity in society (Anand 2019).

The other country (India or Pakistan): narratives of common cultural traits

Elite private school teachers in both Delhi and Lahore labelled India or Pakistan as 'friendly' and 'similar in culture'. In Delhi, teachers expressed the view that both countries share the same culture and speak the same language (Hindi or Urdu). An elite teacher commented as follows:

> We [Hindus and Muslims] can begin with the entire history of its [India/Pakistan] creation in 1947, the political ups and downs we had. Pakistani's social life and Indian social life are comparatively similar. Indians and Pakistanis have the same culture. (Delhi, elite private school teacher 1)

Elite private school teachers believe in the secular nature of India, as do secular nationalists, and allow students liberty to practise their faiths. They equated India with 'diversity' and 'secularism'. The teacher quoted above elaborated this point:

> My students support secularism and diversity. We have different faiths of students in the school. I also support secularism. (Delhi, elite private school teacher 1)

These views were echoed by another elite teacher, who declared

> There is respect for all religions in India. India is a secular nation. I don't listen to people with stories on religions, Muslims and Pakistan. (Delhi, elite private school teacher 2)

Elite teachers in Delhi respect and celebrate diversity. Such views are particularly significant because in India various religions are practised, all of which have their own traditions and views.

Elite teachers were not alone in these views. Both middle government and private school teachers in Delhi made similar responses. They commented that before partition Muslims and Hindus had lived together for centuries, sharing similar cultural values, food, art, music, clothes, poetry, painting, languages and cultural norms. A middle government school teacher expressed this view clearly.

> We [Hindus and Muslims] have been in one state, one soil, one the same water, the same language, almost the same culture we have shared. Now the difference in worship is here in India. We [Indians] have Muslims, Christians, Sikhs, Parsis; we have many religions. (Delhi, middle government school teacher 1)

Another middle government school teacher agreed, commenting that

> Whatever we have read and understood, we [Indians] know much about Pakistan. It was our part only and now it has now been separated [*sic*]. Culture is same as like India, like Gujarat and Rajasthan, because it was a part of them. (Delhi, middle government school teacher 2)

Middle private school teachers echoed similar views. One teacher observed that

India and Pakistan share a lot. Language and culture. There is so much in common. We also used to live together before the partition of India. (Delhi, middle private school teacher 1)

Another was keen to emphasise the modern cultural affinities that exist between people of different religions.

We and Muslims can speak the same language, they can understand us. We are wearing the Kurtas [female dress] made by Pakistanis. They watch Bollywood. (Delhi, middle private school teacher 2)

In their responses teachers referred to the internal unity of India and Pakistan, revealed through the similarity in culture. It seems that they carry a non-biased and impartial outlook towards both Pakistan and India–Pakistan relations.

Similarly, in Lahore, narratives of secularism were echoed by elite private school teachers. Teachers expressed respect for all religions over cultural stereotypes and their narratives imply the dispositions of secularism. One teacher declared

I am not anti-India. The students are also not anti-India. We respect our history and creation. There are a lot of commonalities between Muslims and Hindus. We respect them [India/Hindus]. (Lahore, elite private school teacher 1)

This teacher then evoked the historical context to elaborate their response.

When Pakistan got independence, both countries [India and Pakistan] faced crisis and sacrifices. India is like Pakistan. Muslims and Hindus have a lot of things in common. Culturally, they are alike. (Lahore, elite private school teacher 1)

Another elite private school teacher was keen to emphasise how little influence conventional religious values or social media had in his views of India.

I respect diversity. There should be respect for every faith, religion, and nation. I avoid reading or listening to the media. (Lahore, elite private school teacher 2)

India–Pakistan relations: narratives of migration and narratives of peace and politics

Several elite private school teachers in Delhi mentioned the strong family ties in Pakistan. In their responses they noted the influence that family members had in keeping a positive mindset towards India–Pakistan relations. In describing how her family influenced her attitudes, one teacher commented

> I have been from a family that always connected with people in Pakistan. Some of them migrated from Pakistan, so emotional bonds are attached. Therefore, right from the beginning, there was no feeling of anti-Pakistani in my family. (Delhi, elite private school teacher 1)

She also commented upon the practical difficulties around maintaining a family bond across the two countries – a view shared by several elite private school teachers.

> We should have a better flight and visa system. It is too hard for people to travel to Pakistan. I hope the government does something about this. (Delhi, elite private school teacher 1)

A middle private school teacher echoed her comments.

> The government should have a better visa process. My family wants to go to Pakistan, but it's not possible. It is hard to apply for the visa. (Delhi, middle private school teacher 2)

The general opinion was that improved transport and visa systems between the two countries would contribute to better people-to-people relations.

Another elite private school teacher referred in her response to her [family] migration from Pakistan. She also noted the problems encountered in getting to see relatives who still lived there.

> Attitudes towards Indo–Pakistani relations are based on my family migration from Pakistan. They have narrated many stories. They have good memories. We now have problems meeting them (such as transport and visa process). (Delhi, elite private school teacher 2)

In addition, when asked about India–Pakistan relations, middle private and government school teachers in Delhi blamed politicians for escalating issues between India and Pakistan. Teachers felt that politicians were not supporting or promoting peaceful agreements between India and Pakistan. Opinions on this were divided, however; a middle private school teacher shared

> The politicians, the government, kept on making efforts, treaties, meetings, and conferences, and they try to improve relationships [*sic*]. (Delhi, middle private school teacher 3)

A government school teacher commented that

> Leaders in the country [India] use their political power to affect our relationship [India–Pakistan relations]. It is important to meet the public. If India or some other country [Pakistan] is not wrong, blame the leaders [*sic*]. (Delhi, middle government school teacher 2)

Another government school teacher expressed similar views.

> People in Pakistan and India like each other. We are refugees from Pakistan. We migrated from Pakistan. But after so many years, 65 years of this partition, we felt that countries can live together if the politicians allow it. The media are showing everything [*sic*]. (Delhi, middle government school teacher 3)

Several teachers observed that post-partition problems have been allowed to linger. They have thus created an obstacle to peace between India and Pakistan, and more importance should be paid to the areas of resolution. They emphasised the need for more talks between the politicians of India and Pakistan, relaxing visa restrictions and strengthening people-to-people relationships for conflict resolution. A government school teacher commented that

> Before meeting politicians, I used to like Pakistan. Only it will happen if India and Pakistan and we [Indians and Pakistanis] should avoid politicians [*sic*]. (Delhi, middle government school teacher 4)

Teachers did not blame either Hindus or India or Muslims or Pakistan for the problems in Hindu–Muslim relations and India–Pakistan relations.

They rather blamed the politicians in India and Pakistan. Teachers avoided the marginalisation of Pakistan or Muslims, instead depicting Pakistan or Muslims as legitimate participants in the country's historical establishment.

Similarly, in Lahore, elite private school teachers referred in their responses to their migration from India. Many expressed hopes and aspirations for healthy India–Pakistan relations. One elite private school teacher observed that her views

> ...have been good about India, or Indo-Pakistani relations – they never changed due to ancestral history. We have relatives there [in India]. The media is creating issues between Pakistan and India. People in Lahore don't have bad feelings about India [*sic*]. (Lahore, elite private school teacher 1)

Similar attitudes were expressed in another teacher's responses.

> Attitudes are positive. I have been to India myself. I know a few teachers in India. My parents have migrated from Delhi [India]. Relations are bitter, but should get better by reading more [*sic*]. (Lahore, elite private school teacher 2)

Elite private school teachers in Lahore generally appeared neutral towards India and the subject of India–Pakistan relations. They blamed the media for creating issues between the two nations and thus hampering India–Pakistan relations. The dialogues and sequences in the media show a constructed form of India–Pakistan relations, indicating the existence of 'mental borders' (Tripathi and Raghuvanshi 2020). Teachers shared the narrative of shared cultural traits and migration, serving to hypothesise a perception of collective suffering in migration or a recognition of suffering by the other side (India or Pakistan) to stimulate a secular attitude.

Communal attitude: narrative of blaming the other

The processes of mutual delegitimisation has led to acts of violence in the long-standing conflict between India and Pakistan. In this, the other is described as someone who associates with a set of individuals unknown to the group in which an individual perceives himself or herself (Bar-Tal 1990, cited in Maoz 2000). This acknowledgment of the other as a negative individual has led both sides to perceive each other as 'inhuman, violent and threatening' (Maoz 2000, 732) and creates negative attitudes. The negative narratives are based on actual events, but include their biased selection to meet societal needs (Hobsbawm 1990; Adwan et al. 2014; Liu and Hilton 2005; Southgate 2007). They delegitimise the other and portray the self in glorifying positions as well as for the only victim of the conflict. The narrative of blaming the other also assigns responsibility for the outbreak and continuation of the conflict to the other side, focusing on the violence and atrocities of the other. This leaves little room for recognising the history, culture and future aspirations of the other and for omitting their transgressions (Baumeister and Hastings 1997; Papadakis 2008; Bar-Tal 2013).

In Delhi and Lahore, the narrative of blaming the other (India or Pakistan, Hindus or Muslims) depicts self (India or Pakistan, Hindus or Muslims) as the victim and other (India or Pakistan, Hindus or Muslims) as the perpetrator – a process described as a unilateral perspective. This in turn creates communal attitudes that emphasise the religious differences between self (India or Pakistan, Hindus or Muslims) and other (India or Pakistan or Hindus or Muslims). Such an attitude places blame for the conflict and the massacres inflicted on to a third party, thus creating the unilateral perspective.

The unilateral narratives portray the other (India or Pakistan, Hindus or Muslims) as an enemy and highlight the adverse actions they committed (Banerjee and Stöber 2016). This could be because, in India and Pakistan, the seeds of communalism were sown by British rulers, with the idea that Indians remained divided and unable to challenge British colonial rule – a concept known as a 'divide and rule' policy (Das 1991). After independence, communal forces were active and created issues for both the government and society. Communal ideology results in communal violence (Chandra 2008), a situation that is discussed further below.

The other country (India or Pakistan)

In Delhi, lower SES private school teachers, middle SES government and lower SES government school teachers, along with lower private school teachers in Lahore, shared the unilateral perspective of the other country. This entails negative rather than positive images of the other (India or Pakistan) and provides little information about the religions, culture and life of the other (India or Pakistan). The self-community, by contrast, is characterised in positive terms as a victim that needs to defend itself against the acts and negative intentions of the other (India or Pakistan) and that desires nothing but peace.

When lower SES private school teachers in Delhi were asked for their views of Pakistan, five of them labelled Pakistan as an 'enemy' or a 'terrorist' country. They perceived Pakistan as being responsible for terrorism and the violence connected with the world. One teacher's response emphasised that the role of Pakistan is to spread terrorism and intolerance.

> Pakistan is a country based on religious ideologies. It is not a secular country like India. It has different elements that dominate the political scenario or political systems of that country [Pakistan], and there is not much diversity and tolerance in that country [Pakistan]. Pakistan causes of terrorism in the world [*sic*]. (Delhi, lower SES private school teacher 1)

Another teacher specifically described Pakistan as a terrorist country.

> Pakistan! As a citizen of India, I recommend it is a terrorist country because they don't wish to co-operate with any other country. The politicians don't want to collaborate. Their main ideology is to create terrorism in their country and other countries. (Delhi, lower SES private school teacher 2)

These teachers in Delhi held unilateral and national narratives. Such narratives refer to Pakistan as the enemy and the self (India) in a positive light. Teachers strongly endorsed communal attitudes and viewed Pakistan as a 'threat' to India.

In Lahore, a total of 14 teachers labelled India as the most significant 'threat' to Pakistan. Teachers viewed India as a 'violent enemy', destroying or dominating the self-community (Muslims and Pakistan). A private school teacher commented

> We didn't have many optimistic and positive feelings about India because it is our enemy from the past. I have hatred due to Pakistani reasons [*sic*]. (Lahore, lower SES private school teacher 1)

Responses from a number of teachers revealed how their views continued to be shaped by past family experiences.

> My ancestors were migrated from India. They have told me more stories about India where they used to live together. They have bad memories. It [India] is our enemy [*sic*]. (Lahore, lower SES private school teacher 2)

A middle government teacher was categoric.

> I and my family don't want to go to India ever. My family lost everything there. (Lahore, middle SES government school teacher 1)

Teachers' narratives show the influence of conspiracy theories on attitudes. The term conspiracy is often used in Pakistan Studies textbooks[1] to refer to Hindus and India. In addition, teachers also labelled India as 'cunning' and its intention on creating obstacles for Pakistan both pre-and post-1947. A private school teacher said

> India is just an enemy. They have RAW,[2] which is responsible for terrorism and issues in Pakistan [*sic*]. (Lahore, Lower SES private school teacher 3)

A government teacher echoed similar attitudes on terrorism.

> Terrorism in Pakistan is because India. It is dominating us [Pakistanis]. We are a peaceful nation, but India is destroying us [*sic*]. (Lahore, Lower SES government school teacher 2)

The connection of Pakistan to an ongoing terrorist threat was not uncommon among teachers in these types of school. For some the association was a general one, but others were more specific. In this response a teacher blamed the RAW in India for spreading terrorism in Pakistan, and for training and funding terrorists

> India and India's media creating issues in Pakistan. RAW [Research and Analysis Wing] is their biggest agency which is spreading terrorism [*sic*]. (Lahore, middle SES government school teacher 3)

A few other teachers blamed India for spreading terrorism in Pakistan, while some held both America and India responsible for the threat. Teachers expressing these views labelled India as 'cruel' and saw it as actively engaging in conspiracies against Pakistan. This persistent attitude suggests a prevailing depiction of India and Hindus as the enemy and a threat to Pakistan. In addition, teachers perceived Muslims and Hindus as

---

1   *Pakistan Studies*. Punjab Textbook Board. G.F.H Publishers: Lahore (9th Grade) (P1). *Pakistan Studies*. Punjab Textbook Board. Gohar Publishers: Lahore (10th Grade) (P2).

2   Research and Analysis Wing (RAW) is India's intelligence organisation.

being different, having different religions, customs and traditions, and consequently being unable to live together. These teachers' attitudes seem to be consistent with the textbooks. The textbooks also cover the creation of Pakistan in terms of a conspiracy between Hindus and the British against Muslims, who are presented as victims of the situation. The textbooks' description of the events is one-sided, even as the attitudes of teachers are. A stable relationship between education and violence may thus be perceived (Krueger and Maleckova 2003; Berrebi 2007).

India–Pakistan relations: narratives of blame and politics

As far as India–Pakistan relations are concerned, due to the Kashmir issue and terrorism, teachers in Delhi and Lahore are similar in their views. Teachers' narratives display a recurrent discourse of continually blaming the other country for the situation in Kashmir. The narratives' embeddedness and truth emerge as issues regarding the conflict between Indians and Pakistanis over the land of Kashmir, which arose during partition and to date remain unresolved. One teacher commented:

> My personal views on Indo–Pakistani relations are that unless they solve the Kashmir case Pakistan's ties with India will never be cordial [*sic*]. (Delhi, lower private school teacher 1)

Another observed that Kashmir was effectively the catalyst for many other areas of dispute and suspicion between the two countries.

> They have to change their attitude on Kashmir issue. Otherwise, it is difficult to co-operate with any other neighbouring country [i.e. Pakistan] because the people want terrorism. Their main ideology is to create terrorism in their country and other countries also. So they have to change their minds [*sic*]. (Delhi, lower private school teacher 2)

As mentioned in Chapter 1, Kashmir remains the focal point of tension around India–Pakistan relations. Teachers view the India–Pakistan conflict as a political, religious and bilateral issue. Lower private SES school teachers in Delhi recommended dialogue between the governments of the two countries. One observed

> It [Indo–Pakistan relations] depends on the circumstances. We always try to establish friendly relations with them but they

[Pakistan] are trying to create some problems in my view. For example, the bus on the Wagah border created some problems. They always create some problem [*sic*]. (Delhi, lower private school teacher 3)

Teachers in Lahore similarly felt that Indians were less 'serious' and 'focused' on resolving the Kashmir issue and promoting peace in general. A government school teacher offered a moderate view.

I don't think that our views have changed. We need to be peaceful from our side and India's side. There are never healthy relationships from the beginning. There are always issues between both. Issues have been always problematic between both. As neighbours, India supports us towards development [*sic*]. (Lahore, middle government school teacher 2)

Another teacher provided a more dogmatic response, in which there was little room for compromise.

The conflict between Pakistan and India is due to Kashmir. It is ours and India is not letting it go [*sic*]. (Lahore, lower government school teacher 1)

However, some teachers remained critical of political machinations, which they believed deliberately frustrated hopes of peace. A teacher suggested that

Problems in Pakistan are due to India and its politicians. They should promote peace [*sic*]. (Lahore, lower private school teacher 3)

Despite the communal attitudes, teachers in Lahore suggested that it was important to improve relations between the two nations.

The views of the other (India or Pakistan) are differentiated from views of self. There is one interactive feature that helps to distinguish them from us: religion, a clear commonality or boundary marker. These teachers in Delhi and Lahore characterise the other country (India or Pakistan) as a terrorist enemy and self as the victim. In other words, each blames the other community (Hindus or Muslims). The communal mentality that produces hatred culminates in hostility and mistrust.

Communal attitudes are thus shown to follow the textbooks. Constructing two nations in bipolar opposition accentuates the positive in us and the negative in them, developing a hatred for others. This could be interpreted as being a discourse of nationalism that distorts historical facts in two ways: by glorifying us and by darkening the other (Ahmed 2012).

Blended or mixed attitudes: narrative shifts or clashes

The blended or mixed attitude involves a small shift from the communal attitude to a more secular one, which may indicate a suppressed reconciliatory hypothetical aspect of this narrative (Lambert et al. 2010). It exhibits the shift from secular to communal attitudes that occurs when moving the discussion from the other country (India/Pakistan) to the subject of India–Pakistan relations.

A possible explanation for this change in attitude is the role of emotions or emotional experiences (Lambert et al. 2010). The experience of anger enhances negative attitudes (Lambert et al. 2010). Blended or mixed opinions could thus be due to the influence of the cognitive (legitimacy) and emotional (empathy and anger) aspects (of the narrative of India–Pakistan relations). Lower government SES school teachers in Delhi and middle private SES school teachers in Lahore change their attitudes from secular to communal ones. As noted above, this shift occurs when moving the discussion from the other country (India or Pakistan) to India–Pakistan relations.

The other country (India or Pakistan): narrative of common cultural traits or common suffering

In Delhi, lower SES government school teachers shared secular attitudes towards Pakistani citizens living in Pakistan; such respectful attitudes often change when discussing India–Pakistan relations. Teachers express positive attitudes towards the people of Pakistan, yet blamed politicians in Pakistan for creating problems for India. Many teachers pointed out that Hindus and Muslims have similar cultures and traditions, and have lived together for several centuries. As one teacher noted

> The people who are living there are just like us. They share the same nature as us. In my opinion, if we [Indians] will visit Pakistan, we will be dealt with in the same way as we treat them. We have no differences [*sic*]. (Delhi, lower SES government school teacher 1)

Another expressed similar views, again focusing on the historical background of the two countries.

> Pakistan was a part of India only. However, due to undue circumstances, it has become an independent or separate nation. Until now, we [Indians] only know due to unfair circumstances, our country must be divided. The people living there are like us. They have the same nature as of us [sic]. (Delhi, lower SES government school teacher 3)

Another teacher referred back to family beliefs, based on the lived experience of previous generations.

> Hindus and Muslims were together. They used to live together – my grandparents told me so. Differences between us were created by British people who came here and dominated us. (Delhi, lower SES government school teacher 2)

In Lahore, middle private SES school teachers expressed a favourable attitude towards people-to-people relationships. A few private teachers blamed politicians for maintaining a fragile peace between the two countries, with one observing that

> Forefathers migrated from India. Heard many stories. The stories are upsetting and sad. However, many Hindus helped my grandparents. I blame the Indian government for problems [sic]. (Lahore, middle SES private school teacher 1)

Another teacher in Lahore described India as 'a beautiful country to visit', adding that

> We know the Indians through social media and movies or serials. We are idolising more Indians (like their actresses and cricketers) [sic]. (Lahore, middle SES private school teacher 2)

Direct family experience of partition influenced the responses of another teacher, who explained

> My grandfather migrated from Delhi during Partition. He told me that he had many friends in India. He also told me how Hindus used

to live with them cordially. (Lahore, middle SES private school teacher 3)

Teachers believed in peaceful coexistence based on respect and tolerance between Hindus and Muslims pre-1947, despite religious contrasts and situations of conflict. Oral histories[3] narrated by their families, as evidenced above, seem to play a significant role in developing a positive attitude towards the other country (India or Pakistan).

India–Pakistan relations: narratives of blame towards the other country (India or Pakistan)

The change in views towards Pakistanis that lower SES government school teachers in Delhi expressed when asked about India–Pakistan relations reflects a significant shift in attitude. In moving from secular to communal or directly anti-Pakistan, the change indicates misinterpretations, narrow-mindedness and one-sided sectarian ideologies. Lower government SES school teachers in Delhi believe that the ideology of Pakistan is responsible for spreading terrorism. They suggested the ideology of Pakistan is blended with the Islamic religion to propagate terrorism. One teacher commented that

> Pakistan or Pakistanis fight and get angry whatever happens, they should think of it and should move ahead. They should change their thoughts and ideology [*sic*]. (Delhi, lower government school teacher 1)

Another teacher in a lower government school commented on general views expressed by her colleagues as being 'negative and full of hatred and animosity', adding

> We [India and Pakistan] both are reluctant towards each other. Both countries could not develop friendship and trust with each other. They have been like this for many years. There is a fear to visit

---

3   Oral history is a narrative approach that gathers personal reflections of events, from individuals or groups, and analyses how these events affect the individual group being studied (Creswell 2013, 74). It is extracted from listening to what interviewees say using the interviewee's memories. Using the oral history method, a researcher can view events from a participant's perspective. This facilitates the capturing of the lived experiences of the participants which can contribute to new areas of exploration (Thompson and Bornat 2017).

Pakistan, though I have friends in Pakistan [*sic*]. (Delhi, lower government school teacher 2)

The responses of a few teachers mention specific concerns about terrorism. One teacher commented

Pakistan spreads terrorism and kills a lot of people in Kashmir. They need to stop this. Muslims are always responsible for terrorism. (Delhi, lower government school teacher 3)

These views were shared by another lower government teacher.

On any news channel if there is a terrorist attack, that must have been done by a Muslim. Pakistan's government is responsible for growing terrorism and terrorists. They need to start taking action. (Delhi, lower government school teacher 4)

In Lahore, middle private SES school teachers blamed India's political and media xenophobia for creating issues in Pakistan. Teachers blamed India and Indians for isolating Pakistan in all avenues, including cricket and trade. One reflected that

We become negative when media shows that something said against Pakistan related to LOC, Siachin problems and Kashmir issues. India always raises matters in the cricket series [*sic*]. (Lahore, middle private school teacher 1)

Another teacher blamed India directly for terrorism, commenting that

Terrorism is caused by India and Indians. It has affected our business and economy. We get terrorist attacks. Nobody comes here. That is why our economy gets affected [*sic*]. (Lahore, middle private school teacher 2)

A middle school private teacher bluntly explained his concerns over the situation between India and Pakistan.

Indo–Pakistani relations cannot change. The Indians are not ready to sort out the issues. It is hard to trust them, such as in cricket [*sic*]. (Lahore, middle private school teacher 4)

The blended or mixed attitudes revealed by teachers could be the result of family ties in the other country (either India or Pakistan) or because of a traditional approach to the textbooks as learning material. The dominance of textbooks and learning tasks also led to a partial didactic impact on teachers' individual attitudes.

Sources that influence the attitudes of teachers

When asked about the sources of information that influenced teachers' attitudes towards the other country (India or Pakistan) and India–Pakistan relations, teachers in Delhi and Lahore identified sources such as the family, the media or society, school and textbooks. These sources shaped and refined teachers' attitudes towards India or Pakistan and India–Pakistan relations.

Family or oral history: narratives from survivors

Teachers in Delhi and Lahore recalled oral stories about partition narrated by their parents or grandparents. These oral stories or histories told of the family experiences of partition as secondary sources for teachers in elite SES private schools, lower SES government schools and private schools in both research sites. The oral histories of partition are the memories of history or history of the event, constructed against the state narratives to represent the 'other side of silence' (Butalia 2000, 34). There is a deep sensitivity towards partition and particularly what it meant for the women involved. Butalia highlights how silences speak and how oral histories deeply enrich conventional historical sources in the understanding of partition (Butalia 2000).

Teachers' attitudes towards India–Pakistan relations are constructed and influenced by oral history, significantly responsible for transmitting good or bad memories in teachers' minds. Butalia's partition narratives are both surprising and touching. They reflect the difficulties of remembering the violence that occurred during partition and of speaking about it aloud (Butalia 2000). Some of Butalia's narrators recognise that religious differences were one of the reasons for the partition of India (Butalia 2000).

Teachers in Delhi recalled their parents and grandparents narrating stories when they were growing up. Several mentioned that oral history helped them to understand their roots, as in this response from a teacher in an elite private school.

> I have been from a family that always tied with people there. Some of them migrated from Pakistan – emotional bonds are attached. (Delhi, elite SES private school teacher 1)

Another teacher, this time in a government school, commented that the information came 'from my family'. She explained this further, noting that it came from

> our parents who have come from Pakistan, like my father who has come from there and told us we used to live together. They faced problems, but they don't feel we are different from the Pakistanis [sic]. (Delhi, lower SES government school teacher 1)

Another teacher expressed similar views.

> My notions have developed from grandparents about our house before migration. It has developed by Hindu–Muslim friendship tales narrated by my family [sic]. (Delhi, lower SES private school teacher 1)

The experiences of the historical period of partition also left a bitter and highly debated legacy. This is specifically because of the ways in which the traumatic experience of migration, still embedded in teachers' minds in Delhi, have influenced the lives of many family members.

In Lahore, teachers reported that stories in their families are often narrated on India–Pakistan relations. Elite private school teachers commented

> My grandfather used to live in Shimla; we were Sikh. We had good relations with Hindu family as just as brothers [sic]. (Lahore, elite SES private school teacher 1)

A few other teachers expressed 'bad' experiences; one noted that

> My family told me that how much they faced in partition-killings. Hard to forget [sic]. (Lahore, lower SES government school teacher 1)

The response of another teacher illustrated how feelings of resentment and frustration were passed down through the generations.

Grandparents have told me a lot. How we lived together with Hindus. But they had bitter relations with Hindus. They lost their property because of them [*sic*]. (Lahore, lower SES private school teacher 1)

Although lower SES private school teachers in Lahore do not imitate their parents, they nonetheless credit them with instilling their own values and attitudes. For today's teachers, parents serve as a valuable conduit between narratives of the past, the often impersonal but still important, and the personal and dynamic experiences of individuals. Kaul (2001) argues that rather than considering the events of partition as the national order, there is much to learn about citizenship, the state and mobilisation by studying the local history of separation events. This creates conflict between a narrating state and memories. Oral history has the potential to highlight the personal experiences of historical events and reassert the inherent agency of the individual. As Butalia has observed (2000), a skilled historian must approach oral testimony with a critical eye.

School and textbooks

Schools and textbooks are primary vehicles through which societies formally, intentionally, systematically and extensively transmit national narratives, authority, legitimacy and means, providing conditions in which it can be carried out (Apple and Christian-Smith 1991; Bourdieu, Passeron and Nice 1977). As far as textbooks are concerned, teachers in elite SES private and middle SES government schools in Delhi and Lahore responded consistently regarding the influence of textbooks on their attitudes. When asked about the name of textbooks, for instance, teachers in Delhi listed the textbooks[4] studied in school. One teacher explicitly cited these as sources of influence.

Media, textbooks and interactions with people [*sic*]. I have a few relatives in Pakistan, but interactions impossible to that extent. The school textbooks, *Train to Pakistan* and some research articles. (Delhi, elite SES private school teacher 2)

---

4 *Themes in Indian History*. I, II and III. NCERT. Delhi (12th Grade), 380–1.
Pakistan Studies. Punjab Textbook Board. G.F.H. Publishers: Lahore (9th Grade).
Pakistan Studies. Punjab Textbook Board. Gohar Publishers: Lahore (10th Grade).

In Lahore, Pakistan Studies textbooks act as a significant source of information for teachers on India or India–Pakistan relations. Teachers responded that these textbooks outline the ideologies and values of their society. For some, the textbooks were the only source of information required.

> I read and teach only from Pakistan Studies textbooks. The textbooks have all the information of values of Pakistan society. (Lahore, middle SES government school teacher 2)

Such an opinion was endorsed by another teacher, also working in the middle SES government school.

> Our Pakistan Studies books have everything. They have the right values of Pakistan. I recommend all my students to continue or even read other Pakistan Studies textbooks. (Lahore, middle SES government school teacher 3)

When probed further about the textbooks, this emphasis of some teachers did not change.

> Pakistan Studies have provided us with sufficient information. The textbooks contribute a lot to our understanding of India and Indo–Pakistani relations. (Lahore, middle SES government school teacher 4)

Another teacher, this time from an elite SES private school, shared this view.

> Textbooks are the main source of teaching. We must teach from these textbooks. Textbooks present the values of our society. (Lahore, elite SES private school teacher 1)

Teachers in both Delhi and Lahore were keen to point out the legitimacy of knowledge in the textbooks. Textbooks and teachers thus combine to shape the attitudes and beliefs of students. Textbooks serve to express a society's ideology and ethos, and to transmit the values, goals,and myths that this society seeks to inculcate in new generations (Apple and Christian-Smith 1991; Bourdieu 1973).

In both Delhi and Lahore respondents from middle SES government schools identified their teacher role in the development of values and attitudes. One of them commented that

> My teachers provide a lot of information. I also learned a lot about Pakistan from my school and teachers. (Delhi, middle SES government school teacher 2)

Another remarked upon the enduring effect of information gained from textbooks and teachers at school.

> Teachers also narrated so many stories of Pakistan. Textbooks were important. We used to sincerely read the textbooks. (Delhi, middle SES government school teacher 3)

In Lahore, another teacher cited their Pakistan Studies teacher as a particularly influential source of information.

> I remember she told me how they migrated from India, stories were happy and painful. (Lahore, middle SES government school teacher 1)

This opinion was endorsed by another respondent.

> We get information from our teachers – from curriculum and textbooks! (Lahore, middle SES government school teacher 2)

Teachers play a significant role as a source of views in Delhi and Lahore. Teacher attitudes are extensively regarded as an important focus area for educational research, reform and the education of new teachers. Their values and opinions provide an appropriate filter through which they monitor and interpret their classroom practices and adapt consequent behaviours. Teachers refer to their own actions as 'substantially influenced and even determined by teachers' thought processes' (Clark and Peterson 1984, 255).

Cross-border transgressions: school community projects in Delhi

In Delhi, two middle SES private schools endorsed participation in peace projects and field trips to Pakistan. Teachers claimed that the idea of these educational projects is to start cross-border communication channels between students in India and Pakistan. Historically, during partition, the border established between India and Pakistan shielded a wide amount of land for 'territorializing' and 'nationalizing' native populations and identities (Purewal 2003, 547). The border has been used as a site for the construction of a dominant national consciousness and the location for oppositional expressions. The 'genealogy' of the border also encompasses significant anecdotes of how efforts have been made by the two nations to signify a complex national culture through the border (Purewal 2003, 553). She also considers the impact of border transgressions, actions that seek to contest 'its legitimacy or restrictedness, such as the annually peace vigils, the theatrical production *Ek Thi Naani*, cross-border internet and email communication or business delegations', believing that these 'can serve as catalysts for changing the boundaries of exclusivity that the border represents' (2003, 553).

Purewal goes on to note that communications and interactions based on transgressive actions can build upon the cultural connections separated by borders. In so doing they theoretically present another image of belonging or of nationhood from the borderlands (2003, 553).

In Delhi, cultural and pedagogical exchange programmes (peace projects and field trips to Pakistan) offer a step towards change, encouraging reflection on the intergenerational conflict embedded in their relations. Peace education is a prominent method for encouraging reconciliation. It is dependent on several ways on the requirements and aims of societies (Bar-Tal 2002; Salomon 2004). When communities are associated with an intractable conflict,[5] peace education is a vital means of accelerating peace-making and reconciliation (Bar-Tal 2013, 37).

In 2014, in Delhi, a middle private SES school launched a four-day event for 'spreading harmony' with Pakistan. This occasion involved many of the school's students in a wide variety of activities, including creating welcoming cards, writing articles, celebrating UN Week and Peace Day to praise the United Nations' significant work and encourage everybody to understand the importance of peace in everyday life, and participating in the Aman Ki Asha media campaign to bring about peace between India and Pakistan. The message 'Spreading harmony' reflected the school's determination to promote brotherhood, friendliness and peace with Pakistan. A conference held at the event was joined by the High Commissioner of Pakistan to India, HE Abdul Basit (now retired).

The teacher who organised the event declared that her engagement in peace programmes was a way of countering the long-standing dominant message of intolerance towards Muslims and Pakistan. Asked for more details, she explained

---

5   Intractable conflicts 'are total, viewed as a zero-sum contest, central, protracted, perceived as unsolvable and involve violence and demand extensive investments' (Bar-Tal 2013, 37).

Peace programmes have been organised in our school. They are positive and talk about good things. No conflicts are addressed. Cultural mixture and ambassador-positivity were all around [*sic*]. (Delhi, middle SES private school teacher 3)

She went on to elaborate further.

This peace programme is where we came to one conclusion – every religion asks for peace. Students have been involved in these programmes. The programme was an admirable effort and then we did a formal meeting. Students met different cultures and religions [*sic*]. (Delhi, middle SES private school teacher 3)

This teacher also commented that her school had organised events after the Peshawar school attack that had so alarmed the country.

After the Peshawar attack, there was a prayer meeting. Students were reading one part of the Bible or Quran, because we have a lot of Christian and Muslim students. I prefer doing this way [*sic*]. (Delhi, middle SES private school teacher 3)

She was confident that the school's peace programme served to strengthen bonds with its counterparts in Pakistan.

I met a Pakistani teacher at a conference, and we became friends. I served as a teacher in Pakistan educating teachers about peace in rural areas. I have also taught twenty teachers from the countryside, who doesn't have online teaching awareness [*sic*]. (Delhi, middle SES private school teacher 3)

Teachers at this school observed that these peace programmes act as a vehicle to propagate peace, largely through showing sympathy towards the victims. This helps students to gain factual and conceptual knowledge, develop their competence in using that knowledge to interpret different situations, become aware of their own political agency in the broader development of rights and seize opportunities to tackle misconceptions about the other country.

Another middle private SES school in Delhi is also involved in preparing different national platforms and events for students, enabling them to gain greater knowledge about India or Pakistan. The school organises a meeting for students from both countries to work together and overcome differences and struggles; it encourages them to keep the end goal in mind and to work out the current issues of socio-political and financial measurements. Around a thousand motivated students from Delhi, Mumbai and Bangalore, Indonesia, Pakistan, Sri Lanka, Nepal and Nigeria, meet at these events to discuss and find the best route forward to achieve peace and progress through dialogue and discourse. A teacher at this school commented

> This meeting [Peace] that has been intended to give a broad stage to youthful envoys to obtain and spread peace throughout the world [*sic*]. We used this meeting programme when India and Pakistan suffer a diplomatic crisis, students of both the nations [India and Pakistan] meet for a peace initiative. (Delhi, middle SES private school teacher 4)

She added her own opinion of these platforms' value.

> I think the textbook portrays the Indo–Pakistani relations in a negative light, where two countries have been projected as violent camps. It will instigate change in the minds of children. (Delhi, middle SES private school teacher 4)

This school is trying to develop peace initiatives with Pakistan. Teachers preferred people-to-people contact in their attempt to build a counter-hegemony of civil society, a direct challenge to the hegemony of the state. Such peace initiatives are designed to deconstruct the nation-state system founded on the narrow definition of 'national interest' as envisaged in the National Curriculum Document of 2005 in India.

Pedagogically, these two projects were built on two core ideas. First, the focus sought to engage students in discussions incorporating some of the principles of deliberative democracy (Dryzek 2002). This includes a commitment that coming together for open, honest and respectful conversations across our differences can lead to better, more inclusive outcomes. Whether or not the discussion leads to a consensus, the process of deliberation is transformational: it changes the way in which individuals perceive their own position and that of others, and may well encourage students to review their beliefs to some extent. Deliberative fora typically involve distinct phases of learning in which students deepen their understanding of an issue, often in dialogue with experts. Some commentators have criticised deliberative democratic theorists for failing to develop an adequate account of the role and nature of knowledge (Habibis and Walter 2008).

The media and society

There are diverse epistemological tools and processes related to the production of knowledge, ideas and perceptions. The media is one such tool, with a very important role in disseminating ideas and influencing perceptions. It plays a definitive role in constructing popular imagination regarding issues of identity, a refugee crisis and notions of cultural and psychic frontiers (Tripathi and Raghuvanshi 2020). The effect on collective imagination is achieved through engaging narratives and powerful images that the media can present to viewers. This in turn helps to construct – and deconstruct – popular notions by altering the dialectics of cognitive mapping. Manifestation of this effect can be seen in the way in which the media has impacted mental borders between India and Pakistan (Tripathi and Raghuvanshi 2020).

The jingoistic attitude of the media in the subcontinent undeniably obstructs peace between India and Pakistan. It has been responsible for increasing tension between the two countries and for limiting their governments' abilities to take concrete steps towards peace (Chatterji 2009; Rasul 2002). In 2008, the coverage of the Mumbai attacks was followed by complicated relations between India and Pakistan. Following the attack, neither journalists nor governments were clear about what had happened and the editorial commentary depended on guesswork (Chatterji 2009; Rasul 2002). However, after the identity of the attackers was discovered, both Indian and Pakistani governments hurled accusations at each other, with the national press supporting their governments (Chatterji 2009; Rasul 2002). Although media influences can be manipulative, they have the power to promote controversial ideas through advertising and can contribute to a conflict of national identity. It has also been known to expose bias, stereotypes and sexist or racist ideologies in text, illustrations and photos (van Dijk 1995, 352).

However, the media performance in the India–Pakistan conflict situation deviates from traditional models. The press plays the role of guide, offering solutions for multifaceted issues between the two countries (Chatterji 2009; Rasul 2002). The media can influence the attitudes and beliefs that shape general opinions and behaviour, changing and determining the most basic human actions performed every day (Matsunaga 2010, 71).

As far as the impact of cyberspace on social memories of partition is concerned, communications and interactions based on transgressive actions can build upon the cultural connections separated by borders.

It is exactly the negotiations between the aggressions and transgressions, along with a critical perspective on the displacements that have accompanied the Indo–Pak border's creation and maintenance, that will enable the exploration of any such visions. (Purewal 2003, 553).

The capability of the Indian and Pakistani states indeterminately to uphold the border as a line of separation is a time-consuming task. Media, communication technology and film have all been areas which the state has endeavoured to impact upon and limit access to (Purewal 2003, 553). Technological development, ushered in by the digital age, has provided new formats for transnational communication; it has thus opened a growing number of virtual routes between India and Pakistan (Hartnack 2012). The networks of communication between individuals in India and Pakistan are constructed much more easily, and new South–South interactions have brought about the demise of some miscellanies of colonialism. Telephone calls between Delhi and Islamabad that used to be routed through London, for instance, can now can be made; transnational communication can take place at low or no cost in cyberspace (Hartnack 2012). The concept of a cosmopolitan memory transcends the national memory cultures and sets the stage for a shared memory-scape. Whereas memories narrated in person-to-person communication are collectively constructed and bounded by social – or at most national – borders, memories that pop up in transnational chat rooms are de-territorialised, anonymous and in some sense borderless (Hartnack 2012).

In addition, transnational communication can stimulate the revision of social memory constructs. Inherent in such free-floating communications (including those between India and Pakistan) is the possibility that the patchwork of distorted, narrow-minded social memories might become a publicly argued, cosmopolitan memory-scape (Hartnack 2012). It remains to be seen how such memories will eventually be shaped in cyberspace. On the one hand, the internet offers an unprecedented variety of thoughts, writing and opinions, as well as the potential to bring to light repressions, distortions or amplification of social memories. On the other hand, individuals can choose to be just as parochial as ever, for instance visiting only those chat rooms or forums that confirm and harden their existing prejudices (Hartnack 2012).

Despite the various new alignments between India, Pakistan and Bangladesh, and the array of technological options available through which to develop a shared memory-space, it is far from certain whether Indians, Pakistanis and Bangladeshis will leverage the new technologies in service for refining their collective social memories (Hartnack 2012). Elite private SES and middle private SES school teachers reported that the media is the second source of information for them and their students, playing a key role in 'filling in the gaps'.

Furthermore, the media is the leading source of information in the world today. It helps individuals to stay connected and remain informed, providing the opportunity to construct ideas and personal opinions about the world that surrounds individuals (Matsunaga 2010, 71). Elite SES private and middle SES private school teachers in Delhi and Lahore commented that they rely on the media for their knowledge of the other country (India or Pakistan) and India–Pakistan relations. In Delhi, teachers concurred that there are certain instructive advantages in utilising the media for information about Pakistan. When probed, one explained why.

> Media, textbooks and interactions with people [the sources of information]! I have few relatives in Pakistan, but interactions [with relatives] are impossible to that extent. It keeps me informed [*sic*]. (Delhi, elite SES private school teacher 1)

Another teacher preferred the media to textbooks, but noted that caution and wariness were still required.

> Media provides more information and knowledge of Pakistan than textbooks. We have to use media critically. (Delhi, elite SES private school teacher 2)

Middle private SES teachers also refer to the media for information. Similarly, in Lahore, middle SES private school teachers commented that the media played an integral role in providing information about India, noting that it always had 'updated' and 'accurate' information. As one teacher observed,

> Newspapers and news channels [on television] always have [reports on] India. I daily read them [newspapers] to my knowledge about India and its role in Pakistan [*sic*]. (Lahore, middle SES private school teacher 2)

Another teacher from a middle SES private school in Lahore echoed similar views.

> We have smart media. It is making efforts to motivate us as the citizens of Pakistan. We get a lot of information about Indian people from the media. They are smart [*sic*]. (Lahore, middle SES private school teacher 3)

Such influence by the media fits perfectly into the Gramscian framework of intellectual hegemony. According to Gramsci, the process of hegemony is actualised with the help of intellectual and moral leadership. These tools can present a lopsided view of reality and are instrumental in repetitively reinforcing that view. In this way, ideas and practices favoured by the dominant class are presented in a way that encourages the subordinate class to accept them as their own (Tripathi and Raghuvanshi 2020). Such a situation is complex, leading to

> a society in which subordinate groups and classes appear to actively support and subscribe to values, ideals, objectives, cultural and political meanings, which bind them to, and 'incorporate' them into, the prevailing structures of power. (Storey 2006, 80)

This section elaborates on the various depictions of the India–Pakistan border in the media and analyses the way in which they have reinforced mental borders. Teachers in elite private schools use the media critically to gather information about the other country (India/Pakistan) and India–Pakistani relations, while teachers in middle private SES schools in Lahore may prefer to use the media to authenticate their conspiracy theories (discussed in more detail in Chapter 5).

Conclusion

This chapter has presented teachers' attitudes towards India or Pakistan and India–Pakistan relations. Most elite private SES school teachers in Delhi and Lahore expressed a secular attitude. The narrative of shared cultural traits and migration hypothesised a perception of collective suffering in migration or a recognition of suffering experienced by the other side (India or Pakistan) to elicit a secular or liberal attitude. Middle private and government school teachers in Delhi expressed secular, non-ideological attitudes towards Pakistan. In Lahore, middle SES private and government school teachers shared blended and communal beliefs respectively. In Delhi, lower SES government school teachers expressed a range of opinions; in Lahore, on the other hand, lower SES government school teachers reported a communal attitude towards the other country (India/Pakistan). In both countries, teachers in lower SES private schools projected a communal attitude. Although some prejudices were noted in teachers' behaviours, they were not extreme.

The communal attitudes follow the textbooks. Constructing two nations in bipolar opposition accentuates the positive in us and the negative in them, and so develops a hatred for others. This could be interpreted as a discourse of nationalism that distorts historical facts in two ways: by glorifying us and by darkening the other (Ahmad 2009, Anand 2019). The mixed attitudes could be due to individual teachers having family ties in the other country (India or Pakistan) or because of a traditional approach to the textbooks as learning material.

The dominance of textbooks and learning tasks has also led to a partial, didactic impact on teachers' attitudes. In Lahore, the official textbooks teach the pillars of Islam, and thus violate Pakistan's constitution by teaching the religion to non-Muslims. Beyond that, the Pakistani identity is defined to exclude any other forms of identification – cultural, ethnic, linguistic – and goes along with negative, even hate-filled comments about the 'other', India and Hindus. Many scholars have argued that this exclusionary approach fosters biases, intolerance and bigotry (Nayyar and Salim 2003; Afzal 2015). Afzal (2015) traces the attitudes of high school students towards the government curriculum. In so doing she discovers that students' views on India and Hindus largely mirror those in textbooks and are filled in with societal and media narratives. Such an attitude was not the direct outcome of partition, but the consequence of textbooks that have developed these religious and anti-Indian positions, especially from the 1980s (Hoodbhoy and Nayyar 1985; Afzal 2018). The teachers' fundamental attitudes were formed through family or oral history and the media, but refined through textbooks and their teachers.

The school SES (and the institutional habitus) seem to be closely associated with teachers' attitudes about the other country (India or Pakistan) and India–Pakistan relations. The next chapter presents vivid snapshots of the teachers' classroom practices. In particular it considers how teachers in both countries teach India–Pakistani relations or construct their attitudes, which are then presented through semi-structured interviews and classroom observations.

5
Teachers' pedagogical strategies to India–Pakistan relations: what happens in the classroom?

As discussed in Chapters 1, 2 and 3, teachers play a central role in curriculum use and enactment (Calderhead 1996; Shkedi 1998). Teachers' socio-cultural and political background, the imagination of the 'self' and perceptions of the 'other' may lead them to agree with, submit to, defy, resist or select textbook messages or content (Horner et al. 2015; Durrani, Kaderi and Anand 2020). In practice, teachers have been found to perceive school history through the prism of nationalism, leading them to privilege the nationalisation of students (Durrani, Kaderi and Anand 2020). The consumption of history by students is also subject to negotiation based on their social positioning and axes of identification, as well as the alignment of school history with everyday history – particularly family narratives of the past (Durrani, Kaderi and Anand 2020).

Teachers transmit a curriculum, but what they transmit is not essentially identical to the written curriculum (Shkedi 2009). They also make the final decisions on the curriculum implementation in the classroom (Tyler 1949; Snyder et al. 1992). Teachers' use of peripheral sources varies subject to their attitudes and values, their knowledge of the subject and the settings in which they teach (Johnson et al. 2003); there is sound evidence of teachers' curricular approaches influencing student learning and motivation (Eisner 1990; Erickson and Shultz 1992; King 2002). However, the dominant directive in curricula both challenges teachers' professional autonomy and damages their self-confidence (Rosenholtz 1987; Taylor 2013).

The following sections highlight teachers' pedagogical practices and responses to the teaching of India–Pakistan relations in Delhi and Lahore. The analysis identified three teaching orientations by presenting narrative vignettes to show each style and illustrating the interconnectedness of narrative identity, meaning-making and teaching perspectives through the vignettes. The chapter focuses specifically on the dominant patterns in classroom discourse to understand the ways in which teachers respond to, and interact with, the curriculum and textbooks pedagogically. It also discusses teachers' views about their students' attitudes towards either India or Pakistan and India–Pakistan relations in general, as there is a strong association between teacher and student attitudes (Indoshi et al. 2010; Wirth and Perkins 2013). Finally, the chapter concludes how the socio-economic status (SES) of the school negates teachers' attitudes (presented in the last chapter), dictating their pedagogical responses or classroom strategies in both research sites regardless of their individual attitudes.

Reflective teachers: elite private school teachers

Reflective teachers are those who critically examine their teaching beliefs and practices on an ongoing basis with the goal of enhancing their teaching quality (Borg 2011, 215–28). They avoid routine teaching practices by constantly gaining new insights into their performance and possessing the ability to think reflectively (Braun and Crumpler 2004; Farrell 2016). The concept is clearly defined by Dewey as

> active, persistent and careful consideration of any belief or supposed form of knowledge in light of grounds that support it and the further consequences to which it leads. (Dewey 1933, 9)

Teachers who practise reflective thinking are also opposed to impulsive actions based on trial and error, drawing on individuals' instincts, and to routine actions that mainly rely on 'authority and tradition … undertaken in a passive, largely unthinking way' (Griffiths 2000, 540). In short, reflective teachers 'locate problems, question goals, explore contexts, analyse possibilities and craft appropriate educational experiences to benefit learners' (Baleghizadeh and Javidanmehr 2014, 21). This reflective cycle may cause modifications not only in teachers' classroom practices, but also in their teaching philosophies, principles and theories. Reflective techniques also help teachers to gain a better understanding of how political and social issues may impact their teaching practice, hence the critical dimension of reflection (Farrell 2016).

In both research sites, elite private school teachers were reflective in their teaching practice. In terms of enactment of the curriculum or textbooks in the classroom, elite private school teachers in Delhi and Lahore commented that in the history textbooks social conflicts and violence are included (in Pakistan) or muted (in India). The teachers put forward two claims. First, history textbooks in Delhi and Lahore distort their discussion of the other country (India or Pakistan) and of India–Pakistan relations by omitting individual events, in order to present the events in line with a narrative. Second, textbooks neglect to teach the history, culture, religion and tradition of the other country (India or Pakistan). The shared beliefs of Hindus and Muslims, which could promote trust and familiarity, are either absent (as in Pakistan Studies) or present only in part (as in Indian history textbooks). In Delhi, elite private school teachers commented that the school textbook[1] portrays Pakistan in a 'positive light'.

As discussed in Chapter 2, in the history textbook themes such as 'partition or holocaust?' and 'the power of stereotypes' offer multiple interpretations of how the partition of India was perceived, both at the time and later. When teachers were asked to explain how they enact the textbooks, one of them observed

> The textbook is written to bring the right perspectives by interviewing the people and we bring out the positive aspects of the partition [*sic*]. (Delhi, elite private school teacher 1)

Another teacher revealed a similar perspective in her response.

> Textbook gives positive approach because if you look at sources [oral history], what sources talk about [*sic*], it talks about how Muslims said that he is trying to compensate the *karz*[2] [debt] of his father because how Hindu lady helped his father [*sic*], so how he is

---

1   *Themes in Indian History*. I, II and III. NCERT. Delhi (12th Grade), 380–1.
2   *Karz* is a Hindi word, meaning to settle or pay a debt.

trying to compensate the *karz* of his father, but we handle it critically in the classroom. So I use the textbook in the classroom. (Delhi, elite private school teacher 2)

In Lahore, in semi-structured interviews, elite private school teachers maintained that they critically enact the textbooks.[3] Teachers stated that textbooks present history through a single-sided narrative, with no primary or secondary sources, and are full of stereotypes. Following probing on what amendments should be made to textbooks, one teacher commented

I think textbooks should emphasise more on [*sic*] the issues between Muslims and Hindus in society. This will really help to teach critically. (Lahore, elite private school teacher 1)

Another teacher, also from an elite private school, deplored the limited resources available for teaching.

There are not many secondary sources of information. These sources could have helped in the evaluation and develop discussions in the classroom. (Lahore, elite private school teacher 2)

This teacher also pointed out how controversial topics, such as the negative role of Hindu teachers,[4] the separation of East Pakistan and the creation of Bangladesh in 1971, are presented without explanations or references. She observed

Textbooks[5] describe religion and the culture of Pakistan. We have the history of the creation of Pakistan,[6] which is numerous in the textbook [*sic*]. Hindus are presented in the negative light, but we teach critically. (Lahore, elite private school teacher 2)

---

3   *Pakistan Studies*. Punjab Textbook Board. G.F.H. Publishers: Lahore (9th Grade). *Pakistan Studies*. Punjab Textbook Board. Gohar Publishers: Lahore (10th Grade).
4   'After the establishment of Pakistan, the governments failed to inculcate and create the spirit of Pakistani nationalism. Pakistan's opponent group succeeds in continuing their negative activities. Unfortunately, Bengali Muslims had always been more backward in education than Hindus. Therefore, Hindu teachers were in the majority in schools and colleges, tarnishing the minds of the new generation with the idea of Bengali nationalism. They prepared them to rebel against the ideology of Pakistan. This paved the way for separation from West Pakistan.' (*Pakistan Studies* Textbook, 9th Grade, 126).
5   *Pakistan Studies*. Punjab Textbook Board. G.F.H Publishers: Lahore (9th Grade). *Pakistan Studies*. Punjab Textbook Board. Gohar Publishers: Lahore (10th Grade).
6   *Pakistan Studies*. Punjab Textbook Board. G.F.H Publishers: Lahore (9th Grade).

In their responses many teachers emphasised how they avoided imposing their attitudes or views on their students. Instead, they read from the textbooks,[7] rearticulated particular paragraphs or phrases and asked questions of the students to start discussions. The teacher quoted above gave details of her technique.

> We [teachers] do relate it [textbook] to news, policy or an initiative taken by our [Pakistan] government for developing peace with India. We use classroom debates and discussions. We compare the textbook details on terrorism and teachings of Islam with the news articles. (Lahore, elite private school teacher 2)

The responses showed that elite teachers frequently used group discussions to create a 'relaxed' and 'friendly' atmosphere in the classroom.

In addition to group discussions, elite private school teachers in both research sites critically enacted the textbook in the classroom by employing multiple perspectives in their approach to history teaching. In doing so, they sought to express the equal status of groups (from either India or Pakistan). Elite private school teachers believed that teaching critically is their professional responsibility. To them, the process of critically analysing conflicting perspectives seems to supersede the emphasis on collective identity and building mutual goals or friendly relations. Exposure to traumatic episodes of conflict, however, may have raised feelings of anger, threat and anxiety (Bar-Tal et al. 2010).

When asked about what pedagogical strategies they used to shape students' attitudes, teachers in both research sites referred to non-traditional teaching approaches in their lessons to complement the textbooks. Such approaches included debates and project work, both of which aimed to increase student engagement and promote critical thinking. Teachers reported that their students did not appear to blame one country over the other, but rather demonstrated respect for the other country (India or Pakistan). In terms of promoting critical thinking, a teacher from a school in Delhi shared an example. She explained

> The discussions on Pakistan are always critical in my classroom. All students get engaged in discussions and they [the students] are always secular. No negative feelings towards Pakistan. (Delhi, elite private school teacher 1)

---

7   *Themes in Indian History*. I, II and III. NCERT. Delhi (12th Grade).

Another teacher in Delhi described a similar classroom environment in her elite private school.

> In my classes, when I took this topic about the partition in my class, I found no learners talking against Pakistan or anti-Pakistan, so there were no anti-Pakistani feelings. (Delhi, elite private school teacher 2)

She added that sometimes students used cricket as a tool for voicing attitudes toward Pakistan or Muslims. These were in general positive and unbiased.

> Students support India. But they [students] have sportsmanship and do not burn televisions if India loses to Pakistan. There is no behaviour I felt during matches [*sic*]. (Delhi, elite private school teacher 1)

Cricket was also cited as a positive influence by another teacher from a similar school.

> Their [students'] views are always positive. They [students] are unbiased and secular. We both support the best players, either Indian or Pakistani. (Delhi, elite private school teacher 2)

Similarly, elite private school teachers in Lahore shared positive views of their students' attitudes towards India. Cricket, they said, offers a great opportunity for entertainment and extensive engagement with India. One teacher noted

> Students often say this to me: Pakistan and Indian cricketers should be together [play together]. They [Indian and Pakistani cricketers] are best together. (Lahore, elite private school teacher 1)

While appreciating cricket's ability to connect Pakistanis with Indians, however, teachers recognised that the game is sometimes used to express hostility towards India. One commented

> But we as teachers like in cricket when we had a match everyone watches. I teach them [students] sportsmanship whenever they [students] get upset about losing to India. There is a feeling of loss in a war, however, I try to reduce this feeling [losing]. (Lahore, elite private school teacher 2)

Teachers in Lahore mentioned that students have 'friendly' views of Hindus and are 'tolerant' towards India. Students are free from 'sectarian interpretations'. One teacher explained how she encouraged such views.

> For centuries, cows are worshipping in India [*sic*]. Students asked me, why we [Muslims] slaughter and they [Hindus] worship. I got confused so we tell them by relating it [cow slaughtering or worshipping] to religion. Students understand that it [cow slaughtering or worshipping] is right and they [students] should practise in their way. (Lahore, elite private school teacher 1)

For another teacher, the students' position was clear.

> Students understand the differences in religion between Muslims and Hindus. They [the students] respect the issues between both. (Lahore, elite private school teacher 2)

Teachers in both research sites also found it helpful to use articles (published by authors such as Ayesha Jalal and Khushwant Singh) in the classroom. These sources helped teachers to enact the textbook content on partition to shape students' views.

As far as a hidden curriculum is concerned, elite private school teachers in Delhi explained that the media is a valuable source of information for students' presentations and projects. One commented

> Textbooks[8] do not have a lot of information about Pakistan. I ask students to use the media and evaluate the sources critically. (Delhi, elite private school teacher 1)

Another remarked that

> The media is an active tool for them to know about Pakistan and its people. They [students] cannot go to Pakistan but girls in my class follow their [Pakistan] fashion. (Delhi, elite private school teacher 2)

---

8   Textbooks in India that were selected and analysed are:
     India and the Contemporary World. I. NCERT. Delhi (9th Grade) (T1).
     India and the Contemporary World. II. NCERT. Delhi (10th Grade) (T2).
     Themes in World History. NCERT. Delhi (11th Grade) (T3).
     Themes in Indian History. I, II and III. NCERT. Delhi (12th Grade) (T4).

However, several teachers expressed anger towards the media for propagating feelings of suspicion and mistrust towards Pakistan and Muslims. The response of some was to motivate students to evaluate critically the conflicting views shared by the media. One teacher observed

> Media can influence. It is owned by teachers to make students believe in a balanced view of things. You must put this as you don't have to believe what the other says. I actively challenge the information. Students then change their views critically. (Delhi, elite private school teacher 1)

Another took a similar approach.

> Media is used by my learners critically. They [students] evaluate the sources and then use in their projects or presentations. I get to see many unbiased projects. (Delhi, elite private school teacher 2)

Besides the media, elite private school teachers in Delhi also drew upon a range of different sources, including historical documents, novels and films (such as *Train to Pakistan*[9] and *Earth*[10]), to teach the history of India–Pakistan relations. When teachers were asked to explain how they use these sources, one replied

> We use different books [e.g. *Train to Pakistan*] but tell them it has just one meaning [of partition]. I always ask them questions in the form of discussions. In doing so, I also explore their views received from families. (Delhi, elite private school teacher 1)

These sources help teachers to discuss diverse ideologies so that students can scrutinise the many versions of events from a diversity of perspectives. Another teacher observed

> I use debates and discussions in the classroom in order to teach Indo–Pakistani relations using newspapers. Debates and discussions construct positive thoughts. (Delhi, elite private school teacher 2)

---

9   *Train to Pakistan* is a historical novel by Khushwant Singh, published in 1956. It recounts the Partition of India in August 1947.

10   *Earth* is a 1998 Indian period drama film directed by Deepa Mehta. It portrays the Partition of India.

Vignette 1: A dialogue between elite private school teacher 2 (EPST2) and students in Delhi.

EPST2: What do you know about Pakistan?

Student1: It is our neighbour [Pakistan]. We only have issues due to Kashmir.

EPST2: How can we solve the Kashmir issue?

Student 1: It is due to our politicians.

Student 2: Politicians are creating issues between us. They should sit together and resolve the issue.

Student 3: Sorting out the Kashmir issue. Terrorism can be reduced.

In vignette 1, the teacher gave students the opportunity to examine and debate additional reasons for partition besides those listed in the textbook. This example illustrates an active approach adopted by the teacher. In this way students are encouraged to engage with historical narratives beyond the textbook – including those in the media and informal educational spaces.

Nevertheless, teachers in Lahore acknowledged that the media sometimes inspires students to spread hatred toward India. Articles must therefore be approached with caution, as one teacher observed.

> My students refer to social media and news articles in order to share their attitudes towards India/Hindus and Indo–Pakistani relations. These news articles are useful in educating them. (Lahore, elite private school teacher 1)

Another saw the media in a generally helpful light, but the wariness remained.

> Students use media to communicate and to learn. The media's use and impact are useful for India and Indo–Pakistani relations. They are liberal – sometimes a news article confuses their [students] minds. (Lahore, elite private school teacher 2)

In the classroom, teachers motivated their students to investigate the information in the textbook using the internet. They also brought examples from the local context and personal experiences to shape students' views. Students were encouraged to share their experiences by using the question–answer interaction method to facilitate the discussions (see vignette 2 below).

> Vignette 2: A dialogue between elite private school teacher 1 (EPST1) and students in Lahore.
>
> EPST 1: What are your views on Indo–Pak relations?
>
> Student 1: I am excited to go to India. Politicians are the main cause of tension.
>
> Student 2: Politicians of Pakistan should talk about and resolve the Kashmir issue.
>
> Student 3: Politicians should focus on terrorism.

In vignette 2, the teacher encouraged critical thinking via interactions. Students were critical of politicians who choose to maintain historical grievances and polarise perceptions of hostility and enmity.

The responses of elite private school teachers in both research sites show their efforts to develop students' views beyond the ideas they encountered in their textbook, in the media or at home. In so doing they adopted a participatory approach to history teaching. Such teachers prompted discussions of different views of the partition of India, and the students found participating in the discussions valuable. This is useful because a participatory discussion prepares students to accept their peers' views quickly, to sympathise and to act. The meetings within the history-learning context established conflict at the centre of dialogue, rendering the 'conflict about conflict' redundant (Halabi et al. 2004; Maoz 2000) and repeatedly shadowing India–Pakistan encounters.

Motivated traditional teachers: middle SES government and private school teachers

The teachers discussed in this section are motivated, with critical, thinking-oriented attitudes, but their pedagogical practice remains traditional (Lewin and Stuart 2003; Moloi et al. 2008, 21). The transmission of information involves an established process of review, repetition learning, memorisation, recitation, duplicating from the board, choral reaction and 'chalk and talk' (Lewin and Stuart 2003; Moloi et al. 2008, 21). In Delhi and Lahore, teachers in middle socio-economic status government and private schools are motivated and reflective in ideas. In semi-structured interviews they mentioned teaching critically using structuring practices, which involve summarising the last lesson, reviewing the homework and checking student understanding through questioning in the classroom. However, during the classroom observations, teachers lacked the critical thinking capabilities shown by traditional teachers (see below), and their skills and understanding of critical thinking were lacking. The communicative approach was used only marginally. Teachers simply transmitted the textbook content with minimum levels of student participation; their pedagogy thus remained traditional and teacher-centered.

As far as the enactment of textbooks is concerned, teachers from middle socio-economic status government and private schools in both research sites mentioned that partition is depicted in a positive light in the textbooks. Teachers commented that the syllabus is too long, but the textbook information is appropriate for the students and it fits the intended purpose. They explained that the textbooks are an essential part of their classrooms and discussions, providing the only trustworthy source of information for students. Students are told to rote-memorise the textbooks in order to pass the examinations.

In Delhi, teachers rely heavily on textbooks to teach the partition of India. A middle SES private school teacher commented that

> The textbooks [NCERT] are good. They [textbooks] describe the historical events [partition] with the use of different sources. (Delhi, middle private school teacher 1)

Another private school teacher agreed.

> History textbooks [NCERT] are good. They [the textbooks] seem to have a lot of information. Students say what's in the textbooks. (Delhi, middle private school teacher 3)

Another teacher, this time from a government school, introduced another issue: the need to use available time to best effect.

> Textbooks are enough for students. We don't have time for other information [*sic*]. (Delhi, Middle government school teacher 1)

Another government school teacher noted that

Textbook[11] is important for students. These students just understand about Pakistan from these [NCERT] textbooks. (Delhi, middle government school teacher 2)

Teachers found the NCERT school textbook content on partition generally interesting and useful. They prefer to use textbooks to provide multiple perspectives and opportunities for students to engage critically with the topic. However, in the classroom, rather than allowing the students to think critically about the partition of India, teachers just transmitted the information as predefined truths, without any evaluation or analysis. There was little opportunity for students to 'discover their self about others', or to engage with 'rival perspectives' to form their understanding of the topic, contrary to the pedagogical goal of the National Curriculum Framework (NCF) of 2005 (as discussed in Chapter 2).

In Lahore, middle socio-economic status government and private school teachers similarly used textbooks to teach students about India–Pakistan relations. A private school teacher observed that

I only use the textbook to teach. There is nothing anti-Indian in the textbooks. In the creation of Pakistan, they [textbooks] mention the leaders and their roles. It [the textbook content] is entirely about Pakistan and its culture. Our [Pakistan] things related to government-merits and demerits have been mentioned, which are good. It helps the students to understand which government is good for Pakistan's prosperity and for me to teach. (Lahore, middle private school teacher 1)

Another teacher revealed the extent of the textbooks' influence among learners.

The attitudes of my students are like textbooks. They read and say the same thing as in the textbook. (Lahore, middle private school teacher 1)

One government school teacher described her satisfaction with the textbooks' content and the pedagogical approach they encouraged.

---

11   *Themes in Indian History.* I, II and III. NCERT. Delhi (12th Grade) (T4).

> I rely on textbooks to teach. Textbooks are so nice. Nothing is wrong with India and the Indians. It [textbook] describes the best way. (Lahore, middle government school teacher 3)

When asked to describe what they particularly liked about the textbooks, the same teacher gave a clear response.

> The textbooks [Pakistan Studies] depict the ideology of Pakistan and the creation of Pakistan. There is nothing negative with Hindus or India [*sic*]. (Lahore, middle government school teacher 3)

Other teachers, also supportive of the textbooks, noted their influence on students' attitudes. One gave a guarded response.

> Students receive a lot of information from textbooks. (Lahore, middle government school teacher 1)

Another teacher's comments were more specific.

> In Pakistan, for students, Pakistan Studies textbook has a lot of importance. Views about India are derived from textbooks and teachers. (Lahore, middle government school teacher 2)

Teachers made affirmative assertions about the textbooks they used. They did not comment upon the marginalisation of historical themes such as 'rehabilitation of refugees', 'administrative problems', 'distribution of assets', 'division of the army', 'the river water issue' and 'issues of states' wherever India or Hindus were held responsible, nor the fact that the textbooks offered a wealth of information about India as the enemy (Afzal 2015; Hussain and Safiq 2016). As discussed in Chapter 2, the Pakistan Studies (PS) textbooks continue to encompass anti-Indian or anti-Hindu discourse in the construction of the national identities of students in Lahore. The negative depiction of the other country or faith elucidates the purpose of the hidden curriculum to perpetuate the cause of one own side at the expense of the other (Hussain and Safiq 2016).

As far as teachers' negotiations with the hidden curriculum are concerned, South Asia is a conflict zone where the media has been influential in creating mutually hostile insights. Middle SES private school teachers in Delhi commented that information from newspapers or television influences their own or students' views, not always in a progressive way. Teachers commented that news articles nurture 'anxieties and 'hostile attitudes' among students. At times of terrorist attacks, expressions of hatred and biases frequently intensified. One teacher's response was scathing.

> The media can provide useless stories. They often label Muslims as a terrorist. Students collect negative stories about Muslims, and we have to make them evaluate. (Delhi, middle private school teacher 4)

Another noted that

> The media is negative towards Pakistan and Muslims. There is intolerance in India. Students often comes [sic] with news articles labelling Pakistan as a terrorist country. (Delhi, middle private school teacher 5)

Teachers also mentioned that the newspapers offer young people terms of hatred and labelling for the other religion. The use of derogatory terms such as 'mullahs', 'terrorists' and 'Pakistani Muslim terrorist' by children and young people clearly derives from the media.

In Lahore, teachers' complaints about the media's jingoistic attitude impedes all peace movements in the region. As discussed in Chapter 4, the media has long been responsible for exacerbating the level of tension between the two countries. One teacher observed

> I think family [of students] does not impose that much, but the media influence the minds of learners. Students depend on the internet for information. Most of the TV [television] channels encourage Indo–Pakistani relations. (Lahore, middle private school teacher 2)

Another teacher commented

> The media is very aggressive and adverse, however citizens are more confident about India. Students' views are mostly from the Media [sic]. (Lahore, middle private school teacher 3)

Upon probing further, this teacher offered an example.

> In Kashmir case, students often say India is spreading terrorism and not doing justice to people in Kashmir. When I asked where you [students] saw this [Kashmir case], he [student] said it was on the news channel yesterday. (Lahore, middle private school teacher 3)

Social media thus plays a dominant role in outlining the reactions of the public in Pakistan.

As noted above (pp. 00–00), cricket also shapes the attitudes of all students towards India or Pakistan. A teacher noted its impact in the classroom.

> The cricket match between India and Pakistan is entertaining. Students regularly watch matches with their parents. The views are also derived from the cricket match which they bring to the classroom. (Delhi, middle private school teacher 1)

Another teacher explained how cricket provided a focus for students' opinions.

> My students discuss the cricket matches when I ask them to discuss Indo–Pakistani relations. It is interesting to see how students refer to the cricket match to discuss their views. (Delhi, middle private school teacher 2)

She went on to offer a specific example in her response.

> IPL [Indian Premier League] is entertaining. Students often mention Shoibh Akhtar. They [students] comment that he is such a good person. They have positive views about Pakistan and its population. (Delhi, middle private school teacher 2)

The influence of matches can also be negative. Teachers agreed that cricket in its national avatar may on occasion become an avenue of war between India and Pakistan. The sport presents an opportunity to reflect chauvinism, religious division and the gulf between self and other among the students. One teacher commented that

> Students refer to Pakistan as a terrorist country and show an agreement to their ban on participation in IPL [Indian Premier League]. I can't change their views. (Delhi, lower private school teacher 2)

Another teacher commented

> During cricket matches, students get upset in the classroom when they hear how Pakistani players fight in the playground. They don't

like their behaviour. They say this in the classroom. (Delhi, lower private school teacher 3)

Similarly, in Lahore, teachers remarked that cricket is instrumental in perpetuating the conflict between India and Pakistan. One teacher observed

Cricket matches between Pakistan and India are always heated with controversy. The students do not like Pakistan losing the cricket match to Indians. They talk about this in the classrooms. (Lahore, middle government school teacher 2)

Another teacher noted how individual players could become a focus for students' views.

Students say that India is having success in IPL because of Shoaib Akhtar and Waseem Akhram [Pakistani players]. Indians don't have anyone. (Lahore, middle government school teacher 3)

Cricket has spread anti-social behaviour among youth in Pakistan. The advantages of the sport are not established simply because people from varied cultural backgrounds are brought together. For the game to be successful in dealing with issues of conflict, participants must be defied whenever they engage in unacceptable behaviour. If unacceptable behaviour is not challenged, opportunities to prepare positive attitudes towards people from other cultures are undermined (Khan et al. 2013).

Furthermore, teachers in Delhi used surveys and presentations to allow learners to search and evaluate different sources of information. One teacher remarked

Students think and learn lessons from textbooks [NCERT]. They say Pakistan was part of India. The second point they will say is Pakistan is a religious country. They [Muslims/Pakistan] will go by Quran and religious dictations of Mullah. (Delhi, middle private school teacher 1)

Another teacher commented

Students' views are getting changed. We have worked a lot and students listen very carefully. If you see this school project [peace project] made by students on the partition, whether it was a partition of boundaries or hearts, they [students] performed the survey and conducted interviews. They [students] stated facts. (Delhi, middle private school teacher 2)

In Lahore, teachers from government schools report that their schools lacked resources and books in the library. One response noted the impact of this on the textbooks' status.

I need to rely on textbooks [Pakistan Studies] to teach about India and Indo-Pakistani relations. In the textbook, India is only mentioned in sections on wars and the Mughal period. The media is vast. The media destroys the textbook. Students should have both detailed and practical knowledge [*sic*]. (Lahore, middle government school teacher 4)

Another agreed on the importance of introducing diverse viewpoints.

I do refer to different sources of information and challenge textbooks' narratives. I tell them [students] what is right and show them in the textbooks. Or give them a textbook where they could provide that information. (Lahore, middle government school teacher 2)

A third teacher, also from a middle government school, offered an example of her classroom discourse.

We just talk about the facts. Institution policy and conventional thoughts-issue of sectarianism [*sic*]. Muslims and Hindus have different views and opinions. I always challenge historical evidence. I think we have isolated and have a prolonged history. After we read it, we should bypass it. Should leave the emotional aspect [*sic*]. (Lahore, middle government school teacher 3)

In Delhi and Lahore, teachers point at the supremacy of examinations throughout the education system. As a result they teach according to the state-set syllabus guide that should be completed each month. They do not diverge far from the textbook and ensure that their learners memorise the textbook content by dictating material to them. Adhering so closely to the textbooks means that less time is available in lessons for teacher-student interaction. One middle government school teacher regretted the lack of time available, combined with the need to focus upon examination success.

> I try to use different sources. There is no time. Have you seen the syllabus? Students are also concerned about passing these exams. (Delhi, middle government school teacher 3)

A teacher from a private school shared these views.

> I try but there is so much too [to teach]. These [sources] are in the textbook. It is so much in the textbook. Exams are also important, and students need to pass with good marks.
> (Delhi, middle private school teacher 4)

In Lahore, teachers shared similar issues. One teacher observed that

> We [teachers] can't do much in government schools. It does not involve that much correlation. It is only targeted on textbooks. The point of view is only to pass examinations. We do not have time. (Lahore, middle government school teacher 2)

Another expressed a similar view.

> In my school, I do not have time. Exams are coming. I need to prepare them [students] for exams. (Lahore, middle private school teacher 3)

As a result, critical thinking is rejected in Delhi and Lahore due to examination requirements and a lack of resources. This is inconsistent with the semi-structured interviews, in which teachers commented that they encouraged learners to engage actively in lessons. In reality, classroom observations showed how students' voices were subdued by their teachers. The classroom discourses thus encouraged authoritative trends, not only based on interpretation but also on the fact that teachers controlled the conversation, in which alternative voices were not encouraged.

As a result, teachers in Delhi and Lahore avoid teaching controversial topics in their classrooms. Several teachers expressed concern in interviews about being scrutinised if they discuss contentious topics. Teachers expressed political, national and parental concerns that made them sceptical of teaching controversial topics. In Delhi, teachers also voiced their lack of confidence in using the appropriate teaching strategy (learner-centred approach or teacher-centred approach) to teach students from different backgrounds or faiths. Teachers commented that 'students carry two versions of history in their heads and have loyalty towards

Pakistan which should be valued outside the school' (as illustrated in vignettes 3 and 4 below).

> Vignette 3: A dialogue between middle private school teacher 1 (MPST1) and students in Delhi.
>
> MPST1: What do you know about Indo–Pakistani relations?
>
> Student 1: Relations are not good. Politicians are responsible.
>
> MPST1: Underline the reasons for partition.
>
> Student 1: Why does partition happen?
>
> Student 2: Kashmir.
>
> MPST1: Go to the next page.

> Vignette 4: A dialogue between middle government school teacher 1 (MGST1) and students in Delhi.
>
> MGST1: Underline Indian haters ... Muslim haters.
>
> Students: [smiling]
>
> MGST1: Go to the next page.
>
> Students: [quiet]
>
> MGST1: This is a good paragraph.

After classroom observations, in de-briefing sessions, teachers commented that

> When we receive such topics [partition, Hindu–Muslim conflict], we try to understand them [Hindu students]. We did and understood students who are Muslim are same and sitting with you [Hindu students], what do you think, do you think they are wrong, then why do you think they are bad [sic] ?So, we start debates. Muslim students do not participate in such discussions. (Delhi, middle private school teacher 1)

Another teacher highlighted the problems of dealing with sensitive issues that had affected some students personally.

We have Muslim students who are refugees from Pakistan. I can't. (Delhi, middle government school teacher 1)

Teachers in Delhi expressed confidence in their ability to teach controversial issues in the history classroom by staying silent when dealing with negative attitudes. However, they are distinctly less confident when it comes to dealing with information from family and the media. Several teachers remarked that they face challenges in the discussion of controversial issues, especially when students belong to Muslim communities or have family links with Pakistan. In such cases, teachers created a forum of views within a safe environment. They defended this provision against accusations that they are undermining parental or community views. This also affected students' group work.

Similarly, in Lahore, teachers were reluctant to discuss the multiple perspectives on the partition of India. They feared exposing themselves to scrutiny if they explored controversial issues in the school environment (as illustrated in vignettes 5 and 6 below).

Vignette 5: A dialogue between middle private school teacher 3 (MPST3) and students in Lahore.

MPST3: What are your views on Indo–Pak relations?

Student 1: India is bad. Our enemy.

MPST 3: During the partition, Hindus took furniture from Pakistan. They played a negative role in our society.

Students: [quiet]

Vignette 6: A dialogue between middle government school teacher 1 (MGST1) and students in Lahore.

MGST1: Turn the page to the negative role of Hindu teachers.

Students: [quiet]

MGST1: Underline it and read. Students: [quiet and underlining]

In debriefing sessions (after classroom observations), one teacher explained her professional predicament.

I can't say positive about it [India/Hindus]. It [teaching about India] is not allowed in my school. I want to teach it [India]. But I refer to textbooks [Pakistan Studies] only. (Lahore, middle private school teacher 3)

Another teacher, this time from a middle government school, felt in a similar position.

Textbooks [Pakistan Studies] are not negative about India. In my school, I need to teach from the textbooks only. (Lahore, middle government school teacher 1)

Students' views are understated due to their confusion or a lack of interest in knowing about India. In class they tend either to ask a few questions or to remain silent. A teacher elaborated

We [teachers] are facing difficulties with students. Kashmir issues leave an impact on students' minds. Students start by asking us about the issues. Students think India is creating challenges for us [Pakistanis/Muslims]. (Lahore, middle private school teacher 1)

Teachers related how such students got upset when the historical fact of partition is discussed. This is often due to oral or tragic histories reported to them by their parents or grandparents, for which India is often blamed. As one teacher observed

They [students] often remember the killings in the partition and refer to their stories heard by [sic] their parents or grandparents. They expressed hatred for India and Hindus. (Lahore, middle private school teacher 1)

Another teacher's response related a similar experience.

Students get upset when I teach partition. They often get upset and ask me why India has done this. (Lahore, middle private school teacher 4)

Middle government and private school teachers positioned themselves as agents of the institution and its dominant ideology; their action is confined within regulative institutional contexts and driven by scripted curricula mandated by the state. As professionals. teachers have been motivated to adopt the communicative approach. However, the chosen pedagogical style offered fewer opportunities for students to participate effectively in the debate.

Traditional teachers: lower SES school teachers

Traditional teachers focus on traditional teaching goals, such as covering the material required by the board of education in order to enable students to pass their exams. The overarching aim of traditional teachers is to produce good citizens who will uphold societal norms and become productive members of society. There is less idealism in this orientation, possibly related to teacher burnout, but there is a commitment to the imperative of teaching about the partition of India, not only because it is clearly mandated. Socialising the students into the principles of democracy is at the heart of the topic, but these teachers teach the topic to ensure that all students are familiar with this important event.

The conservative and traditional teachers (in lower socio-economic private and government schools in both Delhi and Lahore) follow the rote-memorisation approach in order to achieve success in the centralised uniform examinations (Zohar 2009). The rote-memorisation approach is characterised by sessions of frontal verbal instruction (or initiation, response, evaluation) (Cazden 2001). This is intended to verify comprehension and memorisation of the correct answers embedded in authorised textbooks (Alexander 2013).

Teachers expressed positive attitudes towards textbooks. They commented that the history textbook plays a critical role in maintaining positive views of Indians or Muslims and in being aware of their country's history. As far as textbooks are concerned, one teacher noted

> Partition is described so nicely. There is nothing negative towards Muslims and Pakistan. There are good oral stories I use stories to teach. (Delhi, lower private school teacher 3)

Another teacher commented that

> The best thing of the textbook is the stories, to describe the partition of India. It is compared with the Holocaust. (Delhi, lower private school teacher 4)

Teachers regarded the textbook as progressive and believe that it provides learning opportunities for students in Delhi. In Lahore, teachers stated that the Pakistan Studies textbook[12] is significant for teaching students about the ideology of Pakistan and the reasons behind the creation of Pakistan. Teachers in Lahore prefer using the textbook as it is neutral and does not incite hatred towards India or Hindus. One commended its contents, observing

> There is nothing harmful about India. There is about relations by focusing on how Britishers came, ruled our nations, discusses the leaders of Pakistan and India such as Quaid-E-Azam and that Indian leader name I forgot, Gandhi. These leaders need to be well presented [*sic*]. (Lahore, lower private school teacher 3)

Another teacher described the textbook as neutral and useful in teaching these topics.

> Pakistan Studies talks about their [Pakistan] relations with India. India is not portrayed in the wrong ways. I teach using the textbook. (Lahore, lower private school teacher 4)

A lower government schoolteacher also endorsed this opinion.

> Hindus do not appear wrong. Textbooks are positive-Indo-Pakistani relations mentioned [*sic*]. (Lahore, lower government school teacher 3)

Teachers in Delhi and Lahore do not find that the textbooks incite hatred of the other country (India or Pakistan). Rather they have determined that the textbook coverage is sufficient for teaching India–Pakistan relations. One of the reasons for sticking to textbooks is the insufficient resources and support from their headteachers. Teachers' responses made it clear that insufficient access to teaching materials is one of the barriers to critical teaching. Consequently the attitude of the teacher becomes an educational tool, along with the text.

Teachers' responses acknowledged that students' views are homogeneous about partition. They noted anger in students' attitudes towards India or Pakistan in the classrooms. According to teachers,

---

12 *Pakistan Studies*. Punjab Textbook Board. G.F.H. Publishers: Lahore (9th Grade) (P1).

students in lower private classrooms in Delhi projected communal attitudes towards Pakistan. Religion and identity are important for students and teachers, yet one of the themes that came through strongly was the students' desire to respect religion. One teacher remarked

> Students want peace in their country [India]. They [students] think Pakistan needs to co-operate with India and stop spreading terrorism. Pakistan is spreading terrorism in the name of religion. (Delhi, lower private school teacher 1)

Another teacher, also from a lower private school, commented that

> Pakistan is a terrorist country and an enemy of India. Hindus and Muslims do not live together again. They [Hindus and Muslims] are religiously different. (Delhi, lower private school teacher 2)

Teachers voiced their reservations about sharing attitudes towards Muslim students in the classroom in the presence of Hindu students. One teacher stated that Muslim students have close ties with Pakistan and were not keen to engage in debate.

> Some Muslim students are quiet in the classrooms. They are not interested in discussions. (Delhi, lower government school teacher 2)

Another teacher offered a similar view.

> Students' views are not much heard. They look blank. I know that they have families in Pakistan. So I do not ask them. (Delhi, lower government school teacher 3)

Students tended to get upset when Pakistan and India–Pakistan relations were discussed, as a teacher from a lower government school teacher observed.

> Honestly speaking, I have a lot of Muslim students. They do have negative views about Pakistan. They are not supporters of Pakistan, but I have to be careful while eliciting their views. (Delhi, lower government school teacher 1)

Another teacher noted that

> We do not have resources. Students are always quiet. They are not interested in discussions. (Delhi, lower government school teacher 5)

Many students remained silent because they had relatives in Pakistan, as a teacher remarked.

> This school is in a Muslim area. So many Muslim families have their friends in Pakistan. They share relationships with them. They are good and in touch with their families in Pakistan. So I think their views are positive, but they are quiet due to their refugee status in India. (Delhi, lower government school teacher 1)

Another teacher from a lower government school agreed that Muslim students' views were positive, claiming that they held 'very good attitudes in their minds', but that most were reticent in expressing them.

> Because they live in India, they are quiet about Pakistan but in their minds they love Pakistan. (Delhi, lower government school teacher 6)

Teachers believed that the students' identity as Indian or Pakistani intersected with their attitudes towards the other country (India or Pakistan) and India–Pakistan relations in the classroom.

Teachers were also aware that students received information from their family members. Their communal views might thus be drawn from the bitter experiences of their families, which were difficult to set aside. One teacher observed

> Students don't come with anti-Pakistan views. These students are from a low-income family. Their family members shape such views. I can't say that your family is wrong. (Delhi, lower government school teacher 1)

Another teacher explained the challenges created by such entrenched family views.

> I ask them why you dislike Pakistan. They tell my parents to think our enemy and we can't trust Pakistan. I can't do anything. (Delhi, lower private school teacher 2)

These narratives indicate biases, stereotypes and hatred among students shaped by their family members. The students also derive stereotypical views and beliefs from wider society, in which a bias towards Pakistan or Muslims is ingrained – then futher developed through politicians or the media. Stereotypes and preconceived notions are associated with the partition of India, which have influenced all areas of Indian and Pakistani society for both good and bad. Expressing concern at this situation, one teacher noted

> Students feel Pakistan as a rival country only because of the influence of our society [*sic*]. You know everywhere people talk about Pakistan. How can I change their views? (Delhi, lower government school teacher 3)

Societal beliefs that are related to patriotism are defined as an emotional attachment. They are formed between the individual and his or her group and country, nurturing loyalty, love, care and readiness for sacrifice. Another teacher offered an example from her own classroom experience.

> My students say Muslims are not loyal and they eat cows. I tried to correct them, but they started laughing at me. (Delhi, lower private school teacher 3)

Another teacher echoed similar concerns.

> When I start teaching about Pakistan, students say their neighbours [Pakistan] share information such as that Kasab is a Pakistani terrorist and Muslim. They think every Muslim is a terrorist. I am not allowed to correct them. (Delhi, lower private school teacher 4)

Another teacher, this time from a lower government school, described the uncompromising views that some students expressed.

> Students say it is a Hindu country. We should not have Muslims in our country. They are terrorists. (Delhi, lower government school teacher 5)

Such messages about Pakistan and India–Pakistan relations in social spaces are delivered to foster contrasting, often conflicting events to those taught by a school textbook (as discussed in Chapter 4).

Sport also acts as a prominent medium for growing issues of social inclusion for refugees because of its capacity to bring people together from different cultural backgrounds. Teachers reported that sport offers the most significant potential for positive impact; nonetheless, they recognised that in contact sports tensions could sometimes run high and deeper conflicts may arise.

> Students support their country [India] and often express prejudice for Pakistan during cricket matches. (Delhi, lower government school teacher 3)

Rivalries on the field may often assume a political cast in a school environment. A government school teacher shared an example from her classroom.

> Students respect government decision to not to have cricket ties with Pakistan. They say it [Pakistan] is a terrorist country and we [India] are a secular country. I agree with them. (Delhi, lower government school teacher 1)

Such a situation appears challenging and stressful for teachers. It also hinders effective curriculum implementation, broadening the gap in student performance.

In Lahore, teachers commented that several students support the two-nation theory that Muslims and Hindus in pre-partition had separate customs and traditions and were unable to live together. One teacher commented

> Overall students are conventional because of killings of people at the border. All students supported Pakistan and considered India not as a friend. In the classroom, it is very difficult to have a discussion. (Lahore, lower government school teacher 2)

Another teacher echoed these concerns.

> Students do not like India. Hindus and Muslims are different in religion. Hindus are responsible for their conditions in Pakistan. I think this is difficult to change. (Lahore, lower government school teacher 1)

Teachers elaborated that the students' views were mostly informed by their teachers' attitudes or textbooks. However, they also highlighted strong parental influence in shaping the students' attitudes towards India and India–Pakistan relations. Oral stories passed down through families can describe friendship or hatred between citizens of the two countries. Teachers reported that many students do not have access to digital tools at home and consequently rely on their families for information. Several of them mentioned parental influence on how children perceive and engage with India–Pakistan relations, suggesting this has a significant impact on them as young people. One teacher noted

> Family tells sad stories about killings and destruction. Students talk about this in the classroom. I am unable to discuss. (Lahore, lower private school teacher 1)

Another described a similar experience.

> Students say Hindus have destroyed their house in the partition. Their family is poor because of Hindus. They are cheaters. (Lahore, lower government school teacher 1)

It thus seems clear that parents influence students' attitudes towards the other country (India or Pakistan) and India–Pakistan relations. Teachers acknowledged that students adopted their parents' views on historical issues uncritically, and they were unable to correct or challenge them.

Students and teachers are the key players in the process of education. One element that enhances the success of a negotiating process is the breaking of old images and the creation of new supportive symbols (Bar-Tal 2007). However, this is not accomplished without a price, manifested through a selective exploration for information as well as perceptual biasing and whitewashing or distortion of the social reality, quick decision-making, unsophisticated and stereotypical thinking (Jost 2006). The philosophies that mature under severe doubt (such as an intractable conflict) are traditional ideas resistant to change (Hogg 2005). There is an important positive association between dogmatic thinking as well as adherence to societal attitudes that comprise the ethos of conflict (Zafran 2002). Due to the distorting effects of prejudice and the lack of resources in lower government and private schools, teachers' interactions thus play a significant role in breaking the stereotypes in these institutions.

As far as teachers' pedagogical decisions to shape the students' attitudes are concerned, in Delhi and Lahore they expect students to participate in the ongoing discussion. However, the delivery of the lecture did not in reality facilitate student participation. The principle of 'read-recall-recite' guided both the classroom discourse and teaching practice. This method encourages students to absorb the textbook content in its entirety. Teachers thought of themselves as a primary source of information, values and attitudes for students. In Delhi, one teacher observed

> Students learn much from us [teachers]. It depends on us [teachers] what to teach. (Lahore, lower government school teacher 4)

Another teacher echoed this belief, acknowledging the responsibilities that it carried.

> I try to be balanced. Students listen to us [teachers] in the classroom but don't talk much. (Lahore, lower government school teacher 5)

In Lahore, a teacher commented that

> Most students just listen and follow teachers blindly. They contest with their parents. They [students] access to the media, but they often discuss with teachers. They agree with teachers. (Lahore, lower government school teacher 4)

Teachers' contributions are thus significant in the students' lives. Students spend a lot of time observing teachers, so it is not surprising that teachers are a primary source of attitudes (Lortie 1975).

Teachers in both research sites have a significant influence on students' views. However, teachers acknowledged that they are cautious of offending students who consider themselves to be of the other faith or students that have different views. Within the context of history education, silences can be institutionally constructed – as when topics are silenced in the history curriculum or the media by governmental pressure. Teachers might be forced by the government, the curriculum or their school director to maintain silence, or they might opt to ignore and resist the norms of silencing (Brauch 2017). However, teachers can also silence topics as an act of self-censorship (Evans et al. 1999), even if the topic appears in the curriculum or does not incur sanctions by society in general (Savenije and Goldberg 2019).

This pedagogical decision suggests that teachers assume that when approaching the other's narrative the members of the minority group express emotional and behavioural enthusiasm, instead of communicating sympathy for the pain of the other. Teachers reported that interactions lead to negative comments. One shared an incident that had occurred in her classroom.

If I start discussing [Indo–Pak relations] in a Muslim class. Hindu students can hurt them by calling 'mullahs' and Pakistanis [*sic*]. I have to stop [discussions]. (Delhi, lower Government school teacher 3)

Another teacher openly declared his position, along with the caution that it imposed.

I have Muslim students in my class. I should be careful sometimes. They can get upset and then they can complain. It can be threatening to me. (Delhi, Lahore government school teacher 2)

In Lahore, in the classroom, teachers similarly distance themselves from the Hindu–Muslim narrative. One observed

I tell them [students] to don't listen to media completely [*sic*]. I ask them to look for different sources [for information]. I can't contest [their views] directly. I wish I could do but I can't. I can't say good things about India sitting in Pakistan. (Lahore, lower private school teacher 1)

Another teacher appeared more resigned to the situation.

Students' views are negative. But I cannot contest the negative opinion. I fear losing my job. (Lahore, lower private school teacher 4)

Teachers' pedagogical interventions in lower private and government schools thus seem to create a paradoxical situation. While their efforts to create some symmetry might be beneficial for promoting mutual respect and understanding, teachers did not find it necessary to discuss partition, nor did they feel comfortable doing so. There is a general concern among teaching staff about the narratives their students hear, as they are still young and can develop radical ideas.

As noted above, several teachers reported avoiding the teaching of sensitive topics – not only because of a lack of time and an already full curriculum, but also because of fear of their superiors' or students' reactions, as well as personal ambivalence. Teachers avoided sensitive issues mainly to prevent intensification of (the idea of) a clash between majority and minority students. In doing so, they protected the belief in peaceful co-existence and the image of the in-group as being tolerant to newcomers and people of different cultural and religious backgrounds

(Bar-Tal 2007). In some cases, it appeared that teachers who were members of the majority group were subjected to a process of silencing, like those who were not there. Their students of minority descent viewed the teacher as unentitled to voice an opinion on sensitive historical issues pertaining to the minority. To do so appeared to the underprivileged students to be upholding the privilege of those who were there against the teacher's privileged professional authority (Winter 2010).

Teachers overtly recognised that their pedagogical purposes could affect student mindsets. India–Pakistani relations are regarded as an unstated paradigm (or mindset) that restricts or distorts discussion of issues between Hindus and Muslims. Teachers also explained that students often get 'upset' and 'emotional' due to family losses when they attempt to teach about India–Pakistan relations.

> Students mostly hate discussing relations with Pakistan in the classroom. There are biases and prejudices in their families. I have to stop sometimes. (Delhi, lower private school teacher 3)

Similar situations arose in Lahore, as a teacher revealed.

> I tell them stories about Hindus. We [Pakistanis] have good friends with Hindus. English people were also responsible. The blame shifts to them. But they [the students] get upset so I have to pause. (Lahore, lower government school teacher 4)

In Delhi and Lahore, teachers agreed that it is difficult to provide reasonable explanations for issues between Hindus and Muslims and to communicate openly in the classroom. Teachers were aware that students are conscious of the classroom environment when it came to responding to teachers' questions; they favoured a private presentation of identity. Students expressed confidence in the competence of their teachers, who play a major role in their students' lives. Teachers also expressed their fear that using multiple sources and information could distract students from the teachings of Islam in Lahore, for instance. Their responses suggested that such knowledge could also undermine the ideology.

In addition, teachers reflected a low-level transmission perspective, with a focus on the role of the teacher in preparing students for exams. Teachers taught based on the examination system, making sure that learners memorised the content from the textbooks. In the classroom teachers repeated sentences from the textbooks, often provided with little explanation, and supported learning with no supplementary learning materials. In their responses teachers were vocal about the critical issue of the exam system. One teacher in Delhi commented

> Students want all answers from us. They worry to pass exams [*sic*]. They don't care about critical thinking. (Delhi, lower government school teacher 3)

Another teacher echoed similar views.

> Finishing syllabus is my priority [*sic*]. I can't go much in-depth about India and Pakistan. (Delhi, lower private school teacher 3)

Another teacher in Lahore experienced the same pressure.

> As a teacher, we received textbooks direct and described the fundamental points of our history. We have to use textbooks. We must make sure they pass the exams. So I just teach so that they pass the exams. (Lahore, lower government school teacher 2)

A teacher from a lower private school in Lahore deplored the limitations of having to take such an approach.

> I only focus on the history and concentrate on completing the syllabus [*sic*]. (Lahore, lower private school teacher 4)

The responses suggested how both classroom teaching and learning can be driven by an examination system that reduces education learning to a product, rather than the process of learning (Watkins 2013). Teachers believed that their job is only to prepare students for examinations. It may be argued that an examination system in this context plays a determining role in shaping teachers' attitudes. It could also be suggested that the curricula and pedagogical methods are used in schools to create and promote discriminatory behaviours against India or Pakistan and India–Pakistan relations.

In both research sites, teachers thus read from the textbook and then paraphrase the text to make it easier for students to understand. They did not encourage multiple perspectives or use reference material other than textbooks to enrich the content. Instead, teachers gave authority to oral history and textbooks. The teaching approach thus remained 'authoritative' (as illustrated in vignettes 7 and 8 below).

Vignette 7: Teacher instruction by lower private SES school teacher 2 (LPST2) in Delhi.

LPST2: Underline paragraph 2 on page 389.[13]

Students: [quiet]

LPST2: Underline paragraphs 1 and 2 on page 391.[14]

Students: [quiet]

LPST2: Read paragraph 1 on page 397.

Vignette 8: Teacher instruction by lower private SES school teacher 1 (LPST1) in Lahore.

LPST1: Page 3. The ideology of Pakistan is essential. It comes in exams.

Students: [quiet]

LPST1: Underline point 1.

Students: [quiet]

LPST1: So, this is the answer to the question on page 16, The ideology of Pakistan.

Vignettes 7 and 8 above show that no opportunity was available for students to acquire and develop the skills necessary to become independent learners, critical thinkers and informed citizens. The skills emphasised reading, writing or underlining, and rote-memorisation that did not bear any relation to the promotion of critical thinking.

The following vignette outlines the pattern of teacher instruction in lower government SES schools.

Vignette 9: Teacher instruction by lower government SES school teacher 1 (LGST1) in Delhi.

LGST1: *Bacho*! [Children!]. Understanding partition is important for exams. Four questions will come [*sic*].

---

13 Topic titled as 'A possible alternative to partition' in *Themes in Indian History*, 389. I, II and III. NCERT. Delhi. (12th Grade).

14 Topic titled as 'Towards partition' in *Themes in Indian History*, 391. I, II and III. NCERT. Delhi. (12th Grade).

Students: [talking to each other]

LGST1: [Shouts] open page 383.[15] Why did partition happen?

Students: [inaudible]

LGST1: Read the first three paragraphs.

LGST1: Underline them.

Vignette 10: Teacher instruction by lower government SES school teacher 1 (LGST1) in Lahore.

LGST1: Open the Two-nation theory on page 9.[16]

Students: [quiet]

LGST1: Read the section on Two-Nation Theory on page 9.

Students: [quiet]

LGST1: Any problem?

Students: [quiet]

Vignettes 9 and 10 above highlight that the dominant communication plan was authoritative and non-interactive. The teacher talk was textbook-oriented and involved no other reference to substantiate explanations. The one-way flow of officially approved textual information was dominant, with students being expected to memorise and reproduce the content in exams. The above vignettes also demonstrate that students were non-participative; they interacted neither with the teacher nor among themselves. Authoritative and non-interactive communication hindered the promotion of critical thinking in the classroom. Overall, the teaching strategy used by lower socio-economic government and private school teachers did not involve democratic processes of active participation that require skills in critical thinking and analysis.

This high rate of closed questioning has been criticised as detrimental to students' independent thinking and learning for three reasons (Apple 2001, 2003; Kelly et al. 1996; Hess 2004). First, the structure positions teachers (and textbooks) as the only legitimate sources of knowledge; the

---

15 *Themes in Indian History*. I, II and III. NCERT. Delhi (12th Grade).
16 *Pakistan Studies*. Punjab Textbook Board. G.F.H. Publishers: Lahore (9th Grade) (P1).

student's role is simply to recall and recite for the evaluation of what they have previously read or been told. Second, the structure tends to produce a rather disjointed lesson overall, with teachers moving from topic to topic with little or no clear line of reasoning. Such a process resembles 'banking education' (Freire 1970, 72), in which students are passive listeners. A third criticism is the limited extent to which participants can engage in more demanding cognitive activities (explaining concepts, relating ideas to one another, challenging and justifying positions).

The engagement with the official textbook noted above illustrates how the conventional-authoritative condition promotes few agreements on the responsibility for critical teaching. It also encouraged participants to adopt the narrative uncritically and reduces their awareness of its one-sidedness. This seems to lend support to the claim that official historical narratives and conventional history education contribute to intergroup conflict (Apple 2003).

Concluding remarks

This chapter shows how teachers systematically shaped their messages according to how they perceived the requirements of their institution. Elite school teachers thus taught India–Pakistan relations differently to teachers in middle and lower socio-economic schools, irrespective of their individual attitudes and positions. In the classroom, teachers from middle and lower SES schools in both countries constructed their attitudes in response to the schools' expectations and assumptions. This shows a close relationship between the socio-economic status (SES) (and institutional habitus) of a school and teachers' pedagogical responses or decisions.

In practice the institutional habitus (as discussed in Chapter 1) of the school thus overrides teachers' attitudes (see Chapter 4) in both countries. Teachers from elite SES schools acted as the mediating agents or referees in their classrooms, often deciding what is right and wrong. They negotiated textbooks' content by organising debates in the classroom in order to develop critical consciousness and to expand the views of students about India–Pakistan relations, extending beyond ideas they encountered in the textbook, media or at home. Teachers from middle and lower SES schools, by contrast, go mechanically across the content in the textbooks. This style of learning also stems from a hierarchical structure of society, which means information is consumed without question from those in positions of authority (in this context, teachers) (Afzal 2018). Teachers in such schools reported fundamental barriers to discussing India–Pakistan relations in both countries. These included concerns about managing conflict in classrooms, sensitivity towards the different views in the classroom, fear of being thought biased or of losing their job and lack of time available to discuss material critically.

The barriers have two propositions: first, teachers place significance on exams and textbooks; and second, teachers select a secular or nationalist reading of the history textbook based on the institutional habitus and the SES of the school. This suggests that both countries need to re-orient their teacher education programmes in ways that promote teacher agency for social cohesion and mitigate conflict through dialogic pedagogies and egalitarian pedagogical relationships (Durrani, Kaderi and Anand 2020). Furthermore, an exam-oriented system impinges on teachers' ability to adopt a critical pedagogy, pushing them to focus on the reproduction of information rather than the creation of knowledge (Kumar 2001; Durrani, Kaderi and Anand 2020, Anand 2019). The socio-economic status (SES) and the institutional habitus of the school profoundly influence or hinder the development of critical historical consciousness and the understanding of India or Pakistan and India–Pakistan relations in both countries. This argument will be discussed further in Chapter 6.

6

Conclusion: socio-economic status of schools and teachers

Introduction

The previous chapters reveal a relationship between the socio-economic status (SES) of a school (and its institutional habitus) and teachers' attitudes towards India–Pakistan relations and their pedagogical responses. Chapters 4 and 5 show that there are significant differences in teachers' attitudes mediated by the SES (and the institutional habitus) of the school, regardless of teachers' individual habitus. In both Delhi and Lahore, teachers find it difficult to articulate and develop critical thinking among their students. In the classroom, teachers conceptualise their attitudes in response to the school's expectations and assumptions. This infers teachers' limited ability to be agents of change in the classroom context. Such agency is either facilitated in elite SES classrooms or constrained in the classrooms of middle and lower SES schools.

The SES of a school thus creates unequal opportunities for students to be educated, teachers to educate and headteachers to fulfil their obligation to secure an equivalent education for all students. This chapter sets out the main conclusions emanating from the research and discusses in more detail the data presented in Chapters 4 and 5. It starts with an overview of the impact of a school's socio-economic status (SES) and institutional habitus on the individual habitus of teachers – an impact that in turn frames their attitudes. The chapter then outlines the ways in which the school's SES and its institutional habitus override the teachers' attitudes and determine their pedagogical responses. The last section summarises the analysis of the fundamental findings.

How institutional habitus of the school negates teachers' attitudes

As presented in Chapter 4, teachers' attitudes in Delhi and Lahore are negated by the institutional habitus of their schools. The institutional habitus has implications not only for understanding the educational practice, but also for appreciating the assimilation of the messages in the work experiences (Bourdieu and Passeron 1990). The attitudes derived from the individual habitus of teachers are influenced by working conditions, support from management and school culture (Opfer and Pedder 2011; Kennedy and McKay 2011). The following sections discuss teachers' attitudes towards India or Pakistan and India–Pakistan relations in Delhi and Lahore.

Chapter 4 shows how the individual habitus (family) of teachers in both Delhi and Lahore influences their positive or secular views towards the other country (India or Pakistan). The individual habitus of elite private school teachers reproduces narratives around the collective suffering of migration or recognition of the other side's suffering. Teachers acknowledge that educational experiences play a major role in the construction of secular views towards the other country (India or Pakistan). As far as teaching practice is concerned, they commented that teaching critically is their professional responsibility – a view that implies their attitudes were influenced, mediated and constructed by their institution. Teachers on the individual level have their views on many social and educational aspects that could influence their daily teaching practice (Burke et al. 2013). However, they do not act independently of their contexts of reference (individual habitus); instead they are embedded in institutional contexts that inevitably affect and influence them.

In this respect, as with an individual habitus (Bourdieu and Passeron 1990), institutional habitus involves a combination of agency and structure, of teachers and institutions. This concept is composed of individual dispositions but goes beyond them; it is negotiated and reinvented in the daily practices of schools (Ingram 2009). The elite schools have reserved their purpose of imparting high-quality 'education to the privileged classes and reproducing Western culture and value systems in the country. The ruling class has always protected these schools as they have served their entrusted interests' (Khattak 2014, 100).

In the classroom, elite school teachers in Delhi and Lahore negotiated and mediated their attitudes within their institutional habitus by critically analysing the sources of information regarding India or Pakistan and India–Pakistan relations. The classroom discourses indicated that interactions with students help teachers to find the critical way of handling the hidden curriculum. They positioned themselves as agents of change within their institutional contexts (classrooms). They were able to do so because, the elite schools provided autonomous status to teachers, enabling them first to develop a distinct status culture, then to draft and implement their institutional policies (Rahman 2006). Elite schoolteachers acknowledged imparting both secular knowledge and praxis and educational discourses as an exclusive and legitimate standpoint for their teaching (derived from their institutions). Furthermore, the institutional habitus influenced knowledge creation through power-sharing strategies (between teachers and students) in the classroom. Here elite teachers allowed the learners to have a voice, raise questions, engage in discussions and take responsibility for their own and others' learning (Bishop et al. 2014; Ladson-Billings 1995). The elite school employees articulate different perspectives vis-à-vis their pedagogy, entirely intended to provide up-to-date knowledge and emerging human capacities of analysis, planning and decision-making (Bishop et al. 2014). Skilful leadership has developed as an unwritten instruction of elite schools since their origin in the subcontinent (Rahman 2006). This has resulted in the process of critically analysing the conflicting perspectives that seems to counter the emphasis on friendly relations between both countries (Bar-Tal et al. 2010).

The institutional habitus of elite school teachers thus allowed both external and internal factors to support critical thinking in order to reduce social marginalisation. The individual habitus of teachers can be transformative in a situation where an individual (teacher) has 'improvisational capabilities' (Mills 2008, 147). Such capabilities allow teachers to acknowledge transformative opportunities in their field (classroom). In the classroom background a teacher's pedagogy, teaching practice and attitudes allow prospects for the growth of the transformative habitus, therefore leading to the transformation of attitudes (Mills 2008).

Chapters 4 and 5 underline the differences between the attitudes of middle private and government schoolteachers in Delhi and Lahore. In Delhi, a discrepancy existed between the attitudes, teaching theory and practice elicited in the semi-structured interviews and observed through classroom observations. In the semi-structured interviews, teachers avoid the marginalisation of Pakistan or Muslims in their narratives and expressed secular attitudes towards Pakistan and India–Pakistan relations. In Lahore, a shift or change in the attitudes of middle private school teachers may be perceived. In the semi-structured interviews, teachers elicited favourable attitudes towards India and Hindus. However, in the classroom they shifted their attitudes from liberal to communal, expressing a unilateral perspective[1] towards India. They blamed Indians and India's political or media jingoism for creating issues in Pakistan. In the classroom, teachers portrayed India in a negative light and provided little information about the Hindu religion, culture and way of life. This seems to be in line with what Bourdieu (1990) found: that the same habitus (middle class of the school) in different social settings (India and Pakistan) could express different standpoints and practices depending on the field (classroom) and dominant culture (of the school).

In terms of individual habitus, middle private or government school teachers in Delhi and Lahore heard different oral histories. Teachers in Delhi commented that the oral histories of their families echoed the common cultural traits; they recognised the collective suffering experienced in migration or acknowledged Pakistan's suffering during the partition of India. These oral histories were persuasive in keeping their mindset towards Pakistan and India–Pakistan relations positive. Teachers mentioned that they analysed different narratives and interpretations of Pakistan by referring to different newspapers and television news channels. The common suffering and migration reinforced the positive attitudes of these teachers in Delhi. Teachers referred to an internal unity between India and Pakistan due to language and culture (Anand 2019).

In Lahore, the oral narratives shared by teachers described India as a 'strong enemy' who is 'destroying or dominating the self-community' (Pakistan). India is labelled as 'cruel' and presented as being always 'engaged in planning conspiracies' against Pakistan. The oral histories shared by teachers and narrated by the families of both teachers and students play a significant role in developing mixed attitudes (both secular and communal) towards India or India–Pakistan relations. The process of transmitting memories of partition and personal narratives of historical events causes functional and intended exchange between older and younger generations (Tripathi 2016). So it is that an image of India is shaped in the minds of young children in Pakistan.

---

1   A unilateral perspective provides negative descriptions of the other country and India–Pakistan relations and little information about the religions, culture and life of the other.

These images of the other country or enemy (India or Hindus) created at an early age stayed in the memories of students. The oral histories led to an affective turn[2] in their attitudes towards the other country (India or Pakistan). Such a narrative of common suffering, along with recollections and memories of wars or losses caused by the conflict, elicited the emotions of anger and anxiety among teachers (Schwarz and Clore 2018). The oral histories (and perceptions) could create barriers to the promotion of a liberal and favourable attitude towards the other country (Tripathi 2016).

In addition, the struggles in acknowledging the narrative of the other were embedded in the production of collective identities in conflict (Kelman 1997). The collective identities are formed with strong beliefs about the self and other. Historical events of collective violence between the groups and collective memory of these events shape attitudes about us and them. Constructing two in bi-polar disagreement serves to stress the positive in us and the negative in them, and to develop a hatred for 'others'. In conflicts, the other's existence is viewed as a threat to one's positive identity (Kelman 1997). To accept the other as legitimate, parties in conflict must liberate themselves from self-validation based on the negation of the other (Kelman 1997).

The oral histories (elicited in the semi-structured interviews) present conflicting narratives or representations of India/Pakistan or India–Pakistan relations. The communal or anti-India attitudes also follow the trends rooted in the textbook.[3] The communal or anti-India attitude is based on the non-reflective attitudes about the other, serving to form a sense of inner rationality and to provide a set of attitudes about the world (Chhabra 2016). The narratives portray India or Pakistan as responsible for the partition. The oral histories explain the dilemma of people from India and Pakistan. The complexity of this topic opposes the teachers' long-lasting attitudes toward the partition of India, of self and other (Chhabra 2016).

Finally, communal attitudes could also be explained by the victim–perpetrator relationship rooted in the oral histories shared by teachers. This is because identity threats to parties in conflict result from their role as victims or perpetrators. Experiencing one's group as a victim poses a threat to the need for power and control, whereas perceiving one's group as a perpetrator threatens that group's members with exclusion from the broader moral community (Shnabel and Nadler 2008). In Lahore, the

---

2   Garagozov (2013) defines affective turn as when the narrative 'common suffering' shifts to the narrative 'blame the other'. This increases the negative effect.

3   *Themes in Indian History.* I, II and III. NCERT. Delhi (12th Grade) (T4).

oral histories suggest that Hindus and the British conspired together against Muslims, who are thus depicted as victims. This seems to be consistent with what Bandura (2001) found the threat to the sense of morality that could lead perpetrators to disengage themselves from uncertain acts which are committed by their group (Pakistan or Muslims). Such an approach lacked empathy for the suffering (to India/Hindus) caused by Pakistan and Muslims (Halpern and Weinstein 2004). Teachers in Lahore were influenced by family routines or oral histories, which may help to egitimate the anti-India sentiments.

As far as institutional habitus is concerned, teachers in Delhi clearly articulated the influence of textbooks on their attitudes. Middle government school teachers recognised the strong belief in the legitimacy of textbooks. For schools the textbook is a significant source of information that includes opportunities to discuss theoretically challenging aspects of the country's cultural traditions and sectarian conflict. It contains a group of powerful and moving personal narratives of victims who suffered during the partition (Aiken 2013). Teachers commented that history textbooks are neutral and present the different perspectives of the conflicting parties. The history textbook covers not only Indian perspectives, but also personal accounts of Pakistani nationals (Tripathi 2016). Such textbook narratives were the significant reason why teachers expressed positive attitudes towards them.

Two private middle schools were supporting participation in peace projects and organising field trips to Pakistan. Teachers proposed the idea of leading these educational projects to start cross-border communication channels between students in India and Pakistan. Through these programmes each country was exposed to the narratives of the conflict held by the other, in an attempt to legitimise or bridge gaps between them. The narratives of mutual understanding and acceptance are therefore likely to be responsible for positive attitudes among teachers (Anand 2019).

Nevertheless, despite such positive attitudes, inconsistency emerged among teachers in Delhi between the theory and practice of teaching, as demonstrated by the semi-structured interviews and classroom observations. In the classroom, teachers repositioned themselves to be in line with the institutional habitus of the school. They integrated the social composition of schools – an inherent element to comprehend their teaching practices, school regulations and methods of organisation. The school culture negated the attitudes of teachers and determined their actions or responses (Burke et al. 2013). Teachers were unable to transmit the positive attitudes (individual habitus) in their classrooms; they could only respond to their institutional requirements.

Such a situation coincides with the teacher-centric approach, which is compounded by the effects of ideological education (Alexander 2013, 498). Furthermore, in the classroom teachers were seen purposely to avoid teaching or discussing the multiple perspectives and views of partition. This is because many felt that they were exposing themselves to unwelcome scrutiny if they dared to discuss controversial issues in their school environment. Teachers thus position themselves as agents of the institution or state, and of its dominant culture or ideology within the institutional contexts and scripted curricula authorised by the state.

In Lahore, teachers highlighted the significance of Pakistan Studies textbooks (PS).[4] These textbooks act as a significant source of information for teachers about other country (India) or India–Pakistan relations more broadly. PS depict the creation of Pakistan by highlighting a conspiracy of Hindus and British against Muslims; the last are thus depicted as victims, as reviewed by Afzal (2015). Middle private and government school teachers voiced the bad intentions of India towards Pakistan, both before and after partition (Hussain et al. 2011, 4–5). The institutional habitus of teachers is dedicated to the overtly biased curriculum of Pakistan Studies (PS).

This seems in line with what Afzal (2015) suggests is the biased content in the PS textbook that influenced teachers' attitudes and guided or dictated their classroom responses or practices. The textbooks' narratives aim to protect Muslim values and to shape the collective memory of learners (Afzal 2015). It is documented (and logical) that educational curricula and textbooks serve ideological purposes around the world (Apple 2004). In so doing PS[5] portrays India as the enemy, deliberately creating problems for Pakistan (such as sharing river water) and lacking any interest in resolving the Kashmir dispute.

The students' views on India and Hindus also mirror the narratives in textbooks, as reviewed by Afzal (2015). In the classroom, teaching critically is relatively muted. Textbooks do not depict India and Indo-Pakistani history using different sources of information (Hussain and Safiq 2016). Besides the textbooks as a primary source of information, teachers' classroom practices, habits, beliefs and attitudes failed to teach the multiple

---

4   *Pakistan Studies.* Punjab Textbook Board. G.F.H Publishers: Lahore, (9th Grade) (P1). *Pakistan Studies.* Punjab Textbook Board. Gohar Publishers: Lahore (10th Grade) (P2).

5   *Pakistan Studies.* Punjab Textbook Board. G.F.H Publishers: Lahore (9th Grade) (P1); *Pakistan Studies.* Punjab Textbook Board. Gohar Publishers: Lahore (10th Grade) (P2).

perspectives of partition. By adopting such an approach, teachers blindly followed the school textbooks which have been designed to promote a sense of patriotism and nationalism as the rationale for creating Pakistan (Hussain and Safiq 2016). They used the textbook to enact the creation of Pakistan as an opportunity to highlight and accentuate alleged animosities and tensions between Muslims and Hindus (or between India and Pakistan).

Lower government and private school teachers in Delhi and Lahore expressed a unilateral perspective that offers negative descriptions of Pakistan/India. From a unilateral perspective, the self is characterised in positive terms, while also being viewed as a victim, required to defend itself against the acts and negative intentions of the other. Teachers from lower government schools in India expressed blended or mixed attitudes (narrative shifts or clashes between liberal and communal attitudes). They acknowledged the influence of the legitimacy of sources and emotional responses (both empathy and anger) on their attitudes. Such blended or mixed attitudes were derived and implemented through their institutional habitus (school culture) (Anand 2019).

In both research sites, teachers referred to oral histories that depict the experiences of the historical period of partition. These have undeniably left a bitter and debated legacy due to migration that is still rooted in their living memory. These oral histories placed blame on either India or Pakistan, a perspective associated with the religious differences. In oral histories, Muslims and Hindus were depicted as mutually incompatible due to differences in religions, customs and traditions that meant they could not live together. The oral histories presented the images of reciprocal distortions and connections. Such reciprocal distortions reinforced the narratives around us versus them and provided a stereotypical depiction of the other country (India or Pakistan) (Anand 2019).

Lower government and private school teachers conceded that their schools' institutional habitus was solely responsible for the reproduction of traditional religious or national scholastic capital. Several teachers voiced the view that their sole responsibility was to prepare students to pass exams. Besides oral histories, teachers referred to textbooks and expressed the issue of limited autonomy in their institutional habitus to use external sources of information. This positioning of teachers presented them as passive agents within regulative institutional contexts and scripted curricula authorised by the institution. Such a situation has occurred because the policies of lower private and government schools are designed to reproduce the scholastic capital approved by the educational bureaucracy (Tripathi 2016).

Teachers in Delhi and Lahore commented that the degree of selectivity overrides the depiction of apparent personalities through textbooks (Tripathi 2016). They voiced difficulties in acknowledging the narrative of the other in their classroom. This is because in order to accept the other as legitimate, parties in conflict must liberate themselves from self-validation dependent on the negation of the other. Historical narratives in the textbooks carried the ideological indoctrination of us and them. Textbooks highlight evident sections of the shared past (in Indian textbooks); however, others were glossed over or even eliminated to suit the nation-building agenda (in Pakistani textbooks). Drawing on Bourdieu's concept of teachers' habitus, the following section explores how teachers' institutional habitus structures knowledge construction about India or Pakistan and India–Pakistan relations through official and hidden curricula.

How institutional habitus of the school overrides teachers' attitudes in the classroom

Both teachers' knowledge of the subject (Hashweh 1987) and their attitudes about teaching (Richardson 1996) affect how they respond to and use textbooks available to them. Teachers' attitudes about learning – operationalised at either the individual or the collective level – are also shaped by the state's policy (Grossman and Thompson 2004; Spillane and Thompson 1997). These attitudes, and the pedagogical responses of teachers, are significantly influenced by the context of the school (institutional habitus) in which they teach (Osler and Starkey 2005). Teachers in both Delhi and Lahore re-conceptualise their pedagogy and enhance critical or independent thinking in their schools.

The following section discusses how and why teachers in this study transformed their classroom practices or pedagogical responses depending on the schools' institutional habitus or socio-economic status (SES) and culture (Solomon et al. 1996). It shows how the SES (and the institutional habitus) of the school overrides the teachers' individual attitudes and determines their pedagogical responses. It presents the field (classroom), sets out the context in which teachers make their pedagogical decisions and reflects on the characteristics of schooling mechanisms that contribute to the legitimisation and dissemination of ideologies or practices.

In the semi-structured interviews, elite school teachers in Delhi voiced concerns regarding omissions[6] (such as the Muslim League and Hindu Mahasabha) from the Indian textbooks.[7] According to teachers, these omissions in the textbooks could be counterintuitive if students seek out alternate sources of information (as instructed by the textbook guidelines). In Lahore, according to elite private school teachers, exposure to traumatic events of conflict results in anger and anxiety among learners. Teachers from these schools in Lahore and Delhi expressed confidence in transmitting their attitudes and adopting professional roles as agents of change. They planned their lessons critically, incorporating non-traditional teaching approaches in their classrooms (such as group discussions, debates and project work) in order to increase student engagement. They critically analysed conflicting perspectives (rooted in textbooks) in order to emphasise collective identity, mutual goals and friendly relations. Teachers' pedagogical responses and decisions are influenced by the institutional habitus of elite schools – including the most modern, secular, progressive and Westernised discourses that are produced and reproduced during school experiences.

Elite school teachers believe that it is their responsibility to provide students with essential skills to draw independent and critical inferences from textbooks. They incorporate different historical narratives to promote critical thinking. This is possible because elite schools are positioned to construct productive and stimulating learning environments, in contrast to other schools (Willms 2010). Elite school teachers discuss multiple perspectives, assisting students to de-categorise and to reduce stereotypes or biases. In the classrooms, teachers thus design and plan their lessons to equip students with the cultural capital of personal expression and an active use of ideas, thoughts and creativity. The elite schools grant absolute leadership to teachers in the classroom. Such a situation supported teachers' capacity to promote students' cognitive capabilities of analysis, reflection, inference, comparison, investigation and making logical decisions.

---

6   As far as textbooks are concerned, elite school teachers put forward the following claims. First, textbooks (in India or Pakistan) misrepresent the description of the other country and India–Pakistan relations by omitting historical events to present them in line with the one narrative. Second, textbooks neglect to teach the history, culture, religion and tradition of the other country. Finally, the shared beliefs of Hindus and Muslims that could promote trust and familiarity are either absent (in Pakistan Studies) or only partially present (in NCERT/Indian) in textbooks.

7   *Themes in Indian History*. I, II and III. NCERT. Delhi (12th Grade).

In addition, in elite schools the student-centred approach is used to develop students' critical thinking abilities and respect for pluralism to reduce the likelihood of violent conflict. In the classrooms of elite schools, knowledge is co-created through power-sharing strategies in which learners have a voice, raise questions, engage in critical reflection and take responsibility for their own and others' learning (Bishop 2012; Ladson-Billings 1995). This creates an inclusive space for teachers and learners to go beyond the textbooks into the process of teaching and learning (National Curriculum Framework 2005).

In Delhi and Lahore, elite schoolteachers act as the mediating agents and negotiate the textbook's content. They do not teach about the other country (Pakistan/India) and India–Pakistan relations only by reading textbooks, but also by using external sources. Teachers admit that discussions help students to develop critical thinking and reasoning skills. The elite schools' classrooms space effectively becomes a hybrid space in which knowledge acquired at school and the students' knowledge of the world gained in their homes and communities intersect. This hybrid space thus becomes an arena to navigate, a place in which students gain competence and expertise (Feldman 2016). By fostering their world knowledge and cultural interests, this space allows learners to achieve success in the standardised school knowledge requirements (Feldman 2016). Elite teachers serve as referees in their classrooms (field), often deciding what is right and wrong. They use debates to develop critical consciousness and to expand students' views beyond ideas encountered in the textbook, media or at home. The multiple-perspective approach to history teaching was used to express the equal status of both groups (Anand 2019).

In Delhi and Lahore, elite school teachers constructed pedagogical choices and responses based on their institutional habitus. This habitus overrides their personal experiences and determines their behaviours within the field (classroom) (Habibis and Walter 2009). It is a vital aspect of the schools' micro-political context that influences teachers' sense of responsibility for their students' learning (Ahmad 2009). In both research sites, the level of autonomy implemented by elite teachers around classroom management procedures, pedagogical choices and discipline governments contributed to the social climate of the field (or classroom). Teachers construct a navigating space in which students gained competence and expertise by discussing their world knowledge and cultural interests. The level of autonomy thus influenced how students, as players, utilised their schools' habitus, as well as the extent of their engagement in constructing discussions in their fields (classroom) (Anand 2019).

The staff of elite schools also have more authority over resource decisions. They are capable of making efficient and effective decisions to use their human or material resources to meet their students' needs (Malik 2012), as they are better resourced than middle or lower SES schools (Darling-Hammond 2013; Tate 1997). Elite teachers thus focus on teaching controversial issues in a democratic setting by encouraging the students' engagement and critical thinking. An open learning environment in their classroom supported discussion of the controversial political and historical problems. This allows students to hear and express different views or opinions (Reay et al. 2001).

In the classroom, teachers from middle government and private schools in Delhi ignore the multiple perspectives on conflict or historical topics. This is because they are wary of risking inspection if they discuss controversial issues in their classroom. This situation could be due to the institutional habitus of schools' teacher-centred pedagogy, compounded by the consequences of ideological education (Alexander et al. 2001, 498). In Lahore, teachers do not deviate from the textbooks; their focus is to ensure that learners have memorised the textbook content. They teach using textbooks and provide less space for teacher-student interactions. In general teachers ignore the fact that these nationalist texts could contribute to exclusionary Pakistani discourse (Afzal 2015; Hussain and Safiq 2016). In the classrooms, teachers do not provide opportunities for students critically to analyse both sides of narratives that could significantly impact their students' lives and their own narratives vis-a-vis the complete picture (Anand 2019).

Teachers in both research sites believe in the legitimacy of the textbooks, which are centralised productions of their respective governments. They signify an official version of history preferred by the state, as well as providing a detailed image of the country's political and ideological agenda (Korostelina 2011; Popson 2001). Teachers are self-absorbed in their professional identities (due to the impact of the institutional habitus). Due to their limited strengths, they tend not to change the surrounding reality or school culture. This can also be due to laissez-faire leadership, a passive form of leadership and its lowest level. Laissez-faire leadership manifests itself in rejecting attempts to influence the system's performance in advance (Avolio et al. 1991).

In Delhi, teachers working in middle SES private and government schools used the teacher-centred approach for teaching about Pakistan or India–Pakistan relations. In the semi-structured interviews, teachers acknowledged that it was important to teach the multiple perspectives of partition. However, they admitted that they were often unprepared to facilitate discussions due to a lack of learning materials (Bellino 2014). The institutional habitus of teachers in Delhi provides a choice of how to teach the textbook and how to ignore using the hidden curriculum in the classroom (Anand 2019).

The hidden curriculum 'consists of those things pupils learn through the experience of attending school rather than the stated educational objectives of such institutions' (Dickerson 2007, 14). Teachers commented that the hidden curriculum influences the students' attitudes. They clarified that recognising others' opinions and attitudes, as well as political affiliations, was not their priority in their classrooms. This indicates that teachers are conscious of the significance of debates but also of the need to maintain a safe atmosphere for debates to protect students from being bullied or humiliated (Anand 2019).

Such a situation can be explained by an example from the semi-structured interviews. In Delhi a teacher from a private, middle SES school responded that their students received much information from the media for making presentations and projects on India–Pakistan relations. However, teachers felt that the news articles could develop anxieties and encourage aggressive attitudes among students in times of terrorist attacks. As a result they tend to avoid teaching controversial topics in their classrooms (Anand 2019).

There is a considerable variation in pedagogical responses of middle private and government SES school teachers in Delhi due to three significant reasons. First, Oliver and Kettley (2010) found that teachers' habitus, their class background and their ethical and political beliefs determined how they intervened in students' choices. However, in Delhi teachers disregarded their cultural capital (attitudes), instead adopting the practices of the school (field) and enacting or delivering the values of education. The data from the semi-structured interviews and classroom observations indicate that teachers from middle SES private and government schools recognise skills per se that are negotiated. This is because a school's institutional or organisational habitus changes when 'school leaders [create] an organisational habitus that [mediates] the relationship between teachers' beliefs and their sense of responsibility' for students' academic outcomes (Diamond et al. 2004, 90). Second, the culture of a school is not a static entity; it is formed by the interactions and actions of the employees directed by state. Teachers commented that the Muslim students in Indian classrooms carried two versions of history in their heads. This reduces the rational analysis in school, meaning that the staff focus their teaching solely on passing examinations. They do not encourage open discussions, debates or expression of different views in their classrooms due to the fear of losing their jobs. Third, Bourdieu

(2005, 45) emphasises that, as a method of 'habitus engagement' that engages with teachers' firmly established pedagogical identities, their 'pedagogical habitus' affects adaptation; it also changes their classroom pedagogy. Teachers in Delhi expressed confusion over choosing a pedagogical approach for presenting controversial issues in the classroom with Muslim students or students with different views and faiths. Teachers were reluctant to discuss contentious issues and nervous of engaging directly with political issues; it was also challenging for them not to reveal their own political views in classroom settings. Teachers thus corroborated with the different school contexts in order to find ways to shift and change their pedagogy (Anand 2019).

In Lahore, middle SES private and government school teachers do not diverge from the textbook to ensure that their learners have memorised its content adequately. Teachers in this study enacted the textbooks in a way that allowed less space for teacher-student interactions. This was due to three reasons. First, the questions in the textbooks require teachers to foster appreciation among students for belonging to 'a member of a Muslim nation' (Nayyar and Salim 2003, 11). Second, as envisioned by Nayyar and Salim (2005, 165)

> What is important in the exercise is the faithful transmission, with no criticism or re-evaluation, of the particular view of the past which is implicit in the coming to fruition of the 'Pakistan Ideology'.

Teachers do not promote critical discussions due to fear of losing their jobs. On the individual level, they voiced concerns on social and educational aspects that affected their classroom practice. However, these views are influenced, negotiated and constrained by the institution. Third, on the fundamental level, the way or method through which learners learn – and through which educational success is measured – is rote-memorisation to pass examinations (Hayes 2009).

Teachers from lower SES private and government schools in both research sites adopted the method of 'read-recall-recite' to guide their pedagogical responses to India–Pakistan relations. They read from the textbooks, then paraphrased the text to make it easier for students to understand. Teachers did not encourage multiple perspectives or the use of the reference material (besides the textbooks) to supplement the textbook content (Anand 2019). In Delhi and Lahore, lower SES private and government school teachers accredit authority to the textbooks. Those in the study adopted a closed questioning approach for three reasons. First, schools (and students) position teachers as the sole legitimate source of knowledge; the students' role was to recall and recite for evaluation what they had previously read or been told. Second, the teaching structure produces a rather disjointed lesson; teachers simply move from one topic to another with no line of reasoning. Teachers assumed that students at lower SES schools might become entangled in a conflict if they attempted to approach the different perspectives of the other's narrative. Third, teachers shared the deficit discourses[8] that outlined their pedagogical decisions within a distinct social or cultural group (Candlin and Crichton 2010, 4). The school culture in lower private and government schools is thus shaped by deficient teaching, learning models and low expectations. The deficit models contribute to a poor classroom climate as well as public behaviour issues (Haydn et al. 2014).

Teachers in this situation, therefore, do not exercise their power or authority to diminish stereotypes by developing empathy and understanding of other groups and their narratives (Steinberg and Bar-On 2002). Oliver and Kettley claim that 'teachers' histories, prior experiences, moral and political beliefs and social capital potentially shape their pro-activity or resignation in engaging with students' expectations and behaviours' (Oliver and Kettley 2010, 739–40). However, the institutional habitus overrides teachers' individual habitus in Delhi and Lahore. Teachers act as gatekeepers, a position that has two consequences. First, it constructs negative attitudes, reinforces negative stereotypes among students or teachers and results in self-fulfilling prophecies among teachers (Castagno and Brayboy 2008). Second, it causes student resistance, alienation, low levels of student engagement and general underachievement (Castagno and Brayboy 2008; Sleeter 2011).

Deficit and pathologising pedagogical approaches

The semi-structured interviews show that teachers in lower SES private and government schools do favour the critical thinking model, if only in theory. Nevertheless, they may have unconscious biases which are revealed in the 'self-fulfilling prophecies' directed toward students. Teachers held misconceptions about co-construction, considering they needed to abdicate their voices and practise authority in the classroom (Anand 2019). Discerning attitudes and deficit dispositions can also be held against racially

---

8   The deficit discourses in schools involve educators who (un)consciously hold deficit assumptions about students. Deficit thinking lowers teacher expectations and reduces teacher agency, as teachers associate the problems of low student achievement with the student's background and culture (Bishop et al. 2014).

marginalised students (Valencia 2010). Pathologising a racially marginalised student should be opposed, as it may lead to re-creating stereotypes about the intellectual capacities of these students (Caplan et al. 2008). This belief is in line with McMahon and Portelli (2012), who argue that the cycle of deficit pedagogy could lead to underachievement by reinforcing the stereotypes about the capabilities of racially marginalised students. Teachers' attitudes towards students' abilities reduce their sense of responsibility for student learning and encourage them to engage such students in rote learning or memorisation (Malik 2011). They believe that the lower SES students serve as a barrier to challenging and cognitively demanding instruction in the classroom (Anand 2019).

This situation is largely due to the schools' socio-economic status (and its institutional habitus), both of which influence teachers' beliefs and interactions with students (Garcia et al. 2010). The lower SES schools have relatively few materials and limited financial resources (Chiu and Khoo 2005). They also have problems with discipline, which diminishes the amount of 'instructional time available to students' (Kahlenberg 2004, 10), and lower teacher hopes and expectations (Rumberger and Palardy 2005). Further issues include less constructive associations between teachers and learners, lower amounts of homework (Rumberger and Palardy 2005) and a less academically challenging curriculum compared with that in middle SES schools (Anyon 1981; Thrupp 1995). Lower SES private and government school teachers also used deficit-orientated and pathologising approaches (Caplan et al. 2008).

Deficit-oriented approach to pedagogy or classroom practices

In the study some teachers voiced low expectations of students and their willingness to contribute to the classroom, consequently labelling their students in 'deficit' terms. Teachers use 'chalk and talk' techniques,[9] in which students are expected to listen and passively absorb. They exercise their authority in the classroom by dictating commands and assigning work-related activities (Lewin and Stuart 2003). The teaching style or approach that was used when teaching lower-class students often involved rote behaviour (Meier 2002). Rote-based learning does not engage with students' identities, however, and often leaves no space to teach critical

---

9   The 'chalk and talk' or teacher instruction still dominates the classrooms, as the government has acknowledged. 'After a number of years of implementing in-service teacher training, it is not clear what type of impact such training has had on improvements in the classroom processes' (Government of India 2010, 35–7).

thinking skills (Meier 2002). The instructional or rote teaching method is rooted in the deficit assumptions that working-class children are not capable of developing critical skills (Meier 2002). In both research sites, teachers expressed concern over the lack of resources in their schools, combined with insufficient support from headteachers (Anand 2019).

In their responses teachers agreed that inadequate access to teaching materials was one of the barriers to critical education. Their positions were recognised by the amount of cultural capital and other types of capital of their school, which influences teachers' pedagogical decisions and encourages them to prefer a deficit-oriented teaching approach in the field (classroom) (Bourdieu 1986). This is due to two reasons. First, the examination systems in India and Pakistan obstruct teaching, learning and educational praxis (Hughes 1993). However, these exam systems dominate secondary education (Zohar 2009), so their influence is substantial. Second, the style of exams has a significant impact on classroom pedagogy, curriculum development and educational policy (Pierce and Larson 1993, 687). In the semi-structured interviews, almost all teachers commented that their job is to prepare students for passing examinations (Anand 2019).

Teachers' beliefs about students from low socio-economic backgrounds reveal 'attitudes of deficit' towards students' abilities to develop critical thinking skills (Delpit 1995). This perception characterised the ethos of low socio-economic students as deficient due to 'weakness in a home environment, family structure, child-rearing patterns, values and attitudes, linguistic capability and cognitive development' (Persell 1981, 27). The attitudes of lower private and government school teachers (created by the institutional habitus) thus became an educational tool, along with the textbook (Anand 2019).

Pathologising-oriented approach to pedagogy

A teacher can become an agent of transformational change by expanding the types of cultural capital available to students through the real-world curriculum and pedagogy (Mills 2008). Such an approach draws a connection between the marginalised players and the field on which they operate. It calls on the teacher to transform the field (in this case, the classroom) by integrating the marginalised into the game (Mills 2008). This is a challenging task, given the context. The schools are populated by students from different faiths or views, and repositioning them as active agents in a school's transformation is both difficult and profoundly democratic. It can only be done by drawing on the cultural knowledge that teachers can gain through reciprocal learning and teaching relationships with their students (Cook-Sather 2006).

In Delhi, teachers explained that they had limited interactions with students from the Muslim neighbourhood. Teachers expressed their concern that Muslim students, or students with relatives in Pakistan, could not be taught effectively due to the lack of intellectual or cognitive dispositions. Low teacher expectations and negative attitudes thus served to promote the alienation of Muslim students in Indian schools. In interviews, teachers confronted biases, assumptions and low expectations of students. In the classrooms, however, the adoption of student-focused approaches that used student-to-student interactions were challenging for many teachers (Anand 2019).

In Lahore, teachers did not find it necessary to discuss controversial topics or different views on the partition of India, nor did they feel comfortable doing so. The interviews highlighted a sense of worry in the narratives of teaching staff, conscious that their students were young and could develop extremist ideas. Teachers in both research sites recognised the need to be cautious and avoid offending students who considered themselves to be of the other faith and who held different views (Anand 2019). In Delhi and Lahore, knowledge in the three types of schools contributes to legitimisation and dissemination of ideologies and practices constitutive of the prevailing socio-economic hierarchy. The knowledge construction differs as per the socio-economic status of schools (Bourdieu 1977; 1984; 1990; 1993). It highlights how the educational practices were constructed by the intersection of the individual and institutional habitus in the classroom (Anand 2019).

Concluding remarks

This chapter shows why, in both Delhi and Lahore, the institutional habitus of the school overrides teachers' attitudes towards India–Pakistan relations and determines their pedagogical responses to the issue. The relationship between the school's socio-economic status (SES) (and the institutional habitus) and teachers' attitudes or pedagogical responses is evident for all schools in both research sites, regardless of teachers' own individual habitus. In capitalist societies teachers in different social classes offer different educational experiences (Anand 2019). Garcia et al. (2010) and Monzo and Rueda (2003) show the ways in which the students' socio-economic class influences how their teachers think about and interact with them.

Classrooms are not the only places in which knowledge and understanding of the past are formulated. Yet schools are venues where fallacies can – and should – be rectified and critical mindsets nurtured. This process seems imperative in empowering schools to influence teachers as rational agents, with the ability to reflect upon and produce changes suited to their own classroom practice (Anand 2019). The SES and the institutional habitus of the school also heavily influence, or hinder, the development of critical historical consciousness and understanding of the other country (India or Pakistan) and India–Pakistan relations in Delhi and Lahore (Anand 2019).

Policy-makers in both countries devise educational policies and curricular content in line with their respective ideological positions or political agendas. These policies will have a limited effect on teachers' attitudes and schools' prescribed pedagogies for history teaching and pupil learning. History teaching has been undermined by a lack of clarity of purpose and rationale on the part of both policy-makers and teachers. This shortcoming has left the teaching and learning about India–Pakistan relations open to politicisation and susceptible to cultural trends. Teachers are central agents of socialisation, transmission and construction of personal or social identities. Policy-makers need to allow the integration of teacher attitudes and their pedagogical attitudes into policy-making processes – a move that could prove instrumental in contextualising progressive pedagogies to history teaching and students' learning outcomes (Anand 2019).

Such a focus on teachers' attitudes and experiences would help to elucidate how schools and communities could nurture learner-centred experiences for pupils and achieve better academic performance. The current norm within the policy discourse is unlikely to result in the anticipated improvement in teaching and learning, particularly in low and middle SES schools. The educational policy thus needs to allow for the uniqueness of local practices that might lead in turn to more practical improvements in the pedagogical practices of both India and Pakistan (Anand 2019).

And finally...

The participant teachers had different teaching approaches, and their school culture and personal understandings influenced the different pedagogies they developed. As previously discussed, however, there were common strands that teachers could perhaps take up to begin to access more democratic practices. These in turn might give opportunities for students to experiment with their own symbolic historical understandings. From the evidence of this study, the author proposes a shift is needed in moving away from teacher perspectives in history teaching towards an approach that authentically listens to, and takes notice of, students' own historical knowledge that they bring with them to school. Some teachers in this study had indeed made that shift; they listened to their students and became advocates for promoting students' historical views.

The author has questioned whether moving to pedagogies that support the historical perspectives of students is possible in India and Pakistan, countries where teachers' voices are rarely heard within a tightly controlled government education system. The author leaves the final important point with the voice of a teacher who participated in the study. In their response this teacher stated and reflected, on more than one occasion

> You have to listen to students' views rather than the student listening to the teacher's attitudes and reading the textbook. For me this is very important. (Lahore, elite private school teacher)

Appendix A
Snapshot of each teacher participant in Delhi and Lahore

Snapshot of each teacher participant in Delhi

Teacher identifier	Gender	Age	Qualification	Teaching experience in years
Elite private school teacher 1	Female	42	BA, MA, B.Ed.	10
Elite private school teacher 2	Female	50	BA, B.Ed., M.Ed.	15
Middle private SES school teacher (MPST) 1	Female	38	BA, B.Ed., M.Ed.	7
Middle private SES school teacher (MPST) 2	Male	45	BA, MA, B.Ed.	8
Middle private SES school teacher (MPST) 3	Female	28	BA, MA, B.Ed.	2
Middle private SES school teacher (MPST) 4	Male	52	BA, MA, B.Ed.	12
Middle private SES school teacher (MPST) 5	Female	48	BA, B.Ed., M.Ed.	4
Middle government SES school teacher (MGST) 1	Male	30	BA, MA, B.Ed.	2
Middle government SES school teacher (MGST) 2	Female	50	BA, B.Ed., M.Ed.	12
Middle government SES school teacher (MGST) 3	Male	55	BA, MA, B.Ed.	12
Middle government SES school teacher (MGST) 4	Female	35	BA, B.Ed., M.Ed.	3

Lower private SES school teacher (LPST) 1	Female	30	BA, MA, B.Ed.	2
Lower private SES school teacher (LPST) 2	Female	30	BA, B.Ed., M.Ed.	3
Lower private SES school teacher (LPST) 3	Female	39	BA, MA, B.Ed.	6
Lower private SES school teacher (LPST) 4	Female	50	BA, B.Ed., M.Ed.	11
Lower private SES school teacher (LPST) 5	Female	45	BA, MA, B.Ed.	9
Lower government SES school teacher (LGST) 1	Male	41	BA, B.Ed., M.Ed.	8
Lower government SES school teacher (LGST) 2	Female	52	BA, MA, B.Ed.	15
Lower government SES school teacher (LGST) 3	Male	50	BA, B.Ed., M.Ed.	18
Lower government SES school teacher (LGST) 4	Female	48	BA, B.Ed., M.Ed.	12
Lower government SES school teacher (LGST) 5	Female	42	BA, MA, B.Ed.	12

Snapshot of each teacher participant in Lahore

Teacher identifier	Gender	Age	Qualification	Teaching experience in years
Elite private school teacher 1	Female	37	BA, MA, B.Ed.	10
Elite private school teacher 2	Male	40	BA, B.Ed., M.Ed.	9
Middle private SES school teacher (MPST) 1	Female	37	BA, MA, B.Ed.	6
Middle private SES school teacher (MPST) 2	Male	34	BA, B.Ed., M.Ed.	4
Middle private SES school teacher (MPST) 3	Female	26	BA, B.Ed., M.Ed.	2
Middle private SES school teacher (MPST) 4	Female	58	BA, B.Ed., M.Ed.	26
Middle private SES school teacher (MPST) 5	Male	56	BA, MA, B.Ed.	21
Middle government SES school teacher (MGST) 1	Male	28	BA, B.Ed., M.Ed.	3
Middle government SES school teacher (MGST) 2	Female	55	BA, MA, B.Ed.	24
Middle government SES school teacher (MGST) 3	Male	58	BA, B.Ed., M.Ed.	26
Middle government SES school teacher (MGST) 4	Female	38	BA, MA, B.Ed.	9

Lower private SES school teacher (LPST) 1	Female	35	BA, MA, B.Ed.	6
Lower private SES school teacher (LPST) 2	Female	33	BA, B.Ed., M.Ed.	5
Lower private SES school teacher (LPST) 3	Male	36	BA, B.Ed., M.Ed.	4
Lower private SES school teacher (LPST) 4	Female	57	BA, MA, B.Ed.	29
Lower private SES school teacher (LPST) 5	Female	48	BA, MA, B.Ed.	5
Lower government SES school teacher (LGST) 1	Female	49	BA, MA, B.Ed.	17
Lower government SES school teacher (LGST) 2	Male	57	BA, B.Ed., M.Ed.	19
Lower government SES school teacher (LGST) 3	Male	56	BA, MA, B.Ed.	23
Lower government SES school teacher (LGST) 4	Female	49	BA, MA, B.Ed.	17
Lower government SES school teacher (LGST) 5	Female	49	BA, MA, B.Ed.	19

References

Achinstein, B. and Ogawa, R. 2006. '(In) fidelity: What the resistance of new teachers reveals about professional principles and prescriptive educational policies', *Harvard Educational Review* 76(1): 30–63.

Adeney, K. and Lall, M. 2005. 'Institutional attempts to build a "National" identity in India: Internal and external dimensions', *India Review* 4(3–4): 258–86.

Adwan, S., Bar-Tal, D. and Wexler, B.E. 2014. 'Portrayal of the Other in Palestinian and Israeli schoolbooks: A comparative study', *Political Psychology* 37(2): 201–17.

Afzal, M. 2015. *Education and Attitudes in Pakistan*. Washington D.C.: United States Institute of Peace.

Afzal, M. 2018. *Pakistan Under Siege: Extremism, Society and the State*. Washington D.C.: Brookings Institution Press.

Ahearn, L.M. 2001. 'Language and agency', *Annual Review of Anthropology*: 109–37.

Ahmad, M. 2009. 'The problematique of education in Pakistan', *IBT Journal of Business Studies (JBS)* 1(1); *Journal of Management and Social Sciences* 5: 13–21.

Ahmed, M. 2012. 'Factors affecting initial teacher education in Pakistan: Historical analysis of policy network', *International Journal of Humanities and Social Science* 13(2): 104–13.

Ahmed, Z.S. and Baxter, M.A. 2007. *Attitudes of teachers in India and Pakistan: Texts and contexts* (Vol. 1). Women in Security Conflict Management and Peace, Foundation for Universal Responsibility of His Holiness the Dalai Lama. New Delhi: WISCOMP.

Aiken, N. 2013. *Identity, Reconciliation and Transitional Justice: Overcoming intractability in divided societies*. New York: Routledge.

Alavi, H. 1982. 'State and class under peripheral capitalism'. In *Introduction to the Sociology of 'Developing Societies'*, edited by H. Alavi and T. Shanin, 209–307. New York: Monthly Review Press; London: Palgrave Macmillan.

Alexander, K.L., Entwisle, D.R. and Kabbani, N.S. 2001. 'The dropout process in life course perspective: Early risk factors at home and school', *Teachers College Record* 103(5): 760–822.

Alexander, K. and Alexander, M.D. 2018. *The Law of Schools, Students and Teachers in a Nutshell*. St. Paul, MN: West Academic Publishing.

Alexander, R., 2013. *Essays on Pedagogy*. Oxford; Boston, MA: Routledge.

Alexander, J.C. and Dromi, S.M. 2011. 'Trauma construction and moral restriction: The ambiguity of the Holocaust for Israel'. In *Narrating Trauma: On the impact of collective suffering*, edited by Ron Eyerman, Jeffrey C. Alexander and Elizabeth Butler Breese, 107–32. Boulder, CO: Paradigm Press.

Anand, K. 2019. *Teaching India and Pakistan Relations: Teachers' pedagogical responses and strategies* (PhD thesis, UCL (University College London)).

Anand, K. and Lall, M. 2022. 'The debate between secularism and Hindu nationalism – how India's textbooks have become the government's medium for political communication', *India Review* 21(1): 77–107.

Anderson, B. 1991. *Imagined Communities: Reflections on the origin and spread of nationalism* (rev. and extended ed.). London: Verso.

Andrabi, T.R., Das, J. and Khwaja, A.I. 2010. *Education Policy in Pakistan: A framework for reform*. London: International Growth Centre.

Anitha, S. 2011. 'Legislating gender inequalities: The nature and patterns of domestic violence experienced by South Asian women with insecure immigration status in the United Kingdom', *Violence Against Women* 17(10): 1260–85.

Anyon, J., 1981. 'Social class and school knowledge', *Curriculum Inquiry* 11(1): 3–42.

Apple, M.W. 1990. 'The text and cultural politics', *The Journal of Educational Thought (JET)/ Revue de la Pensée Educative* 24: 17–33.

Apple, M.W. 1990. 'Is there a curriculum voice to reclaim?', *The Phi Delta Kappan* 71(7): 526–30.

Apple, M.W. 1993. 'What post-modernists forget: Cultural capital and official knowledge', *Curriculum Studies* 1(3): 301–16.

Apple, M.W. 2001. 'Comparing neo-liberal projects and inequality in education', *Comparative Education* 37(4): 409–23.

Apple, M.W. 2003. 'The state and the politics of knowledge'. In *The State and the Politics of Knowledge*, edited by Apple, M.W., Aasen, P., Cho, M.K., Gandin, L.A., Oliver, A., Sung, Y.-K. et al., 9–32. New York: Routledge Falmer.

Apple, M. 2004. *Ideology and Curriculum*. Routledge, New York.

Apple, M.W. 2018. 'The struggle for democracy in education'. In *The Struggle for Democracy in Education*, edited by Michael Apple, 1–19. New York: Routledge.

Aronowitz, S. and Giroux, H. 1985. 'Radical education and transformative intellectuals', *CTheory* 9(3): 48–63.

ASER. 2014. 'Annual Status of Education Report (Rural) 2014'. New Delhi: Annual Status of Education Report (ASER). Accessed 25 December 2018. Retrieved from: http://img.asercentre.org/docs/Publications/ASER%20Reports/ASER%202014 /fullaser2014mainreport_1.pdf.

ASER. 2017. 'Annual Status of Education Report (Rural) 2017: Beyond Basics'. New Delhi: Annual Status of Education Report (ASER). Accessed 25 December 2018. Retrieved from: http://img.asercentre.org/docs/Publications/ASER%20Reports/ASER%202017/ aser2017fullreportfinal.pdf.

ASER. 2018. 'Annual Status of Education Report (Rural) 2018: Provisional'. New Delhi: Annual Status of Education Report (ASER). Accessed 15 January 2019. Retrieved from: http://img. asercentre.org/docs/ASER%202018/Release%20Material/aserreport2018.pdf.

Atkinson, W. 2016. 'From sociological fictions to social fictions: Some Bourdieusian reflections on the concepts of "institutional habitus" and "family habitus"'. In *Theorizing Social Class and Education*, edited by Diane Reay and Carol Vincent, 127–44). London: Routledge.

Avolio, B.J., Yammarino, F.J. and Bass, B.M. 1991. 'Identifying common methods variance with data collected from a single source: An unresolved sticky issue', *Journal of Management* 17(3): 571–87.

Ayaz Naseem, M. 2006. 'The soldier and the seductress: A post-structuralist analysis of gendered citizenship through inclusion in and exclusion from language and social studies textbooks in Pakistan', *International Journal of Inclusive Education* 10(4–5): 449–67.

Aziz, K. 1993. *The Murder of History: A critique of history textbooks used in Pakistan*. Lahore: Vanguard.

Baart, J.L. 2003. 'Sustainable development and the maintenance of Pakistan's indigenous languages'. In *Proceedings of the Conference on the State of the Social Sciences and Humanities: Current scenario and emerging trends*. Islamabad, September 26–27 2003.

Baldauf, S. 2001. 'Pakistan's two schools of thought', *Christian Science Monitor* 93(217), 7–17.

Baleghizadeh, S. and Javidanmehr, P.D.S.Z. 2014. 'Exploring EFL teachers' reflectivity and their sense of self-efficacy/İngilizce Öğretmenlerinde Yansıtıcılığın Özyeterliklerini Yordama Gücü', *e-Uluslararası Eğitim Araştırmaları Dergisi* 5(3): 19–38.

Ball, S.J. and Bowe, R. 1992. 'Subject departments and the "implementation" of National Curriculum policy: An overview of the issues', *Journal of Curriculum Studies* 24(2): 97–115.

Ball, D.L. and Cohen, D.K. 1996. 'Reform by the book: What is – or might be – the role of curriculum materials in teacher learning and instructional reform?', *Educational Researcher* 25(9): 6–14.

Bandura, A. 1999. 'Social cognitive theory: An agentic perspective', *Asian Journal of Social Psychology* 2(1): 21–41.

Bandura, A. 2001. 'Social cognitive theory: An agentic perspective', *Annual Review of Psychology* 52(1): 1–26.

Banerjee, B.K. and Stöber, G. 2016. 'The portrayal of "the other" in Pakistani and Indian school textbooks'. In *(Re)constructing Memory: Textbooks, identity, nation, state*, edited by J.H. Williams and W.A. Bokhorst-Heng, 141–76). Rotterdam, NL: Sense Publishers.

Bar-Tal, D. 1990. 'Causes and consequences of delegitimization: Models of conflict and ethnocentrism', *Journal of Social Issues* 46(1): 65–81.

Bar-Tal, D. 2002. 'Conciliation through storytelling: Beyond victimhood'. In *Peace Education: The concept, principles, and practices around the world*, edited by Gavriel Salomon and Baruch Nevo, 109–116. Mahwah, NI: Lawrence Erlbaum.

Bar-Tal, D. 2007. 'Socio-psychological foundations of intractable conflict', *American Behavioural Scientist* 50(11): 1430–53;

Bar-Tal, D. 2001. 'Why does fear override hope in societies engulfed by intractable conflict, as it does in the Israeli society?', *Political Psychology* 22(3): 601.

Bar-Tal, D., Halperin, E. and Oren, N. 2010. 'Socio–psychological barriers to peace making: The case of the Israeli Jewish society', *Social Issues and Policy Review* 4(1): 63–109.

Bar-Tal, D. 2013. *Intractable Conflicts: Socio-psychological foundations and dynamics*. Cambridge: Cambridge University Press.

Batra, P. 2005. 'Voice and agency of teachers: Missing link in national curriculum framework 2005', *Economic and Political Weekly* 40(40):4347–56.

Batra, P. 2006. 'Building on the National Curriculum Framework to enable the agency of teachers', *Contemporary Education Dialogue* 4(1): 88–118.

Batra, P. 2011. 'Teacher education and classroom practice in India: A critique and propositions'. In *EpiSTEME-4 Conference*, Mumbai.

Baumeister, R. and Hastings, S. 1997. 'Distortions of collective memory: How groups flatter and deceive themselves'. In *Collective Memory of Political Events: Social psychological perspective*, edited by J. Pennebaker, D. Paez and B. Rimé. 227–93. Mahwah, NJ: Lawrence Erlbaum.

Behera, N.C. 1996. 'Perpetuating the divide: Political abuse of history in South Asia', *Contemporary South Asia* 5(2): 191–205.

Behuria, A. and Shehzad, M. 2013. 'Partition of history in textbooks in Pakistan: Implications of selective memory and forgetting', *Strategic Analysis* 37(3), 353–65.

Bellino, M.J. 2014. 'Whose past, whose present?: Historical memory among the 'postwar' generation in Guatemala. In *(Re)constructing Memory*, edited by James H. Williams, 131–53. 129–51). Rotterdam, NL: Sense Publishers.

Ben-Peretz, M. 1990. *The Teacher-Curriculum Encounter: Freeing teachers from the tyranny of texts*. Albany: State University of New York Press.

Bentrovato, D. 2017. 'History textbook writing in post-conflict societies: From battlefield to site and means of conflict transformation'. In *History Education and Conflict Transformation*, edited by M. Carretero, C. Psaltis and S. Cehanic-Clancy, 37–76. Cham: Palgrave Macmillan.

Bernstein, B. 2000. *Pedagogy, Symbolic Control and Identity: Theory, research, critique* (Vol. 5). Lanham, MA: Rowman & Littlefield.

Berrebi, C. 2007. 'Evidence about the link between education, poverty and terrorism among Palestinians', *Peace Economics, Peace Science and Public Policy* 13(1): 18–53.

Bhattacharya, N. 2008. 'Predicaments of secular histories', *Public Culture* 20(1): 57–73.

Bhattacharya, N. 2009. 'Teaching history in schools: The politics of textbooks in India', *History Workshop Journal* 67(1): 99–110. Biddle, B.J. 1986. 'Recent developments in role theory', *Annual Review of Sociology* 12: 67–92. https://doi.org/10.1146/annurev.so.12.080186.000435.

Biesta, G.J.J. and Tedder, M. 2006. How is Agency Possible? Towards an Ecological Understanding of Agency-as-Achievement' (Working Paper 5). Exeter: The Learning Lives Project. Bishop, P. and Hines, A. 2012. *Teaching About the Future*. Basingstoke: Palgrave Macmillan.

Bishop, R., Ladwig, J. and Berryman, M. 2014. 'The centrality of relationships for pedagogy: The whanaungatanga thesis', *American Educational Research Journal* 51(1): 184–214.

Bourdieu, P. 1973. *Cultural Reproduction and Social Reproduction* London: Tavistock, 71.

Bourdieu, P. 1977. *Outline of a Theory of Practice*. Cambridge: Cambridge University Press.

Bourdieu, P. 1984. *Distinction: A social critique of the judgement of taste*. Cambridge, MA: Harvard University Press.

Bourdieu, P. 1986. 'The force of law: Toward a sociology of the juridical field', *Hastings Law Journal* 38(5): 805.

Bourdieu, P. 1990. *The Logic of Practice*. Redwood City, CA: Stanford University Press.

Bourdieu, P. 1991. *Language and Symbolic Power*. London: Polity.

Bourdieu, P. 1993. *The Field of Cultural Production: Essays on art and literature*. Columbia, NY: Columbia University Press.

Bourdieu, P. 1998. *Practical Reason: On the theory of action*. Redwood City, CA: Stanford University Press.

Bourdieu, P. 2005. 'Habitus'. In *Habitus: A sense of place*, edited by J. Hillier and E. Rooksby, 43–9. Farnham, UK: Ashgate.

Bourdieu, P. and Passeron, J.C. 1977. *Education, Society and Culture*. Trans. Richard Nice. London: SAGE Publications.

Bourdieu, P. and Passeron, J.C. 1990. *Reproduction in Education, Society and Culture* (Vol. 4). London: SAGE Publications.

Borg, S. 2011. 'Language teacher education'. In *The Routledge Handbook of Applied Linguistics*, edited by J. Simpson. London: Routledge.

Brauch, N. 2017. 'Bridging the gap: Comparing history curricula in history teacher education in Western countries'. In *Palgrave Handbook of Research in Historical Culture and Education*, edited by M. Carretero, M.S. Berger and M. Grever, 593–611. London: Palgrave Macmillan.

Braun Jr., J.A. and Crumpler, T.P. 2004. 'The social memoir: An analysis of developing reflective ability in a pre-service methods course', *Teaching and Teacher Education* 20(1): 59–75.

Brinkmann, S., 2016. 'The role of teachers' beliefs in the implementation of learner-centred education in India'. PhD thesis, UCL (University College London).

Buchanan, R. 2015. 'Teacher identity and agency in an era of accountability', *Teachers and Teaching* 21(6): 700–19.

Bukor, E. 2015. 'Exploring teacher identity from a holistic perspective: Reconstructing and reconnecting personal and professional selves', *Teachers and Teaching* 21(3): 305–27.

Burke, C.T., Emmerich, N. and Ingram, N. 2013. 'Well-founded social fictions: A defence of the concepts of institutional and familial habitus', *British Journal of Sociology of Education* 34(2): 165–82.

Butalia, U. 2000. *The Other Side of Silence: Voices from the Partition of India*. London: Hurst and Company.

Byrne-Armstrong, H., Higgs, J. and Horsfall, D. 2001. *Critical Moments in Qualitative Research*. Oxford: Butterworth-Heinemann Medical.

Calderhead, J. 1996. 'Teachers: Beliefs and knowledge'. In *Handbook of Educational Psychology*, edited by D. Berliner and R. Calfee. New York: Macmillan.

Calvert, L. 2016. 'The power of teacher agency', *The Learning Professional* 37(2): 51.

Campano, G., Ghiso, M.P., Badaki, O. and Kannan, C. 2020. 'Agency as collectivity: Community-based research for educational equity', *Theory into Practice* 59(2): 223–33. Accessed 18 October 2021. https://doi.org/10.1080/00405841.2019.1705107.

Candlin, C. and Crichton, J. 2010. *Discourses of Deficit*. Basingstoke: Palgrave Macmillan.

Caplan, R., Siddarth, P., Stahl, L., Lanphier, E., Vona, P., Gurbani, S., Koh, S., Sankar, R. and Shields, W.D. 2008. 'Childhood absence epilepsy: Behavioral, cognitive and linguistic comorbidities', *Epilepsia* 49(11): 1838–46.

Castagno, A.E. and Brayboy, B.M.J. 2008. 'Culturally responsive schooling for Indigenous youth: A review of the literature', *Review of Educational Research* 78(4): 941–93.

Cazden, C.B. 2001. *The Language of Teaching and Learning*. Portsmouth, NH: Heinemann, 348–69.

Chakrabarty, D. 2002. *Habitations of Modernity: Essays in the wake of subaltern studies*. New Delhi: Permanent Black.

Chandra, B. 2008. *Communalism in Modern India*. New Delhi: Har Anand Publications.

Chatterji, A.P. 2009. *Violent Gods: Hindu nationalism in India's present: Narratives from Orissa*. Gurgaon: Three Essays Collective.

Chaudhuri, D. 2020. 'In the "New India", all the values of the values of the righteous – as enumerated in The *Bhagavad Gita* – appear to have become penal offences', *Punch Magazine*.

Accessed 10 April 2020. Retrieved: http://thepunchmagazine.com/the-byword/non-fiction/about-values-why-hinduism-loving-citizens-tolerate-the-unrighteous-or-the-devilish.

Chhabra, M. 2016. 'A social-psychological perspective on teaching a historical event of collective violence: The case of the 1947 British India partition'. In *History Can Bite: History education in divided and post-war societies,* edited by D. Bentrovato, K.V. Korostelina and M. Schulze, 243–56. Göttingen: V&R Unipress.

Chiu, M.M. and Khoo, L. 2005. 'Effects of resources, inequality, and privilege bias on achievement: Country, school, and student level analyses', *American Educational Research Journal* 42(4), 575–603.

Clandinin, D.J. and Connelly, F.M. 1992. 'Teacher as curriculum maker'. In *Handbook of Research on Curriculum,* edited by P. Jackson, 363–401. New York: Macmillan.

Clandinin, D.J. and Connelly, F.M. 1998. 'Stories to live by: Narrative understandings of school reform', *Curriculum Inquiry* 28(2): 149–64.

Clark, C.M. and Peterson, P.L. 1984. 'Teachers' thought processes'. Occasional Paper No. 72. East Lansing: Institute for Research on Teaching, Michigan State University.

Coburn, C.E. and Woulfin, S.L. 2012. 'Reading coaches and the relationship between policy and practice', *Reading Research Quarterly* 47(1): 5–30.

Cochran-Smith, M. 2005. 'Studying teacher education: What we know and need to know', *Journal of Teacher Education* 56(4): 301–6.

Cohen, D.K., Raudenbush, S.W. and Ball, D.L. 2003. 'Resources, instruction, and research', *Educational Evaluation and Policy Analysis* 25(2): 119–42.

Conley, S. 1991. 'Chapter 6: Review of research on teacher participation in school decision making', *Review of Research in Education* 17(1): 225–66.

Cook-Sather, A. 2006. 'Sound, Presence, and Power: "Student Voice" in Educational Research and Reform', *Curriculum Inquiry* 36(4): 359–90.

Corbin, J. and Strauss, A. 2008. *Basics of Qualitative Research: Techniques and procedures for developing grounded theory.* 3rd edition. London: SAGE Publishers.

Creswell, J. 2013. 'Steps in conducting a scholarly mixed methods study', DBER Speaker series. University of Nebraska Discipline-Based Education Research Group. Accessed 21 January 2018. Retrieved: https://digitalcommons.unl.edu/cgi/viewcontent.cgi?referer=http://www.eajournals.org/wp-content/uploads/Mixed-Methods-Theory-and-Practice.-Sequential-Explanatory-Approach.pdf&httpsredir=1&article=1047&context=dberspeakers.

Cuban, L. 1998. 'How schools change reforms: Redefining reform success and failure', *Teachers College Record* 99(3): 453–77.

Darling-Hammond, L. and Lieberman, A., eds. 2013. *Teacher Education Around the World: Changing policies and practices.* New York: Taylor and Francis.

Das, S. 1991. *Communal Riots in Bengal, 1905–1947.* Delhi: Oxford University Press.

Davis, E. 2006. 'Preservice elementary teachers' critique of instructional materials for science', *Science Education* 90(2): 348–75.

Day, C., Kington, A., Stobart, G. and Sammons, P. 2006. 'The personal and professional selves of teachers: Stable and unstable identities', *British Educational Research Journal* 32(4): 601–16.

Dean, B. 2005. 'Citizenship education in Pakistani schools: Problems and possibilities', *International Journal of Citizenship and Teacher Education* 1(2): 35.

De Baets, A. 2015. 'Post-conflict history education moratoria: A balance', *World Studies in Education* 16(1): 5–30.

Debs, M. 2013. 'Using cultural trauma: Gandhi's assassination, partition and secular nationalism in post-independence India', *Nations and Nationalism* 19(4): 635–53.

Delpit, L. 1995. *Other People's Children: Cultural conflict in the classroom.* New York: New Press.

Denzin, N. and Lincoln, Y. 1998. *Strategies of Qualitative Inquiry.* Thousand Oaks, CA: SAGE Publications.

Devine, N. and Irwin, R. 2005. 'Autonomy, agency and education: *He tangata, he tangata, he tangata', Educational Philosophy and Theory* 37(3): 317–31.

Dewey, J. 1933. *How to Think: A re-statement of the relation of reflective thinking to the education context.* Washington, D.C.: Heath and Company.

Diamond, B. and Randolph, A. 2004. 'Teachers' expectations and sense of responsibility for student learning: The importance of race, class, and organizational habitus', *Anthropology & Education Quarterly* 35(1): 75–98.

Dickerson, L. 2007. 'Postmodern view of the hidden curriculum', *Electronic Theses and Dissertations* 455. Accessed 21 May 2019. Available at: https://digitalcommons.georgiasouthern.edu/cgi/viewcontent.cgi?article=1455&context=etd.

Dickson-Swift, V., James, E., Kippen, S. and Liamputtong, P. 2007. 'Doing sensitive research: What challenges do qualitative researchers face?' *Qualitative Research* 7(3): 327–53.

Dover, A. G., Henning, N. and Agarwal-Rangnath, R. 2016. 'Reclaiming agency: Justice-oriented social studies teachers respond to changing curricular standards', *Teaching and Teacher Education* 59, 457–67.

Dryzek, J.S. 2002. *Deliberative Democracy and Beyond: Liberals, critics, contestations.* Oxford: Oxford University PressDuFour, R. 2002. 'The learning-centered principal', *Educational Leadership* 59(8): 12–15.

Durand, J.L. and Kaempf, S. 2014. 'Reimagining communities: Opening up history to the memory of others', *Millennium* 42(2): 331–53.

Durrani, N. 2008. 'Schooling the "other": The representation of gender and national identities in Pakistani curriculum texts'. *Compare: A Journal of Comparative and International Education* 38(5): 595–610.

Durrani, N. and Dunne, M. 2010. 'Curriculum and national identity: Exploring the links between religion and nation in Pakistan', *Journal of Curriculum Studies* 42(2): 215–40.

Durrani, N. and Halai, A. 2018. 'Dynamics of gender justice, conflict and social cohesion: Analysing educational reforms in Pakistan', *International Journal of Educational Development* 61: 27–39.

Durrani, N., Kaderi, A. S. and Anand, K. 2020. 'National identity and the history curriculum: Nation making in the shadow of Partition'. In *Handbook of Education Systems in South Asia,* edited by P.M. Sarangpani and R. Pappu, 1–27. Singapore: Springer. Retrieved on 10 April 2020 from https://doi.org/10.1007/978-981-13-3309-5_41-1.

Dyer, C., Choksi, A., Awasty, V., Iyer, U., Moyade, R., Nigam, N. and Sheth, S. 2004. 'Knowledge for teacher development in India: The importance of "local knowledge" for in-service education', *International Journal of Educational Development* 24(1): 39–52.

Eisner, E. 1990. 'Creative curriculum development and practice', *Journal of Curriculum and Supervision* 6(1): 62–73.

Eisner, E.W. 1999. 'The uses and limits of performance assessment', *Phi Delta Kappan* 80(9): 658.

Engineer, A. 2007. *Islam in Contemporary World.* New Delhi: Sterling Publishers Pvt. Ltd.

Erickson, F. and Shultz, J. 1992. 'Students' experience of the curriculum'. In *Handbook of Research on Curriculum,* edited by P.W. Jackson, 465–85. New York: Macmilan.

Evans, P.M. and Mohr, M. 1999. 'Professional development for principals: Seven core beliefs', *Phi Delta Kappan* 80(7): 530.

Farrell, T.S.C. 2016. 'The practice of encouraging TESOL teachers to engage in reflective practice: An appraisal of recent research contributions', *Language Teaching Research* 20: 223–47.

Feldman, J. 2016. *Eliciting pedagogical learning among teachers in a professional learning community.* PhD thesis (Stellenbosch University, Stellenbosch).

Fitzduff, M.E. and Stout, C.E. 2006. *The Psychology of Resolving Global Conflicts: From war to peace. Vol. 2.* Santa Barbara, CA: Praeger Security International.

Foote, L., Smith, J. and Ellis, F. 2004. 'The impact of teachers' beliefs on the literacy experiences of young children: A New Zealand perspective', *Early Years* 24(2): 135–47.

Foucault, M. 1982. 'The subject and power', *Critical Inquiry* 8(4): 777–95.

Foucault, M. 1995. *Discipline and Punish: The birth of the prison.* New York: Vintage Books.

Freire, P. 1970. *Pedagogy of the Oppressed.* London: Bloomsbury.

Freire, P. 1998. 'Cultural action and conscientization', *Harvard Educational Review* 68(4): 499.

Frost, D. 2008. '"Teacher leadership": Values and voice', *School Leadership & Management* 28(4): 337–52.

Ganguly, S. and Bajpai, K. 1994. 'India and the crisis in Kashmir', *Asian Survey* 34(5): 401–16.

Garagozov, R. 2013. 'Implicit measures of attitude change via narrative intervention in the Karabakh conflict', *Dynamics of Asymmetric Conflict* 6(1–3), 98–109.

García, E., Arias, M., Harris Murri, N. and Serna, C. 2010. 'Developing Responsive Teachers: A challenge for a demographic reality', *Journal of Teacher Education* 61(1–2), 132–42.

Gardezi, H. 1970. 'Neo-colonial alliances and the crisis of Pakistan', *Pakistan Forum* 1(2): 3.

Gellner, E. 1983. *Muslim Society* (Vol. 32). Cambridge: Cambridge University Press.

Giesen, B. 2004. 'The trauma of the perpetrators: The holocause as the traumatic reference of German national identity'. In *Cultural Trauma and Collective Identity*, edited by J. Alexander, 112–54. Berkeley, CA: University of California Press.

Giroux, H. A. 1988. *Teachers as Intellectuals: Toward a critical pedagogy of learning*. Granby, MA: Bergin and Garvey.

Gottlob, M. 2007. 'India's unity in diversity as a question of historical perspective', *Economic and Political Weekly* XLII(9): 779–89.

Government of India. 2010. *Government of India*, 35–7. Sarva Shiksha Abhiyan: Framework for implementation. D.o.S.E. a. Literacy, India: Controller of publications.

Government of Pakistan. 1998. *Percentage Population by Religion, Mother Tongue and Disability*. Islamabad: Ministry of Pakistan.

Government of Pakistan. 2006. *National Curriculum Document*. Islamabad: Ministry of Education.

Government of Pakistan. 2009. *National Education Policy*. Islamabad: Ministry of Education.

Greenberg, J. 2005. 'Generations of memory: Remembering Partition in India/Pakistan and Israel/Palestine', *Comparative Studies of South Asia, Africa and the Middle East* 25(1): 89–110.

Griffiths, V. 2000. 'The reflective dimension in teacher education', *International Journal of Educational Research* 33, 539–55.

Grossman, P. and Thompson, C. 2004. 'District policy and beginning teachers: A lens on teacher learning', *Educational Evaluation and Policy Analysis* 26(4): 281–301.

Guerra, P. L. and Wubbena, Z.C. 2017. 'Teacher beliefs and classroom practices', *Issues in Teacher Education* 26(1): 35–51.

Guichard, S. 2010. *The Construction of History and Nationalism in India: Textbooks, controversies and politics*. London: Routledge.

Guichard, S. 2013. 'The Indian nation and selective amnesia: Representing conflicts and violence in Indian history textbooks', *Nations and Nationalism* 19(1): 68–86.

Gulzar, H., Bari, F. and Ejaz, N. 2005. *The role of NGO in basic education in Pakistan*. Lahore: LUMS-McGill Social Enterprise Development Programme.

Gupta, A. 2015. 'Pedagogy of third space: A multidimensional early childhood curriculum', *Policy Futures in Education* 13(2): 260–72.

Gyurko, J. 2012. 'Teacher voice'. PhD thesis, Columbia University, New York.

Habib, I. 2005. 'How to evade real issues and make room for obscurantism', *Social Scientist* 33(388–9): 3–12.

Habibis, D. and Walter, M. 2009. *Social Inequality: Discourses, realities and futures*. South Melbourne: Oxford University Press, South Melbourne.

Halai, A. and Durrani, N. 2018. 'Teachers as agents of peace? Exploring teacher agency in social cohesion in Pakistan', *Compare: A Journal of Comparative and International Education* 48(4): 535–52.

Halabi, R., Sonnenschein, N. and Friedman, A. 2004. *Liberate the oppressed and their oppressors: Encounters between university students*. New Brunswick, N.J.: Rutgers University Press, 59–78.

Halpern, J. and Weinstein, H. 2004. 'Rehumanizing the Other: Empathy and reconciliation', *Human Rights Quarterly* 26(3): 561–83.

Hameed, S. 2017. 'Two sisters – Lahore and Delhi'. Accessed 2 January 2019. Retrieved: at: http://tns.thenews.com.pk/two-sisters-lahore-delhi/#.XFbu5y2cY_M.

Hamidi, S. 2019. 'Don't overlook the root cause of the latest India–Pakistan flare-up', *The Diplomat*. Accessed 12 January 2021. Retrieved: https://thediplomat.com/2019/03/dont-overlook-the-root-cause-of-the-latest-india-pakistan-flare-up/.

Hansen, J. 2012. 'De-nationalize history and what have we done? Ontology, essentialism, and the search for a cosmopolitan alternative'. In *History Education and the Construction of National Identities*, edited by M. Carretero, M. Asensio and M. Rodriguez-Moneo, 17–32. Charlotte, NC: Information Age Publishing.

Hargreaves, A. 1996. 'Revisiting voice', *Educational Researcher* 25(1): 12–19.

Hartnack, C. 2012. 'Roots and routes: The partition of British India in Indian social memories', *Journal of Historical Sociology* 25(2): 244–60.

Hashweh, M. 1987. 'Effects of subject-matter knowledge in the teaching of biology and physics', *Teaching and Teacher Education* 3(2): 109–20.

Haydn, T., Stephen, A., Arthur, J. and Hunt, M. 2014. *Learning to Teach History in the Secondary School: A companion to school experience*. London: Routledge.

Haydock, K. 2015. 'Stated and unstated aims of NCERT social science textbooks', *Economic and Political Weekly* 50(17): 109–19.

Hayes, L. 1987. *The Crises of Education in Pakistan*. Delegate brief. Lahore: Vanguard Books.

Herndl, C. and Licona, A. 2007. 'Shifting agency: Agency, kairos, and the possibility of social action'. In *Communicative Practices in Workplaces and the Professions: Cultural perspectives on the regulation of discourse and organizations*, edited by M. Zachary and C.G. Thralls, 133–54. Amityville, NY: Baywood Publishing Company. Hess, D. 2004. 'Controversies about controversial issues in democratic education', *Political Science and Politics* 37(2): 257–61.

Hitlin, S. and Elder, G. H. 2007. 'Time, self and the curiously abstract concept of agency', *Sociological Theory* 25(2): 170–91.

Hobsbawm, E. 1990. *Nations and Nationalism since 1780: Programme, myth, reality*. Cambridge: Cambridge University Press.

Hogg, M.A. and Van Knippenberg, D. 2003. 'Social identity and leadership processes in groups'. In: *Advances in Experimental Social Psychology* 35, 1–52. San Diego, CA: Academic. Hoodbhoy, P. and Nayyar, A. 1985. 'Rewriting the history of Pakistan'. In *Islam, Politics and the State: The Pakistan experience*, edited by A. Khan, 164–77. London: Zed Books.

Horner, L., Kadiwal, L., Sayed, Y., Barrett, A., Durrani, N. and Novelli, N. 2015. *Literature Review: The role of teachers in peacebuilding, research consortium, education and peacebuilding*. Brighton: Centre for International Education, University of Sussex.

Hughes, T. 1993. *Networks of Power: Electrification in Western society, 1880–1930*. New York: JHU Press.

Hursh, D. and Ross, E. (eds) 2000. *Democratic Social Education: Social studies for social change*. Falmer: New York.

Hussain, A. and Safiq, I. 2016. *Teaching Intolerance in Pakistan: Religious bias in public school textbooks*. Washington, D.C.: United States Commission on International Religious Freedom.

Hussain, F., Sajjad, S., Shafique, K., Majoka, S. and Ahmed, M. 2011. *Social Studies 5*. Lahore: Punjab Textbook Board.

Hussain, N. and Boquérat, G. 2012. 'Enlightened moderation: Anatomy of a failed strategy'. In *Pakistan: From the rhetoric of democracy to the rise of militancy*, edited by Ravi Kalia, 177–93. London: Routledge India.

Indoshi, F., Wagah, M. and Agak, J. 2010. 'Factors that determine students' and teachers' attitudes towards art and design curriculum', *International Journal of Vocational and Technical Education* 2(1), 9–17.

Indurthy, R. 2005. 'The turns and shifts in the US role in the Kashmir conflict since 1947: Today's propitious times for a facilitator to resolve it;, *Asian Affairs*, 16 July 2005, 31–56.

Ingersoll, R.M. 2007. 'Short on power, long on responsibility', *Educational Leadership* 65(1): 20–5.

Ingram, N. 2009. 'Working-class boys, educational success and the misrecognition of working-class culture', *British Journal of Sociology of Education* 30(4): 421–34.

Johnson, T., Thompson, L., Smagorinsky, P. and Fry, P. 2003. 'Learning to Teach the Five-Paragraph Theme', *Research in the Teaching of English* 38(2): 136–76.

Jost, J. 2006. 'The end of the end of ideology', *American Psychologist* 61(7): 651–70.

Juma, S.S. 1987. Social structure, educational disparities and elite schooling in Pakistan. Phd thesis. Edmonton: University of Alberta.

Kahlenberg, R.D. 2004. *All Together Now: Creating middle-class schools through public school choice*. Washington, D.C.: Brookings Institution Press.

Kahlenberg, R. D. and Potter, H. 2015. 'Why teacher voice matters', *American Educator* 38(4): 6–7.

Kaul, S. (ed.) 2001. *The Partitions of Memory: The afterlife of the division of India*. Delhi: Permanent Black. Kayi-Aydar, H. 2015. 'Teacher agency, positioning and English language learners: Voices of pre-service classroom teachers', *Teaching and Teacher Education* 45: 94–103.

Kelly, A.V. 2009. 'The curriculum: Theory and practice.' London: SAGE Publications.

Kelly, P., Gutmann, A. and Thompson, D. 1996. 'Democracy and disagreement: Why moral conflict cannot be avoided in politics, and what should be done about it', *The British Journal of Sociology* 48(3): 529.

Kelchtermans, G. 2009. 'Who I am in how I teach is the message: Self-understanding, vulnerability and reflection', *Teachers and Teaching* 15(2): 257–72.

Kelman, H.C. 1999. 'The interdependence of Israeli and Palestinian national identities: The role of the other in existential conflict'. *Journal of Social Issues* 55(3): 581–600.

Kennedy, A. and McKay, J. 2011. 'Beyond induction: The continuing professional development needs of early-career teachers in Scotland', *Professional Development in Education* 37(4): 551–69.

Ketelaar, E., Beijaard, D., Boshuizen, H.P. and Den Brok, P.J. 2012. 'Teachers' positioning towards an educational innovation in the light of ownership, sense-making and agency', *Teaching and Teacher Education* 28(2): 273–82.

Khan, A.N. 2020. 'Amid the hideous pandemic, praying wise souls will avoid "another bout of fighting"'. Accessed 11 February 2021. Retrieved: http://citysentinel.com/2020/05/amid-the-hideous-pandemic-praying-wise-souls-will-avoid-another-bout-of-fighting/.

Khan, S., Khan, A. and Khan, I. 2013. *Cricket Cauldron: The turbulent politics of sport in Pakistan.* London: I.B. Tauris.

Khattak, S. 2014. 'A comparative analysis of the elite-English-medium Schools, state Urdu-medium schools and dini-madaris in Pakistan', *International Journal of Multidisciplinary Comparative Studies* 1(1): 92–107.

King, M. 2002. 'Professional development to promote schoolwide inquiry', *Teaching and Teacher Education* 18(3): 243–57.

Klerides, L. 2008. 'The discursive (re) construction of national identity in Cyprus and England with special reference to history textbooks: A comparative study'. PhD thesis, Institute of Education, University of London.

Korostelina, K. 2011. 'Shaping unpredictable past: National identity and history education in Ukraine', *National Identities* 13(1): 1–16.

Kronstadt, K. 2004. *Education Reform in Pakistan.* Washington, D.C.: Library of Congress Washington DC Congressional Research Service.

Krueger, A. B. and Malečková, J. 2003. 'Education, poverty and terrorism: Is there a causal connection?', *Journal of Economic Perspectives* 17(4): 119–44.

Kumar, A. 2018. *Curriculum in International Contexts: Understanding colonial, ideological, and neoliberal influences.* Canada: Palgrave Macmillan.

Kumar, K. 2001. *Prejudice and Pride: School histories of the freedom struggle in India and Pakistan.* New Delhi: Penguin.

Kumar, K. 2005. *Political Agenda of Education: A study of colonialist and nationalist ideas.* New Delhi: SAGE Publications India.

Kutty, B.M. 2004. 'Pakistan–India relations: Non-governmental initiatives for peace', *Pakistan Horizon* 57(3): 41–53.

Ladson-Billings, G. 1995. 'Toward a theory of culturally relevant pedagogy', *American Educational Research Journal* 32(3): 465.

Lall, M. 2008. 'Educate to hate: The use of education in the creation of antagonistic national identities in India and Pakistan', *Compare: A Journal of Comparative and International Education* 38(1): 103–19.

Lall, M. and Vickers, E. (eds). 2009. *Education as a Political Tool in Asia.* London; New York: Routledge.

Lall, M. and Saeed, T. 2019. *Youth and the National Narrative: Education, terrorism and the security state in Pakistan.* London: Bloomsbury.

Lall, M. and Anand, K. 2020. 'How the Covid 19 crisis is exacerbating and embedding communal inequalities in India and Pakistan'. UCL blogs. Accessed 22 June 2012. Retrieved: https://blogs.ucl.ac.uk/ceid/2020/04/27/lall-anand/.

Lambert, A., Scherer, L., Schott, J., Olson, K., Andrews, R., O'Brien, T. and Zisser, A. 2010. 'Rally effects, threat and attitude change: An integrative approach to understanding the role of emotion', *Journal of Personality and Social Psychology* 98(6): 886–903.

Lasky, S. 2005. 'A sociocultural approach to understanding teacher identity, agency and professional vulnerability in a context of secondary school reform', *Teaching and Teacher Education* 21(8): 899–916.

Laurence, P. 1983. *The Reading of Silence*. Stanford, CA: Stanford University Press.

Leming, J.S. 1994. 'Past as prologue: A defence of traditional patterns of social studies instruction'. In *The Future of Social Studies*, edited by M. Nelson, 17–23. Boulder, CO: Social Science Education Consortium.

Lerch, J., 2016. 'Embracing diversity? Textbook narratives in countries with a legacy of internal armed conflict, 1950 to 2011'. In *History can Bite: History education in divided and postwar societies*, edited by D. Begtrovato, K.V. Korostelina and M. Schulze, 31–43.

Lewin, K.M. and Stuart, J.S. 2003. *Researching Teacher Education: New perspectives on practice, performance and policy*. MUSTER Synthesis Report (no. 666-2016-45491). London: DFID.

Lipsky, M. 1980. *Street Level Bureaucrats*. New York: Russell Sage Foundation.

Liu, J. and Hilton, D. 2005. 'How the past weighs on the present: Social representations of history and their role in identity politics', *British Journal of Social Psychology* 44(4): 537–56.

Llewellyn, K. and Ng-A-Fook, N., eds. 2017. *Oral History and Education: Theories, dilemmas, and practices*. New York: Palgrave Macmillan. Lortie, D. 1975. *Schoolteacher: A sociological analysis*. Chicago: University of Chicago Press.

Magnuson, K A. and Duncan, G. J. 2006. 'The role of family socioeconomic resources in the black–white test score gap among young children', *Developmental Review* 26(4): 365–99.

Malik, A. 2011. *Policy Analysis of Education in Punjab Province*. Islamabad: UNESCO.

Malik, A. 2012. 'A comparative study of elite-English-medium schools, public schools and Islamic madaris in contemporary Pakistan: The use of Pierre Bourdieu's theory to understand inequalities in educational and occupational opportunities', unpublished PhD thesis. University of Toronto, Department of Sociology and Equity Studies in Education. .

Maoz, I. 2000. 'Power relations in intergroup encounters: A case study of Jewish–Arab encounters in Israel', *International Journal of Intercultural Relations* 24(2): 259–77.

Marlow-Ferguson, R. 2002. *World Education Encyclopaedia*. Detroit, MI: Gale Group.

Matsunaga, T. 2010. 'The role of English media in modern Japan: Through the history of English-language newspapers issued by Zumoto Motosada', *Lifelong Education and Libraries* 10: 71–7.

McCutcheon, R.T. 1997. *Manufacturing Religion: The discourse on sui generis religion and the politics of nostalgia*. Oxford: Oxford University Press.

McLachlan, C., Carvalho, L., de Lautour, N. and Kumar, K. 2006. 'Literacy in early childhood settings in New Zealand: An examination of teachers' beliefs and practices', *Australasian Journal of Early Childhood* 31(2): 31–41.

McMahon, B.J. and Portelli, J.P., eds. 2012. *Student Engagement in Urban Schools: Beyond neoliberal discourses*. Charlotte, NC: Information Age Publishers (IAP).

Meier, D. 2002. *The Power of their Ideas: Lessons for America from a small school in Harlem*. Boston, MA: Beacon Press.

Merriam, S.B. 1998. *Qualitative Research and Case Study Applications in Education*. San Francisco, CA: Jossey-Bass Publishers.

Miller, D. 1988. 'The ethical significance of nationality', *Ethics* 98(4): 647–62.

Mills, C. 2008. 'Reproduction and transformation of inequalities in schooling: The transformative potential of the theoretical constructs of Bourdieu', *British Journal of Sociology of Education* 29(1): 79–89.

Mishra, I. 2019. 'Won't take Jammu and Kashmir students: Private college', *The Times of India*, 19 February 2019. Accessed on 21 February 2019. Retrieved from: https://timesofindia .indiatimes.com/city/dehradun/wont-take-jk-students-pvt-college-forced-to-give-in -writing/articleshow/68054506.cms.

Molla, T. and Nolan, A. 2020. 'Teacher agency and professional practice', *Teachers and Teaching* 26(1): 67–87.

Moloi, F., Morobe, N. and Urwick, J. 2008. 'Free but inaccessible primary education: A critique of the pedagogy of English and Mathematics in Lesotho', *International Journal of Educational Development* 28(5): 612–21.

Monzó, L.D. and Rueda, R. 2003. 'Shaping education through diverse funds of knowledge: A look at one Latina paraeducator's lived experiences, beliefs and teaching practice', *Anthropology and Education Quarterly* 34(1): 72–95.

Muhammad, M. 2002. *Decentralization of education system in Sind: A critical review*. Islamabad: Ministry of Education.

Mumtaz, C. and Bluth, U. 2020. *India–Pakistan Strategic Relations*. ibidem-Verlag, Jessica Haunschild und Christian Schon. BoD–Books on Demand.

Murali, K. 2004. 'Lahore is Delhi, Karachi is Mumbai', *Hindustan Times*, 11 March 2004. Accessed 20 November 2017. Available at: https://www.hindustantimes.com/india/lahore-is-delhi-karachi-is-mumbai/story-Lpn28XPjWUBlttapRzaoLL.html.

Nash, S. 2005. 'Learning objects, learning object repositories and learning theory: Preliminary best practices for online courses', *Interdisciplinary Journal of e-Skills and Lifelong Learning* 1: 217–28.

National Council of Educational Research and Training. 2005. *National Curriculum Framework*. New Delhi: NCERT.

National Council of Educational Research and Training. 2000. National Curriculum Framework. New Delhi: NCERT. Accessed 21 November 2021. http://www.ncert.nic.in/html/framework2000.htm.

Naveed, A., Sakata, N., Kefallinou, A., Young, S. and Anand, K. 2017. 'Understanding, embracing and reflecting upon the messiness of doctoral fieldwork', *Compare: A Journal of Comparative and International Education* 47(5): 773–92.

Nayyar, A.H. and Salim, A. 2003. *The Subtle Subversion: A report on curricula and textbooks in Pakistan*. Islamabad: Sustainable Development Policy Institute.

Nayyar, A.H. and Salim, A. 2005. *The Subtle Subversion: The state of curricula and textbooks in Pakistan-Urdu, English, social studies and civics*. Current Issues in Comparative Education series. Islamabad: Sustainable Development Policy Institute.

Novelli, M. and Sayed, Y. 2016. 'Teachers as agents of sustainable peace, social cohesion and development: theory, practice and evidence', *Education as Change* 20(3): 15–37.

Oliver, C. and Kettley, N. 2010. 'Gatekeepers or facilitators: The influence of teacher habitus on students' applications to elite universities', *British Journal of Sociology of Education* 31(6): 737–53.

Opfer, V. and Pedder, D. 2011. ,Conceptualizing teacher professional learning', *Review of Educational Research* 81(3): 376–407.

Osler, A. and Starkey, H. 2005. *Changing Citizenship: Democracy and inclusion in education*. New York: Open University Press.

Papadakis, Y. 2008. *History education in divided Cyprus: A comparison of Greek Cypriot and Turkish Cypriot school books on the history of Cyprus*. PRIO report, February 2008. Oslo: International Peace Research Institute.

Paris, C. and Lung, P. 2008. 'Agency and child-centred practices in novice teachers: Autonomy, efficacy, intentionality, and reflectivity', *Journal of Early Childhood Teacher Education* 29(3): 253–68.

Parise, L.M. and Spillane, J.P. 2010. 'Teacher learning and instructional change: How formal and on-the-job learning opportunities predict change in elementary school teachers' practice', *The Elementary School Journal* 110(3): 323–46.

Parker, S. 1997. *Reflective Teaching in the Postmodern World: A manifesto for education in postmodernity*. Buckingham, UK: Open University Press. Persell, C. 1981. 'Genetic and cultural deficit theories: Two sides of the same racist coin', *Journal of Black Studies* 12(1): 19–37.

Pierce, F. and Larson, W. 1993. 'Developing criteria to evaluate sustainable land management'. In *Proceedings of the Eighth International Soil Management Workshop: Utilization of soil survey information for sustainable land use*, edited by J.M. Kimble, 7–14.

Pinar, W.F. 1993. 'Notes on understanding curriculum as racial text'. In *Race, Identity and Representation in Education*. New York: Routledge.

Pollard, A.J. and Triggs, P.A. 1997. *Reflective Teaching in Secondary Education*. London: Cassell.

Popson, N. 2001. 'The Ukrainian history textbook: Introducing children to the "Ukrainian nation"', *Nationalities Papers* 29(2): 325–50.

Powell. C. 1996. 'Consolidating – and defending – democracy.' In *Juan Carlos of Spain*, edited by C. Powell. 157–80. London: Palgrave Macmillan.

Powell, R., Cantrell, S.C. and Correll, P. 2017. 'Power and agency in a high poverty elementary school: How teachers experienced a scripted reading programme', *Journal of Language and Literacy Education* 13(1): 32.

Priestley, M., Biesta, G. and Robinson, S. 2013. 'Teachers as agents of change: Teacher agency and emerging models of curriculum'. In *Reinventing the Curriculum: New trends in curriculum policy and practice*, edited by M. Priestley, G.J.J. Biesta and S. Robinson, 187–206. Retrieved from http://books.google.nl/.

Pritchett, L. and Beatty, A. 2012. *The Negative Consequences of Overambitious Curricula in Developing Countries*. Cambridge, MA: Harvard Kennedy School.

Purewal, N. 2003. 'The Indo-Pak border: Displacements, aggressions and transgressions', *Contemporary South Asia* 12(4): 539–56.

Qadeer, M. 2006. *Pakistan: Social and cultural transformation in a Muslim nation*. New York: Routledge.

Rahman, T. 2004. *Denizens of Alien Worlds: A study of education, inequality and polarization in Pakistan*. Oxford: Oxford University Press.

Rahman, T. 2006. '"One step forward, two back"', *Dawn*. Accessed 10 November 2017. Retrieved: http://www. dawn.com.

Ramachandran, R., Vasavi, A.R., Sinha, A. and Narasimha, R. 2000. 'Science in Society: A new social contract', *Science, Technology and Society* 5(1); 93–116. Report on the Bangalore Symposium.

Rasul, A. 2002. 'Media and foreign policy: A critical analysis of the coverage of Kashmir issue in elite English-language newspapers of Pakistan'. Unpublished MPhil thesis. University of the Punjab, Lahore.

Ray, L. 2018. *Violence and Society*. London: SAGE Publications.

Reardon, B.A. and Cabezudo, A. 2002. *Rationale for and Approaches to Peace Education*. New York: The Hague Appeal for Peace.

Reay, D. 2004. '"It's all becoming a habitus": Beyond the habitual use of habitus in educational research', *British Journal of Sociology of Education* 25(4): 431–44.

Reay, D. 1998. 'Setting the agenda: The growing impact of market forces on pupil grouping in British secondary schooling', *Journal of Curriculum Studies* 30(5): 545–58.

Reay, D., Davies, J., David, M. and Ball, S. 2001. 'Choices of Degree or Degrees of Choice? Class, "Race" and the Higher Education Choice Process', *Sociology* 35(04): 855–74.

Rehman, S. and Zia, A. 2010. *The Impact of Educational Policies on the Religious Minorities of Pakistan 1947–2010*. Karachi: South Asia Forum for Human Rights.

Reitlinger, G. 1953. *The Final Solution: The attempt to exterminate the Jews of Europe 1939–1945*. Cranbury, NJ: Thomas Yoseloff.

Resh, N. and Benavot, A. 2009. 'Educational governance, school autonomy and curriculum implementation: Diversity and uniformity in knowledge offerings to Israeli pupils', *Journal of Curriculum Studies* 41(1): 67–92.

Richardson, V. 1996. 'The role of attitudes and beliefs in learning to teach'. In *Handbook of Research on Teacher Education*, edited by J. Sikula, 102–19. nd ed. New York: Simon and Schuster/ Macmillan.

Rivalland, C. 2007. 'When are beliefs just "the tip of the iceberg"? Exploring early childhood professionals' beliefs and practices about teaching and learning', *Australian Journal of Early Childhood* 32(1): 30–7.

Rosenholtz, S. 1987. 'Education reform strategies: Will they increase teacher commitment?', *American Journal of Education* 95(4): 534–62.

Rosser, Y.C. 2003. *Curriculum as destiny: Forging national identity in India, Pakistan and Bangladesh*. Austin, TX: University of Texas Press.

Rotberg, R. 2006. *Israeli and Palestinian Narratives of Conflict*. Bloomington, IND: Indiana University Press.

Rumberger, R. and Palardy, G. 2005. 'Does segregation still matter? The impact of student composition on academic achievement in high school', *Teachers College Record* 107: 1999–2045. Retrieved from htpp://www.tcrecord.org/content.asp?contentid-12152.

Sadgopal, A. 2005. 'On the pedagogy of writing a National Curriculum Framework: Reflections from an insider', *Social Scientist* 33(9/10): 23–36.

Saigol, R. 1993. *Education, Critical Perspectives*. Lahore: Progressive Publishers.

Saigol, R. 2000. *Symbolic Violence*. Lahore: Society for the Advancement of Education.

Saigol, R. 2005. 'Enemies within and enemies without: The besieged self in Pakistani textbooks', *Futures* 37(9): 1005–35.

Saleem, M. 2009. *The Development and State of the Art of Adult Learning. National Report of Pakistan*. Islamabad: Project Wing Ministry of Education.

Salomon, G. 2004. 'Comment: What is peace education?', *Journal of Peace Education* 1(1): 123–7.

Sandhu, A. 2009. 'Reality of "Divide and Rule" in British India', *Pakistan Journal of History & Culture* 30(1).

Sarangapani, P.M. 2003. 'Childhood and schooling in an Indian village', *Childhood* 10(4): 403–18.

Savenije, G.M. and Goldberg, T. 2019. 'Silences in a climate of voicing: teachers' perceptions of societal and self-silencing regarding sensitive historical issues', *Pedagogy, Culture & Society* 27(1): 39–64.

Schwartz, N. and Clore, G. 2018. 'Feelings and phenomenal experiences'. In *Social Psychology: Handbook of basic principles*, edited by A. Kruglanski and E.T. Higgins, 385–407. 2nd edition. New York: Guilford.

Schwartz, S.H. 1997. 'Values and culture'. In *Motivation and Culture*, edited by D. Munro, S. Carr and J. Schumaker, 69–84. New York: Routledge.

Sebastian, J., Huang, H. and Allensworth, E. 2017. 'Examining integrated leadership systems in high schools: Connecting principal and teacher leadership to organizational processes and student outcomes', *School Effectiveness and School Improvement* 28(3): 463–88.

Sen, A. 1985. 'Well-being, agency and freedom: The Dewey lectures 1984', *The Journal of Philosophy* 82(4): 169–221.

Setalvad, T. 2005. 'Comments on National Curriculum Framework 2005', *The South Asian*. Available online at: http://www.thesouthasian.org/archives/2005/comments_on_national _curriculu.html.

Shakil, A. and Akhtar, S. 2012. 'Consideration of Islamic values in the educational policies of Pakistan', *Journal of Educational and Social Research* 2(1): 297–308.

Shawer, S.F. 2010. 'Classroom-level curriculum development: EFL teachers as curriculum-developers, curriculum-makers and curriculum-transmitters', *Teaching and Teacher Education* 26(2): 173–84.

Sherman, B. and Teemant, A. 2021. Agency, identity, power: An agentive triad model for teacher action', *Educational Philosophy and Theory* 1–25.

Shkedi, A. 1998. 'Can the Curriculum Guide both emancipate and educate teachers?', *Curriculum Inquiry* 28(2): 209–29.

Shkedi, A. 2009. 'From curriculum guide to classroom practice: Teachers' narratives of curriculum application', *Journal of Curriculum Studies* 41(6): 833–54.

Shnabel, N. and Nadler, A. 2008. 'A needs-based model of reconciliation: Satisfying the differential emotional needs of victim and perpetrator as a key to promoting reconcilation', *Journal of Personality and Social Psychology* 94(1): 116.

Skocpol, T. and Somers, M. 1980. 'The uses of comparative history in macrosocial inquiry', *Comparative Studies in Society and History* 22(2): 174.

Sleeter, C. 2011. 'The academic and social value of ethnic studies: A research review', *National Education Association Research Department*.

Sloan, K. 2006. 'Teacher identity and agency in school worlds: Beyond the all-good/all-bad discourse on accountability-explicit curriculum policies', *Curriculum Inquiry* 36(2): 119–52.

Smail, A. 2014. 'Rediscovering the teacher within Indian child-centred pedagogy: Implications for the global child-centred approach', *Compare: A Journal of Comparative and International Education* 44(4): 613–33.

Smith, A.D. 2002. 'When is a nation?' *Geopolitics* 7(2): 5–32.

Snyder, L.L. 1990. *Encyclopedia of Nationalism*. New York: Saint James Press.

Snyder, J., Bolin, F. and Zumwalt, K. 1992. *Curriculum Implementation, Handbook of research on curriculum*, 402–35. 4th ed. New York: Simon and Schuster/Macmillan.

Solomon, D., Battistich, V. and Hom, A. 1996. 'Teacher beliefs and practices in schools serving communities that differ in socioeconomic level', *The Journal of Experimental Education* 64(4): 327–47.

Soreide, G.E. 2006. 'Narrative construction of teacher identity: Positioning and negotiation', *Teachers and Teaching* 12(5), 527–47.

Southgate, B. 2005. *What Is History For?* New York: Routledge. Ltd.

Southgate, B. 2007. 'Memories into something new: Histories for the future', *Rethinking History* 11(2): 187–99.

Spillane, J. and Thompson, C. 1997. 'Reconstructing conceptions of local capacity: The Local Education Agency's capacity for ambitious instructional reform', *Educational Evaluation and Policy Analysis* 19(2): 185.

Spring, J. 2011. *The Politics of American Education*. New York: Routledge.

Sriprakash, A. 2012. *Pedagogies for Development: The politics and practice of child-centred education in India*. London: Springer.

Stake, R. 1995. *The Art of Case Study Research*. Thousand Oaks, CA: SAGE Publications.

Staub, E. 2005. 'The origins and evolution of hate, with notes on prevention'. In *The Psychology of Hate*, edited by R.J. Sternberg, 51–66. Washington, D.C.: American Psychological Association.

Steinberg, S. and Bar-On, D. 2002. 'An analysis of the group process in encounters between Jews and Palestinians using a typology for discourse classification', *International Journal of Intercultural Relations* 26(2): 199–214.

Storey, J. 2006. *Cultural Theory and Popular Culture: A reader*. Athens, GA: University of Georgia Press.

Talbot, C. 1995. 'Inscribing the other, inscribing the self: Hindu-Muslim identities in pre-colonial India', *Comparative Studies in Society and History* 37(4): 692.

Talbot, P. 1998. *Pakistan: A modern history*. London: Hurt and Company.

Taneja, N. 2003. 'BJP's assault on education and educational institutions'. *CPIML*. Accessed 10 January 2019. Retrieved:: www.cpiml.org/liberation/year_2001/september/saffronimp .htm.

Tao, J. and Gao, X. 2017. 'Teacher agency and identity commitment in curricular reform', *Teaching and Teacher Education* 63: 346–55.

Tate, W. 1997. 'Race-ethnicity, SES, gender and language proficiency trends in Mathematics achievement: An update', *Journal for Research in Mathematics Education* 28(6): 652.

Taylor, M. 2013. 'Replacing the "teacher-proof" curriculum with the "curriculum-proof" teacher: Toward more effective interactions with mathematics textbooks', *Journal of Curriculum Studies* 45(3): 295–321.

Thapar, R. 1993. 'Durkheim and Weber on theories of societies and race relating to pre-colonial India'. In *Interpreting Early India*, edited by Romila Thapar, 25–39. New Delhi: Oxford University Press.

Thapar, R. 2005. 'Syndicated Hinduism', *Hinduism Reconsidered* 4: 54–81.

Thompson, P. and Bornat, J. 2017. *The Voice of the Past*. New York; Oxford: Oxford University Press.

Thrupp, M. 1995. 'The school mix effect: The history of an enduring problem in educational research, policy and practice', *British Journal of Sociology of Education* 16(2): 183–203.

The Times of India. 2019. 'Days after Doon college suspends Kashmiri dean, it says took action under pressure of mob, dean can come back', *The Times of India*, 19 February 2019. Accessed 20 February 2019. Retrieved from: http://timesofindia.indiatimes.com/articleshow /68070200.cms?utm_source=contentofinterest&utm_medium=text&utm_campaign= cppst.

Tripathi, D. 2016. 'Sustainable peace between India and Pakistan: A case for restructuring the school education system'. In *History Can Bite*, edited by B. Denise, M.S. Karina and V. Korostelina, 125–38. Gottingen: V & R Unipress.

Tripathi, D. and Raghuvanshi, V. 2020. 'Portraying the "other" in textbooks and movies: The mental borders and their implications for India–Pakistan Relations', *Journal of Borderlands Studies* 35(2): 195–210.

Turnbull, M. 2006. 'Student teacher professional agency in the practicum', *Asia-Pacific Journal of Teacher Education* 33(2): 195–208. Accessed 18 November 2021. https://doi.org/10.1080 /13598660500122116.

Tyler, R. 1949. *Basic Principles of Curriculum and Instruction*. Chicago: University of Chicago Press.

UNESCO. 2006. *Education for All: Literacy for fife, Paris*. EFA Global Monitoring Report 2006 [online]. USAID. Accessed 23 June 2018. Available at: http://www.usaid.gov/pk/sectors /education/.

United States Commission on International Religious Freedom. 2016. *Teaching Intolerance in Pakistan: Religious Bias in Public School Textbooks*. [online]. Islamabad: Peace and Education Foundation. Accessed 9 June 2018. Available at: https://hsdl.org/?view&did=794028.

Valencia, R.R. 2010. *Dismantling Contemporary Deficit Thinking: Educational thought and practice*. New York: Routledge.

van Dijk, T. 1995. 'Power and the news media', *Political Communication and Action*, 6(1): 9–36.

van Dijk, T., Ting-Toomey, S., Smitherman, G. and Troutman, D. 1997. 'Discourse, ethnicity, culture and racism'. In: *Discourse as Social Interaction*, edited by T.A. van Dijk, 144–80. London: SAGE Publications.

van Lier, L. 2010. 'Forward: Agency, self and identity in language learning'. In *Language Learner Autonomy: Policy, curriculum, classroom*, edited by B. O'Rourke and L. Carson, ix–xviii. Oxford: Peter Lang.

Vogt, W. 1997. *Tolerance and Education: Learning to live with diversity and difference*. Sage Publications, Thousand Oaks, CA: SAGE Publications.

Vollhardt, J. 2009. 'The role of victim beliefs in the Israeli-Palestinian conflict: Risk or potential for peace?', *Peace and Conflict: Journal of peace psychology* 15(2): 135–59.

Vygotsky, L. 1980. *Mind in Society: The development of higher psychological processes*. Cambridge, MA: Harvard University Press.

Watkins, K. 2013. *Education without Borders: A summary: Report from Lebanon on Syria's out of school children*. London: A World At School.

Webb, J., Schirato, T. and Danaher, G. 2002. *Understanding Bourdieu*. Crows Nest, Australia: Allen & Unwin.

Wells, C.G. 1999. *Dialogic Inquiry*, 137–41. Cambridge: Cambridge University Press.

Wilcox-Herzog, A. 2002. 'Is there a link between teachers' beliefs and behaviors?', *Early Education & Development* 13(1): 81–106.

Willis, G. and Turner, E. 2007. 'Primary and secondary features of Parkinson's Disease improve with strategic exposure to bright light: A case series study', *Chronobiology International* 24(3): 521–37.

Wilms, J.D. 'School composition and contextual effects on student outcomes', *Teachers College Record* 112(4): 1008–37.

Winter, J. 2010. 'Thinking about Silence'. In *Shadows of War: A social history of silence in the twentieth century*, edited by E. Ben-Ze'ev, R. Ginio and J. Winter, 3–31. Cambridge: Cambridge University Press.

Wirth, K. and Perkins, D. 2013. *Learning to Learn*. [online] Accessed 28 June 2018. Available at: http://www.macalester.edu/academics/geology/wirth/learning.doc.

Wohl, M. and Branscombe, N. 2008. 'Remembering historical victimization: Collective guilt for current ingroup transgressions', *Journal of Personality and Social Psychology* 94(6): 988–1006.

Yilar, M.B. and Çam, İ.D. 2021. 'Who are we? and Who are they? The construction of Turkish national identity in textbooks within the context of the Turkish War of Independence', *Middle Eastern Studies* 57(6): 880–903.

Yin, R. 2004. *The Case Study Anthology*. Thousand Oaks, CA: Sage Publications.

Yoo, J. and Carter, D. 2017. 'Teacher emotion and learning as praxis: Professional development that matters', *Australian Journal of Teacher Education* 42(3): 38–52.

Zafran, A. 2002. 'Measuring the ethos of the Jewish-Arab conflict: Antecedents and outcomes'. Unpublished master's thesis. Tel Aviv University, Tel Aviv. In Hebrew.

Zia, R. 2006. 'Islamic education: From ancient to modern times'. In: *Globalization, Modernization and Education in Muslim Countries*, edited by R. Zia, 31–46. New York: Nova Science Publishers.

Ziring, L. 2005. *Pakistan at the Crosscurrent of History*. New Delhi: Manas Publications.

Zohar, A. 2009. *Report on Education for Thinking (Pedagogical Horizon) 2006–2009: Out-line insights and recommendations*. Jerusalem: Publications Department, Israeli Ministry of Education.

Index

Abou Hamdan, Mazen 146, 158–60
abuse, forms of 145
activism 1–3, 71–6, 134, 136, 291
Adam 208–12
advocacy 5
aesthetics 20–4, 80–6, 127–8, 131–2, 135, 137–8
as a dimension of religion 129
of persuasion 136–8
of religion 129–31, 139
of science and politics 129–31
of the secular 131–4, 139
of speech
Abou Hamdan, Mazen 146, 158–60
abuse, forms of 145
activism 1–3, 71–6, 134, 136, 291
Adam 208–12
advocacy 5
aesthetics 20–4, 80–6, 127–8, 131–2, 135, 137–8
as a dimension of religion 129
of persuasion 136–8
of religion 129–31, 139
of science and politics 129–31
of the secular 131–4, 139
of speech 135
affect 20, 149–58, 164, 167, 246, 254, 310
affordances 40,
Afghan, 29
Afghanistan, 27 n.2
agency
teachers, 55, 56, 57, 58, 59, 62-4, 70, 71, 81, 90, 136-8
Aman Ki Asha, 93
America, 81
Annual Status of Education Report (ASER), 14
Apple, 19-22, 55, 58, 60
Ayesha Jalal, 107

Bangalore, 95
Bangladesh, 49, 97, 104
Balochistan, 45
Bengal, 32
Bengali, 104
    Muslims, 104 n.4
    nationalism, 104 n.4

Bharatiya Janata Party (BJP), 4, 6-7, 23-5, 28, 31, 68-9
Bourdieu, 9, 16-7, 21, 55, 60, 90-1, 138, 140, 145, 149, 153-4
British, 3-4, 30-2, 42-4, 46-7, 49, 79, 82, 85, 142-3

capital, 10 n.3, 12, 16, 144, 153
    physical, 13
    human, 13
    social, 21
    cultural, 149, 153
case study methodology, 4, 10
caste, 11, 27, 31 n.4, 42, 65
chalk and talk, 110, 152
child labour, 65
child-centred pedagogy, 71
Childhood education, 40
Christians, 74
citizenship, 37, 39, 90
classroom management, 147
classrooms, 69-72, 92, 100, 109, 111, 112, 115, 128-131, 134-5, 137, 139, 143, 145-9, 151-4
    climate, 151
    discourse, 128
    experience, 126
    interaction, 68
    observation, 142
    pedagogy, 153
    practices, 143, 145, 150-2, 154
    responses, 143
    settings, 150
    space, 147
    teaching, 132,
cohesion, 25, 40-1, 66
    social, 2, 25, 51, 60, 136
conflict, 3-6, 8, 21, 24, 34-6, 48-53, 56-7, 60, 71-2, 77-9, 82-3, 86, 90, 93, 96, 105, 110, 113, 116, 119, 128, 135-6, 141-2, 145-6, 148, 150, 160
Congress, 24, 25, 26, 31, 35, 36, 42, 69
Constitution of India, 23
constructivism, 27, 62
contrast of contexts, 9, 11
conspiracy theories, 81, 99
Covid-19 pandemic, 5

174   TEACHING INDIA–PAKISTAN RELATIONS

Cricket, 87, 106, 115-6, 126-7
critical thinking, 2, 15, 24, 26, 69, 105, 110, 111, 118, 132-4, 137, 139, 146-7, 151-3
culture, 36, 40, 46, 50, 64, 66, 73-5, 79, 84, 97, 103, 112, 139, 140 n.1, 143, 145, 148, 149, 151, 155
curricula, 1-2, 19, 37-8, 41, 55, 57, 59-62, 102, 121, 132, 143
curriculum, 1, 5-6, 8-9, 12, 19-24, 26, 28, 37, 40-1, 50, 53, 58, 61, 64, 66, 67, 69-71, 92, 100-103, 107, 129-30, 152
   adaptation, 61
   development, 59, 62
   enactment, 61-2
   fidelity, 59
   hidden, 46, 113, 139, 148
   implementation, 127
   innovation, 64
   planning, 36
   transmission, 59

data processing, 9, 15-6
Dalits, 25
decentralisation, 41
deficit discourses, 151 n.8
Delhi, 14, 29, 33, 51, 73-95, 97-99, 102-33, 137-42, 144-50, 153-5
diversity, 27, 34, 38-9, 44, 73-5, 80, 108
divide and rule policy, 30, 79

Earth, 43, 108
Education, v, 1-3, 5-10, 13, 16-23, 25-7, 34, 37-8, 40-1, 55, 57, 59, 60, 64, 67-70, 82, 92, 104, 122, 128-9, 135, 137-8, 149, 153
   development, 39
   systems, 11, 21, 23, 37, 40, 59, 64-5, 69, 117
Educational
   discourse, 11,139
   goals, 22
   inequality, 16
   landscape, 26
   philosophy, 38
   policies, 19-21, 23, 37, 43, 153
   practice, 138, 154
   projects, 92, 142
   research, 19, 55
   reforms, 38, 71
   spaces, 62, 109
   theory, 54
English language, 10 n.3
English-medium schools, 15, 23 n.9, 36, 46, 52
examinations, 40, 67-8, 111, 117-8, 122, 132, 149-50, 153
exclusion, 41, 46, 141

family, 17-8, 20, 73, 76, 80-1, 85, 88-9, 100-1, 114, 120, 125, 128, 131, 138, 142, 153
Foucault, 55, 57
field, 13, 16, 17, 39, 127, 139, 140, 145, 147, 149, 153

Gandhi, Mahatma, 32-3, 42-3, 83
General Zia-ul-Haq (Zia), 37, 46

gender, 11, 20, 27, 38, 65, 73
government schools, 13-4, 68, 88, 90-1, 117-8, 122, 130, 144, 148-51
Gramsci, 90
Gujarat, 74

Habitus, 16-8, 100, 140, 145, 147
   Institutional, 135-9, 142-9, 151-2, 154-5
   Individual,137-8, 140, 142, 151
headteachers, 123, 137, 152
Hindi, 13-4, 73
Hindus, 2, 3, 9-10, 14-5, 19, 23, 27, 29-33, 35-8, 41-50, 73-75, 77, 79, 81-6, 90, 100, 103-4, 107, 109, 113, 117, 120-1, 123-4, 127-8, 131, 140-44, 146
Hindu Mahasabha, 31, 83, 146
Hindu Nationalist Ideology, 23
Hindutva, 23
History, 22, 34, 129
   education, 22, 34, 129, 135
   textbooks, 6-7, 23-5, 27-8, 51, 103, 111, 142
Holocaust, 29-30, 103, 122
homework, 111, 152

ideology, 6, 13, 23, 37, 38, 80, 86, 113, 143
   Hindu nationalist, 23
   of Pakistan, 38, 45, 86, 123, 133
   Pakistan ideology, 41, 150
Imran Khan, 5
Indonesia, 95
India-Pakistan relations, ix, 1-3, 5, 7-12, 15, 16, 18, 19, 23, 28, 32, 34, 37, 51, 52, 58, 72, 75-78, 82, 84, 86, 88, 89, 91, 98, 99, 100-3, 108, 112, 123, 124-8, 131, 132, 135-41, 143-5, 147-50, 154-5
Indian National Congress (INC), 31 n.6
Islam, 5 n.2, 11, 19, 37-9, 41, 46, 50, 66, 100, 105, 131
Islamabad, 97
Islamic education, 40
Islamic nationalism, 6

Jammu and Kashmir, 3-4, 47 n.24

Kashmir, 3-5, 29, 47, 82-3, 87, 109-10, 114, 119, 121, 143
Khushwant Singh, 107
Khyber Pakhtunkhwa, 45

labelling, 44, 114, 152
Lahore, 46, 51, 73, 75, 78-92, 98-9, 102, 104-7, 109-10, 112-4, 116-8, 120-23, 127-32, 134, 137-41, 143-7, 150-1, 154-6
languages, 10 n.3, 74
Lessons, 43, 67, 105, 116-8, 140, 146
liberation, 55
Lord Mountbatten, 3, 38, 42
Lucknow Pact, 31

mathematics, 68 n.1
marginalisation, 37, 78, 113, 139
media, 9, 34, 64, 73, 75, 77, 78, 81, 85, 87-8, 90, 93, 96-100, 107-110, 113-5, 117, 120, 125, 129, 130, 135, 140, 147, 149

INDEX   **175**

methodological design, 2, 9, 18
middle class, 140
migration, 33, 65, 73, 76, 78, 89, 99, 138, 140, 144
Ministry of Education, 50, 64
minorities, 25
   religious, 5, 25, 40, 46, 49
moral values, 40
Muhammad Ali Jinnah (Jinnah), 30-1, 42, 45, 83
Mumbai, 10 n.3, 95, 96
Muslims, 2-3, 5, 9-10, 14-5, 23, 25, 28-32, 35-8, 41-50, 73-5, 77-87, 93, 100, 103-4, 106-8, 114, 116-7, 121-22, 124-7, 131, 139, 142-44, 146
Muslim League, 3, 30, 31-2, 42, 145
Muslim Ummah, 38-9, 70

Narendra Modi (Modi), 5
National Council of Educational Research and Training (NCERT), 26
National Curriculum Framework (NCF) 2000, 24
National Curriculum Framework (NCF) 2005, 26-7, 34, 36, 65, 69, 112, 147
national identity, 5, 19-22, 30, 37, 41, 51, 53, 65, 71, 96
   construction, 18-20, 23-5
Nation-states, 6
nationalism, 4-7, 10, 19-20, 26, 30, 37, 68, 84, 100-1, 104, 144
nation-building, 5-6, 22, 145
Nepal, 95
New Delhi, 10 n.3,
non-governmental organizations (NGOs), 5, 54
NVivo, 17,

oral history, 33-4, 86, 88, 90, 100, 103, 132, 140
oral narratives, 140

Pakistan High Commission, 33
Pakistan Studies, 91-2, 103, 113, 117, 120-23, 134, 143, 146
Partition, 2-4, 7, 9-10, 15, 29-36, 41-4, 46-7, 49, 51, 74-5, 77, 82, 85, 88-90, 92, 96, 100, 103, 106-12, 116-7, 119-23, 125, 127-8, 130, 133, 140-4, 148, 154
Parsis, 74
patriotism, 15, 126, 144
pedagogy, 24, 27-9, 36, 55, 111, 136, 139, 145, 150, 152-
pedagogical practices, 2, 102, 155
Pervez Musharraf (Musharraf), 38-9
pluralism, 146
positionality, 9, 12, 15
postcolonial societies, 6
poverty, 44
praxis, 139, 153
Pulwama, 4
Punjab, 7, 10 n.3, 29, 32, 45
Punjab Schools Roadmap, 69
Punjabi, 10, 29, 33

quality, 102, 138

qualitative research, 15

Rajasthan, 74
Rashtriya Swayamsevak Sangh (RSS), 4, 31 n.7
reflexivity, 12, 15-6
religions, 24, 45, 74, 75, 79, 94, 140 n.1, 144,
Research and Analysis Wing [RAW], 81
Rote memorisation, 50, 68-9, 122, 133, 150
Rote learning, 69, 152

Saffronisation, 23, 26
Sangh Parivar, 23, 31
schools, 1-2, 5-6, 8, 10-14, 16-7, 19, 21, 27, 34, 38, 53-4, 60, 62, 64, 68-70, 72-3, 88, 90-2, 99-100, 104, 110-11, 117-18, 122, 128, 130, 132-33, 135, 137-9, 141-55
sciences, 38, 69
secularism, 11, 13, 26-7, 36, 74-5
self-efficacy, 65-6
Siachin, 87
Sikhs, 7, 10 n.3, 33,
Sikhism, 165
Sikkim, 89 n.30
Simple Education Foundation, 83
Simplilearn, 155
Sindh, 45
Sir Radcliffe, 47
Socio Economic Status (SES), 12, 17, 73, 102, 110-2, 135-7, 139, 141, 143, 145, 147, 152-5
socialisation, 16, 18, 20, 72, 155
South Asia, 5, 27, 32, 70, 113
sports, 13, 126
Sri Lanka, 95
standardised testing, 57

teachers, ix, 1-2, 8-13, 16, 22, 26-7, 31-2, 34-5, 38-41, 43, 51-67,
   attitudes, 1-2, 15, 18
absenteeism, 69
agency of, 8, 53-4, 56, 59, 62-5, 70- 1, 81, 90, 136-8,151
autonomy of, 59
classroom practices, 8
curricular approaches, 59
confidence, 67, 102, 120, 131
education programmes, 136
efficacy, 65
identity, 54, 56-8
individual habitus, 17
institutional habitus, 17
leadership, 62
of history, 67, 69
pedagogical responses, 10, 12, 22
power, 54
self-efficacy, 65-6
state controls and, 103–5
training of, 64, 68, 70, 81
voices of, 7-9
teaching practice, 67-9, 72, 102-3, 128, 138-9, 142, 169
teacher-centered, 111
technology, 97
terrorism, 81-2, 86-7, 105, 109-10, 114, 124

textbooks, 1-2, 5-8, 14, 19-20, 22-8, 34-8, 41-53, 58, 60, 64, 67-69, 71, 73, 81-3, 88, 90-2, 98, 100, 102-7, 111-3, 116-8, 120-3, 127, 131-3, 134-6, 142-60
  culture, 27, 64, 68 n.1, 69,
tolerance, 49, 60, 80
Train to Pakistan, 90, 108
Two-nation theory, 3, 30, 45-6, 127, 134

UNESCO, 68
United Progressive Alliance (UPA), 25-6, 35
Universalization of Elementary Education, 27
Urdu, 10 n.3, 31, 38, 73

water, 13-4, 47-9, 74, 113, 143
West Bengal, 49
women, 25, 29, 88

Zulfikar Ali Bhutto (Bhutto), 37

Milton Keynes UK
Ingram Content Group UK Ltd.
UKHW021315290724
1069UKWH00079B/1529